The View from Xanadu
William Randolph Hearst and United States Foreign Policy

The Hearst newspaper chain, at its peak the largest in the history of American journalism, was a mouthpiece for William Randolph Hearst. He used the editorial page to expound his views on national and world events, becoming a major and ever-present figure in the political arena. Despise and hate him as they might – and many of them did – American presidents and politicians could not ignore him, even during his later years. In *The View from Xanadu* Ian Mugridge evaluates Hearst's attitudes toward u.s. foreign policy issues and the effect of his views on national foreign policy in the first half of the twentieth century.

Hearst is usually remembered as a flag-waving, jingoistic patriot who was anti-British, anti-French, anti-Oriental – anti-almost everything except the United States. He was regarded as an admirer of Hitler and Mussolini, and a staunch isolationist who believed that minimizing American contact with the rest of the world was the only sure way to achieve security.

Using all the journalistic apparatus at his disposal, Hearst trumpeted his views about the conduct of other nations and peoples and, more particularly, about the conduct of his own country in relation to them. The Spanish-American War of 1898 was often described as "Mr Hearst's war" because of the role he apparently played in pushing the United States into the war. Mugridge investigates Hearst's journalistic tactics, which seldom varied, and concludes that ultimately Hearst's flamboyant style militated against his being taken seriously by those responsible for the nation's affairs.

Exploring the personal side of this very public figure, Mugridge argues that Hearst was a far more complex individual than previous biographers have assumed. He probes beneath Hearst's largely self-created image to delineate the aspirations, anxieties, and vanities that led Hearst to embrace and advance his positions on u.s. foreign relations.

IAN MUGRIDGE is senior consultant, higher education, at the Commonwealth of Learning and is responsible for policy and program development at the Open Learning Agency in Vancouver, BC.

The Gentleman Who Got a
Hundred - Dollar Watch for
Thirty Dollars Thinks That
"Examiner" Want Ads Are
Worth Reading. Do You
Read Them?

The Examiner.

VOL. LXVI.   SAN FRANCISCO, SATURDAY MORNING, FEBRUARY 19, 1898.   NO. 50.

THE SPIRIT OF WAR PERVADES THE BREASTS OF ALL AMERICANS.

Patriotic Citizens Advocate Recourse to Arms to Wreak Vengeance Upon Spain for the Cruel and Cowardly Destruction of the Maine.

WASHINGTON

MILITIAMEN READY TO TAKE THE FIELD.

Governors of States Voice the Patriotic Willingness of the National Guard.

NEW YORK, February 18.—"Examiner" correspondents 18, 32 of the State militia to be mustered "Examiner" or command- ing officers with willing to do its strength of the State militia, it loses a great re- public to mobilize it and be confident for entire duty. All officers report worn bones ean and pavilion. Among them were the following.

ALBANY, BY T.L. February 18.—Gov- ernor Black will investig- that the State service, considering 12,000 bones, can be in command of war. There is a willing instruct-

UPHOLD THE NATION'S HONOR.

W. R. Hearst, "The Examiner"—It is the duty of the United States to make an immediate and thorough investigation into the cause of the disaster and take necessary steps to uphold the honor of our nation regardless of cost.

JAMES H. BUDD.

AVAILABLE FORCES IF WAR SHOULD ENSUE.

Strength of the Military and Naval Arms of the United States Now Ready to Meet an Enemy.

WASHINGTON, February 18.—Con-

The View from Xanadu

*William Randolph Hearst
and United States Foreign Policy*

IAN MUGRIDGE

McGill-Queen's University Press
Montreal & Kingston • London • Buffalo

Legal deposit third quarter 1995
Bibliothèque nationale du Québec

Printed in Canada on acid-free paper

This book has been published with the help of a grant from the Social Science Federation of Canada, using funds provided by the Social Sciences and Humanities Research Council of Canada.

McGill-Queen's University Press is grateful to the Canada Council for support of its publishing program.

Canadian Cataloguing in Publication Data

Mugridge, Ian
    The view from Xanadu: William Randolph Hearst and United States foreign policy
    Includes bibliographical references and index.
    ISBN 0-7735-1281-0 (bound)
    ISBN 0-7735-1295-0 (pbk.)
    1. Hearst, William Randolph, 1863–1951 – Views on international relations.   2. United States – Foreign relations – 20th century.
    3. Hearst, William Randolph, 1963–1951 – Influence.   4. Press and politics – History – 20th century.   I. Title.
    PN4874.H8M84 1995   070.5'092   C95-900179-4

This book was typeset by Typo Litho Composition Inc. in 10/12 Palatino.

All cartoons are published courtesy of the *San Francisco Examiner*.
Cover illustration of Hearst Castle (Hearst Monument/John Blades) published courtesy of Department of Parks and Recreation, California.

More years ago than I care to recall or record, I received a letter from Stuart Bernath's father asking if I would consider finishing the project on which his son was working when he died. I agreed but soon discovered that much more than I had expected – almost all the research, in fact – remained to be done. The years that followed involved for me a number of career changes, most of which effectively removed opportunities for historical research and writing, and Hearst lay unnoticed for long periods. I regret this profoundly, most particularly because both Stuart's parents, who asked me to take on his work, have not lived to see its completion. Even so, although this book is not at all what he would have written, the project that Stuart Bernath began is at last finished.

Stuart Bernath's death in his early thirties was a tragedy for those who knew him and for his profession. The promise he already showed would almost certainly have enabled him to become a distinguished historian of u.s. foreign relations as well as a notable teacher. He was a decent, gentle, and civilized man, and he was also my friend. I dedicate this book to his memory.

Contents

Acknowledgments   ix

Introduction   3

1 Prologue: The Spanish-American War   7

2 Hearst and His Newspapers   19

3 Hearst and Europe   30

4 Hearst and the Yellow Peril   46

5 Hearst, the Czar, and the Bolsheviks   60

6 Hearst and the Red Menace   77

7 Hearst and Peace   90

8 Hearst and War   108

9 America First   127

10 Hearst and United States Foreign Policy   144

11 Epilogue: 1941–1951   153

Notes   163

Bibliography   207

Index   217

Acknowledgments

As I indicated in the dedication, this book has been a long time coming, and it has benefited from the contributions of many people and institutions during that time.

Librarians at my own institutions, Simon Fraser University, the British Columbia Open Learning Agency, and the Commonwealth of Learning, have answered requests for materials and for help in locating them with great patience and competence. Heather Schwabe of the *San Francisco Examiner* provided valuable help in locating the cartoons that appear in this book. I am very grateful for their help, as I am for the generous and informed assistance of staff in the archives I visited in the course of research. In particular I would like to thank staff at the Bancroft Library at Berkeley, where Hearst's papers and several other important collections are deposited, at the Library of Congress, and at the National Archives in Washington, DC. At the latter John Taylor, who called my hotel at midnight to tell me that he had just realized where, after a couple of days of dead ends, we should have been searching, was only one memorable example of the very high level of staff provided by these repositories. Particular thanks are also due to the Hoover Institution for the Study of War, Revolution and Peace at Stanford University, which gave me a home and facilities for almost a year while I undertook a good deal of the research for this book.

Stephen Duguid, then a graduate student at Simon Fraser University, undertook much of the basic research assistance for this book, and I much appreciate his help. Brian Wilson, then vice-president, academic, at the same institution, provided the funds to support this assistance. In another place I have acknowledged with gratitude and affection the continuing wise counsel and assistance of Alex DeConde, and I do so again here. Geoff Smith, like me a former DeConde student, intervened at a critical point in the progress of this work, and, having learned the generosity of our mentor, he provided thoughtful and detailed comments on the manuscript as well as timely and valuable help, for which I am extremely grateful.

The Watkinses of Atherton, California – Bill, Jean, and Louisa – gave me a home in their guest house during my year at the Hoover Institution and put up with Hearst's and my vagaries for all that time. There are no words to express my gratitude for their hospitality and support. The same comment applies in rather different ways to my wife, Pat, who came into the Hearst project part way through when we married and has done much by her encouragement (and occasional needling) to ensure its completion.

Norah Kembar has edited the entire manuscript twice. The first occasion began with what must have been the rather disconcerting discovery that I thought that "vilify" had two l's and was uncertain about the difference between "that" and "which." But she stayed with the task, and whatever merit the prose has owes a great deal to her. Joan McGilvray and Susan Kent Davidson of McGill-Queen's University Press have, with efficiency, patience, and humour, shepherded the manuscript through its preparation for publication.

The View from Xanadu

Introduction

One of the obstacles to writing a balanced assessment of prominent figures in the recent past is that they are still hedged about with the prejudices they attracted during their lifetime. For William Randolph Hearst, who died in 1951, the problem is compounded because he elicited such strong emotions in his lifetime, emotions that still exist forty years later in those who are old enough to remember him – "a monster" was a recent reaction to the news that Hearst was the subject of this study.

Not only this, but the literature surrounding Hearst – if the term is rather loosely applied – is enormous. Much of it can be dismissed as vilification or sycophancy, or as the memoirs of fellow journalists telling their readers what fun it was to work for "the Chief" or, conversely, what harm he did to their profession. Amateur psychologists have left a mass of speculation, much of which tells us more about them than about Hearst. Finally, one must add the huge volume of writing produced by Hearst during an amazingly long and productive journalistic career. All this makes the task of sifting through the material about his life an unusually intimidating one.

There are, in fact, few worthwhile Hearst studies – for example, there are only two biographies of real value – so that Hearst has been left largely to the myth-makers. Chief among these is Orson Welles, as I became more than ever aware writing parts of this study in the summer of 1991, when *Citizen Kane* received its fiftieth anniversary reissues. Thus, for most literate Americans – and probably other English speakers, too – Hearst is almost certainly viewed as someone who looked like the young Orson Welles and behaved like Charles Foster Kane. This was not the case: he was short, inclined to be chubby, and had a high-pitched voice. Even though his behaviour came close to that of the flamboyant and domineering Kane – and Welles undoubtedly had him in mind as he created the publisher in his monumental film – the similarities are perhaps only superficial.

It is not my intention, however, to write a biography or a psycho-history. The study that follows will attempt to assess Hearst's views of United States foreign policy during the period of his national prominence, when his opinions were constantly before the American people and their rulers, their friends and enemies, and to examine how his interpretation of domestic and international politics influenced the conduct of American foreign policy.

In the sphere of U.S. foreign relations Hearst is most usually remembered as the flag-waving, jingoistic patriot of the Spanish-American War, anti-British, anti-French, anti–Oriental, anti-almost everything but, as he might have printed it in an editorial, PRO-AMERICAN. He is recalled as the virulent red-baiter, the admirer of Hitler and Mussolini who supported Germany at least until American entry into both world wars. He is regarded as the model isolationist, who believed that American contact with the rest of the world should be minimal and that a strong and aloof nation relying on its own resources was the only sure way to achieve security. At the same time he is remembered as someone who changed his mind so often that predicting his position was impossible, who, like John Dryden's Achitophel, was "stiff in opinions, always in the wrong; / everything by starts and nothing long."

Some of these impressions are correct; others are not. For example, it will be one of the contentions of this study that Hearst's views about American foreign policy, while they exhibited some of these features, were nothing if not consistent – often in the face of great changes in the world he wrote about and the views of the American public, and, ultimately, in the face of irrelevance. But it is first necessary to say something about William Randolph Hearst the man, who for more than fifty years bestrode the world of American journalism and, in some ways, American life as no other has before or since. It is not too much to say that, relevant or not, and even in glowering and bad-tempered retirement at San Simeon, Hearst was a major and ever-present figure in the life of the nation he prized so highly. Thus, on his death, "as the vast Hearst publicity machine unlimbered, sparing none of the devices it had developed in sixty-four years in the business ... millions of Hearst readers must surely have doubted that the nation would survive the blow."[1]

Flippant as this comment may be, it is nevertheless clear that, despise and hate him as they might – and many did both – American politicians from the presidents down could not ignore him, even during his later years. The amount of material related to Hearst in both official and private correspondence of the first half of this century is sufficient evidence of that.

Many of the conflicts and contradictions in Hearst's character and attitudes will appear in the course of this study. These contradictions were real and often obvious: it is significant that, in the last chapter of his biography, W.A. Swanberg composed two completely contradictory and entirely correct obituaries. Swanberg claimed that the two Hearsts were irreconcilable, Prospero and Caliban shackled together in a single body.[2] This view is arguable, for there still seems a unity to the man that can be explained. From the time of his appearance on the public stage, the interpretations of his character and the explanations of his actions have been many – and many of them far from the truth. The one that comes closest, however, appeared a dozen years after his death in an article by Frank MacShane entitled "The Romantic World of William Randolph Hearst."

MacShane places Hearst firmly in the context that explains him best – that of California in the later years of the last century and of his magnificent, vulgar house at San Simeon: "If he is viewed primarily as a Californian and in terms of the decades in which his predominantly Western character was formed, he will be seen to be a natural product of the area possessing a coherent (if not especially attractive) attitude towards its future."[3] MacShane also – I think correctly – notes that "it is undeniable that San Simeon has a distinct personality and character. Despite the contrast of the grotesque with the delicate and of the tasteless with the exquisite, it is unified through the personality of its builder."[4] Far from being the man of irreconcilable contradictions described by Swanberg, Hearst "was like his own San Simeon – a collection of individual ideas and impulses held together only by his own personality."[5]

If William Randolph Hearst is seen in this way, it is possible to explain him as a late nineteenth-century Californian, formed when San Francisco, for all its pretensions, was still a frontier town and the country around it as wild and outrageous as the young Hearst.[6] In this context, the comparison with Charles Foster Kane is not a superficial one, and the views on America's place in the world that Kane often expressed seem to have come straight from the editorials of the Hearst papers, justifying the connection implied in the title of this book.

Such an upbringing, in Hearst's words, gave a man room to stretch, but it also gave him the impression that life in America could be lived as it was in California and led him perhaps to misunderstand the nation he so loved. It also helped to produce the irony that Hearst, while dreaming of and yearning for the simplicity of earlier times in America, was partly instrumental in turning the nation into the mass society he abhorred. Such an upbringing gave him, too, the source of his persistence in carrying his message to the American people and their leaders. MacShane compares Hearst to Gatsby, who had "an extraordinary gift for hope, a romantic readiness such as I have never found in any other person." Hearst's entire career in politics and in journalism reflected this hope and kept him going through a long series of defeats that would have discouraged most men.[7] It was, I think, this hope, springing from a profound belief in his country and what it stood for, that led Hearst to trumpet for more than fifty years his views on the right conduct of the United States in its relations with the rest of the world. Later chapters will document the consequences of his campaigns and some of the inevitable conclusions about Hearst's methods that they produced. At least at the beginning, however, it is as well to record the source of his views about the foreign policies of the United States.

1 Prologue:
The Spanish-American War

The Hearst press, which dominated American journalism for at least forty years, may be said to have come into existence in 1895. In that year, after eight years of perfecting – on his first newspaper, the *San Francisco Examiner*, a gift from his father – the techniques that were to revolutionize the American newspaper industry, William Randolph Hearst returned to the eastern United States, where he had spent a brief and undistinguished career at Harvard and a short spell studying Joseph Pulitzer's *New York World*, and bought the *New York Journal*. In the same year, the first Hearst syndicate was established, to supply features to other newspapers.[1]

Thus the Hearst chain, consisting initially of two newspapers and a small syndicate, was launched. For good or bad, the journalistic world was never to be the same again. Hearst at once set to work to boost the circulation of his New York newspaper by the same aggressive methods he had used in San Francisco to replace the *Chronicle* with his own *Examiner* as the city's leading newspaper.[2] He began a competition with Pulitzer for the mass readership of New York, a struggle climaxing in their treatment of the Cuban crisis that, in 1898, led to the Spanish-American War.

The Hearst press operated – at least on issues "the Chief" considered important – as a unit, fighting the same battles through both its news coverage and its editorial and cartoon comment.[3] In 1898 this meant that two major cities on opposite sides of the country carried Hearst's message on the Cuban situation, but later, as the newspapers he controlled grew into the largest chain in the United States, it was to mean that his views were carried into almost every major centre in the country. Before 1898, however, only the *Examiner* and the *Journal* represented Hearst in the fight for Cuban independence.

The crisis in Cuba had been growing since the depression of 1893 and an American tariff that greatly increased the duty on raw sugar the following year. These factors produced a renewed poverty that only exacerbated years of Spanish misrule and led to the outbreak of rebellion in Cuba early in 1895. Cuban exiles were already finding it easy to arouse American sympathy when a Spanish gunboat fired on an American freighter, the *Alliance*, off the Cuban coast in early March. The rebellion became headline news across the country as Americans demanded revenge and their discontent was fed by further incidents. Hearst, already engaged in a circulation war in New York with Pulitzer's *World*, marched into action with sensational headlines and editiorial comment.

In August 1895 an *Examiner* editorial noted that "there is a growing feeling in favor of the recognition by the United States of Cuban belligerency." It indicated that the public statements of the Spanish authorities were not altogether truthful – "Spain is being drained of men and money. The work of keeping Cuba under is exhausting her strength. And yet she would have the world believe that she is dealing with nothing but a riot" – and it concluded with a discussion of the possibilities of, and reasons for, American intervention:

Of course if we should think best to interfere our intervention would be purely benevolent. We are not looking for new territory, especially when it is inhabited by over 1,600,000 Spaniards, Creoles and negroes. We should be glad to see Cuba independent, or annexed to Mexico, or even in the enjoyment of an autonomous local government under the sovereignty of Spain. But the present condition of the island is an international scandal, and a reproach to the premier republic of the world.[4]

In this editorial most of the elements of the succeeding campaign have been established, either explicitly or implicitly. The writer hints at the oppression and misrepresentation being practised by the Spanish authorities, notes the increasing popular sentiment in the United States for intervention or at least for recognition of the rebels, and emphasizes the obligation of the United States to take steps to secure a solution acceptable on humanitarian grounds and in America's national interest.

Later in the month Hearst took notice of the obduracy of the Spanish and the heroism of the Cubans: "The reports indicate that Cuba is likely to gain her independence, but not before many battles have been fought, many lives have been lost, much property has been destroyed and not until Spain has been convinced that Cuba is too expensive a luxury to hold as a reminiscence of the conquest ... Already recognition by the United States of the insurgents as belligerents is asked, and such recognition seems fairly earned by vigorous fighters."[5] Hearst emphasized that the Cubans were not the sort to accept defeat after one unsuccessful campaign. A September 1895 editorial noted that, allied to the rains and the yellow fever, the rebels would in the end prevail.[6]

A week later the righteous wrath of the *Examiner* came down on a manifesto issued by the Spanish authorities, indicating their firm intention to put down the rebellion at whatever cost: "This document announces that the whole eastern end of Cuba will be freed from all rebels and their adherents, that it will be war to extermination, that no foes will be allowed to remain to create further disturbances, that Spain will enter the fall campaign with only one object in view – the immediate and absolute subjugation of the island – and that the portion of the rebels will be death". If this unthinkable event occurred, then the United States would be obliged to review its relationship to the rebellion, for (referring to the massacre of Armenians in Turkey that year) "it may not be our duty to interfere in Turkey, but we certainly cannot permit the creation of another Armenia in this hemisphere."[7]

It was to this aspect of hostilities that the Hearst papers returned repeatedly, mentioning atrocities committed by the rebels but concentrating on those of the Spaniards and – in February 1896 – on the actions of the new Spanish commander in Cuba, General Valeriano Weyler, named, not perhaps altogether justly, "the Butcher." On his announcement of a campaign of extermination, the *Examiner* commented: "General Weyler need not think that he and the insurgents will be allowed to engage in a competition in savagery" and "we draw the line at systematized massacre,"[8] referring again to the duty of the United States to prevent a catastrophe from occurring in its own hemisphere:

Cuba is our Armenia, and it is at our doors. The powers of Europe admit that it is their duty to restore order to Armenia, but they cannot control their mutual jealousies sufficiently to permit anything to be done. We have a similar duty towards Cuba, and we have no balance-of-power fetish to interfere with its performance. We have no jealousy of our neighbors. All we want is for Cuba to be free and prosperous. We are not figuring on stealing its territory – we are willing that it shall belong to Mexico if its people choose. But we are determined that no more butcheries and arsons shall be laid to our door. Cuba must not stand in the relation to us that Armenia does to England.[9]

In the spring and early summer of 1896 pressure from Hearst and other editors, resisted by President Grover Cleveland, grew for American intervention. By June, Hearst was maintaining that American and Cuban freedom were irrevocably linked. "No American," the *Examiner* proclaimed, "can be true to the freedom of his own country without feeling such a sympathy for Cuba as will urge him to interfere for its liberation."[10] Having reached this conclusion, Hearst proceeded to interfere.

During the summer and fall of 1896, however, interest in Cuba was subordinated to the American presidential election. Hearst, unlike most eastern Democratic newspapers, supported the first candidacy of William Jennings Bryan, but the result was the first election of William McKinley.[11] With the election out of the way, the Hearst papers returned to the Cuban problem: "Now that the election is over interest in Cuban affairs may be expected to revive. Already the talk of war between the United States and Spain has become sufficiently audible to distract the sensitive nerves of the New York Stock Market. It is not at all likely, however, that Spain will be foolish enough to attack us if our Government acts with firmness and courtesy. The trouble all along has been that there has been too much talking on our part and too little acting."[12] While the new president began his administration with firm statements against aggression, the Hearst papers stepped up the campaign for war over Cuba, attacking both the Spanish authorities for their actions in Cuba and the American authorities for their inaction.[13]

The campaign of parading the iniquities of the Spanish administration of the island escalated as Hearst sent Richard Harding Davis, the well-known war correspondent, and artist Frederick Remington to Cuba to report on the situation. Together, in graphic reporting and harrowing pictures, they detailed the crimes of Spain against the people of the island. Early in February, for example, both Hearst papers carried an account of the execution of one Adolfo Rodriguez. Headlines blazed across the front page —"SHOOTING OF A BRAVE CUBAN PATRIOT ON THE PLAINS OF SANTA CLARA" — and below them a Remington picture bore the caption, "With Boyish Face Uplifted to the Rising Sun, Fearlessly and Calmly Awaiting Death, a Peasant Hero Is Sacrificed to the Vengeful Lust of the Cruel and Merciless Spaniards."[14]

Now, in early February, Remington sent Hearst his famous telegram, claiming that the situation was quiet and there was no trouble, and asking to return to the United States. In reply Hearst is said to have sent the even more famous message, "Please remain. You furnish the pictures and I'll furnish the war."[15] This story has been repeated many times, but it is doubtful that such a reply was ever sent. As one of Hearst's biographers (admittedly a friendly one) points out, it is unlikely that such a telegram would have got past the rigorous Spanish censorship in Havana;[16] it seems even less likely that Spanish authorities would have failed to make propaganda use of such a missive. There is no question, however, that by this time Hearst wanted war. Through the spring and summer of 1897 his campaign increased in violence until, in August, an opportunity occurred that was second in publicity value only to the later sinking of the u.s. battleship *Maine* in Havana harbour.

On 16 August 1897 Hearst heard the story of Evangelina Cisneros, "a report of a situation that was to provide a story to satisfy even Hearst's craving for the sensational mixed with the sentimental."[17] Evangelina Cisneros was eighteen years old and had been imprisoned for more than a year, apparently for resisting the advances of one of General Weyler's aides. Hearst ordered not only a campaign to right this wrong but also an attempt, ultimately successful, to rescue her – an event that took place in mid-October, by which time all the world knew of Evangelina Cisneros. A group of prominent American women pleaded with the Spanish queen, and even the Pope interceded for her.[18] After her rescue she was brought to New York, fêted, and, when no longer newsworthy, dropped. She had been merely another device employed in Hearst's righteous war with Spain.[19]

Alongside the pillorying of Spain and the American government, Hearst used other means to further his campaign. Early in February 1898, when the Spanish ambassador, Enrique Dupuis de Lôme, made slighting remarks about President McKinley in a private letter to a friend, Hearst, along with other editors, used this incident to whip up anti-Spanish feeling. Dupuis de Lôme resigned as the United States government demanded his recall, having seriously damaged Spanish-American relations.[20] At about the same time Hearst sent to Cuba what was grandly called a congressional commission – three senators and two congressmen, none very prominent but all with strong interventionist sympathies. They reported that "the future of Cuba is American" and that the island was already lost to Spain.[21] But none of these campaign-bolstering opportunities had the compelling power and possibilities of the sinking of the *Maine*.

On the night of 15 February 1898 the *Maine*, moored in Havana hbour, blew up, killing 260 men. The cause of the explosion was never clearly established, although in early March a naval inquiry gave its view that a submarine had destroyed the vessel; but by then the facts of the case were irrelevant. The sinking of the *Maine*, milked

THE GOVERNMENT READY FOR WAR

VICTIMS OF SPANISH CRUELTY AT THE FUNERAL OF THE MAINE'S GALLANT CREW.

San Francisco Examiner, 24 February 1898

of every drop of its sensational value, gave Hearst and other publishers campaigning for war the final and overwhelming opportunity to get what they wanted. The events of the next two months, between the sinking and the declaration of war, seem now to have about them an awful quality of doom and inspire the conviction that neither the United States government nor that of Spain was in control of the situation and that war was inevitable. After the *Maine* there could be no turning back. Reviewing the events of these weeks, it is impossible to escape the feeling that Hearst not only had his circulation, but he had his war, too.[22]

As the fighting began, news of the triumphs of American arms was blazoned across the front pages of the two Hearst papers. Banner headlines announced Admiral George Dewey's victory in Manila Bay and other engagements.[23] At the same time Hearst and his editorial writers began to pay attention to the settlement that must follow the war. With the overwhelming confidence and sense of American superiority that had characterized the campaign for war and the treatment of the war itself, they started to make known their terms for that settlement.

The two major issues were the fate not only of Cuba but also of the Philippines, Spain's remaining Pacific colony. The attitude of the Hearst papers to the making of the peace was that it was to be an American peace, arrived at without reference to or interference from European powers. In an editorial discussing the fate of the Philippines in the summer of 1898, the *Examiner* set out this attitude very clearly: "The United States will determine the fate of the Philippines, and they will determine it without the aid of any European power or European Congress. They will fulfill their obligations to humanity and the world by securing good government for the people whom the fortunes of war have brought under their power. And, whether we keep the islands or make other disposition of them, our action will be determined by our ideas of right, and not by the threats of other nations."[24]

It quickly became obvious to Hearst that the Philippines, beginning as a side-show in the war, an almost accidental problem alongside the major question of Cuba, would be the main issue of the future. "Our amiable friends, for whose benefit in part we are waging war, appear to be difficult people to get along with," he said, referring to the Filipino rebels and their leader, Emilio Aguinaldo, who showed an alarming tendency to take matters into their own hands and to ignore the wishes of their deliverers. "[But] the United States will go through with their work, whether with or without the help of their native allies ... To the Philippines they are under no pledges, and will do for them what statesmanship and humanity require."[25] Two weeks later Hearst prepared, on behalf of the people and government of the United States, to shoulder the white man's burden: "We are morally responsible for the future of the islands. Interest and duty go hand in hand. Let us not surrender the Philippines in the terms of peace."[26]

The Cuban problem was different. Clearly, Spain had to be relieved of the island as she did of everything else within reach of the American mainland.[27] The nation was, however, bound by pledges to the Cubans, on whose behalf the war had been started. In an editorial already quoted the *Examiner* noted that, in contrast to the Philippines, "to Cuba, they [the American people] have promised independence and self-government, and these they will provide."[28]

In a remarkably short time Spanish resistance was virtually destroyed, so that, at the end of July, the president was able effectively to dictate terms to the Madrid government. These were largely confirmed by the formal peace treaty, signed in Paris on 19 December, which gave independence to Cuba, ceded Puerto Rico, and surrendered the Philippines for $20 million. The Hearst papers greeted these terms with pleasure and took up the paternal and protective attitude towards the three countries that never varied during the next fifty years. In 1899, with the long-term fate of Cuba still uncertain, an editorial entitled "Home Rule for Cuba" noted: "It is the duty of the United States to carry out their promises to the Cubans, and to carry them out as soon as it becomes certain that no wrong will be done to any class of the population of the island by a Cuban government."[29] But in 1902, when the civilian government of Cuba replaced a United States military government, Hearst applauded this event, both for the sake of the Cubans themselves and for the good work that the nation had done: "The United States have set to the nations of the earth a high example of honorable fidelity to promise by withdrawing from the island. The representative of the American Republic with his own hands yesterday hauled down our flag and raised that of Cuba libre. It was a noble spectacle."[30]

However, warned the same editorial, the young nation still depended on the United States, which must always be ready to support its progress and guard against any backsliding from the course along which the American administration had set it. Hence, in 1906, when rebellion broke out and the possibility of American intervention to uphold the legitimate government was discussed, the *Examiner* – cautioning that, if disorder continued and grew, "it will be the duty of the United States to take a hand and restore order" – gave its opinion that "President Palma should be given a fair opportunity to show what he can do toward maintaining his government." The paper expressed the hope that, partly because "rebel-chasing in the Cuban mountains is a heart-breaking military exercise, ... the Cubans will be able to settle their own troubles and we shall be spared the bloodshed, the cost and the humiliation of a campaign."[31] This same view of the situation reappeared throughout the years as the Hearst papers maintained that "the American intention to help the Cubans govern themselves is based on a national pledge," a pledge that must be exercised responsibly and delicately, but nevertheless exercised when the need arose.[32]

As the Hearst papers had earlier recognized, the post-war situation in the Philippines was rather different from that in Cuba, but the American attitude towards those islands should nevertheless be informed by the same ideals. Apparently, the Filipinos were not yet fit to govern themselves and must be led along the road to self-government and responsibility by the American authorities. Again, this was not a task to be entered into lightly or for the sake of profit but an opportunity to spread enlightenment and democracy among a people less fortunate than those of the United States:

The United States with all its vast power has not oppressed this dependent and alien people. With an expenditure of hundreds of millions of dollars and the infinitely greater cost of thousands of lives, this country stands as the only nation among the Aryan races which has administered an Oriental colony upon any other policy than that of aggrandizement or exploitation.

The humblest peasant in the Philippines long ago learned that the Americans did not seek to reduce him to peonage. And gradually he has learned that they are not taking his lands, nor subjecting him to harsh taxation or military service or military oppression.

The United States has not only protected its wards from the greed and rapacity of other nations and enlightened them with education, but it has performed an infinitely greater service to the world in maintaining its American ideals in an alien land.[33]

One of the problems encountered by the American authorities in the Philippines was, of course, that the "humblest peasant" had learned nothing of the sort and tended to regard American government of the islands as a slightly different, not much better substitute for that of Spain. None the less, the Hearst papers held to their belief that American ideals would finally triumph and show the Filipinos the way to freedom. It would be unfortunate if this were to take a little longer than had been anticipated, but that should not deter the nation from its ideals or its duty. [34] If, as time went on, other factors were added to the reasons for not granting independence to the Philippines, and the interests of the United States were seen to take a more prominent place in discussions of the future of the islands, there was still a strong sense that duty to the islands and their welfare indicated that they be retained and strengthened. America should not be allowed to forget her duty either to herself or to the lesser breeds for whom she had assumed responsibility.[35]

The role of the press among the causes of the Spanish-American War has been examined and re-examined with great frequency. Whatever yardstick is used to measure press influence, it is clear that certain newspapers – the "yellow press," particularly in the eastern United States – played a part, if not in actually bringing on the war, then in causing it to occur when it did.

But the focus of this study is on Hearst and his newspapers. The best discussion of the role of the press in the war notes that "the press could have helped bring on the war only if the people were ready for it" because "the press – the newspapers and the correspondents – acted as if it were" responsible for the war.[36] The press, and the

Hearst press in particular, sometimes acted as if it were the government of the United States and not merely responsible for reporting what was happening. "Commissioners" were sent to Cuba to confer with the rebels. Dispatch boats carrying them in and out also carried messages, both official and unofficial. Hearst's action in sending a "congressional commission" to Cuba before the outbreak of war has already been mentioned; later, he went so far as to arrange an attempt, subsequently called off, to sink a ship in the Suez Canal to stop the Spaniards from sailing a fleet through to relieve the Philippines. "All these activities may have been in the interests of getting the news, but it was hard to tell when the press was functioning in its legitimate capacity and when it was acting in a governmental capacity – with or without the cooperation of officials."[37] Another writer notes:

The power of the press in fomenting American intervention in 1898 was indefinable. The Cubans themselves held that, however valuable it was to them, it merely fed a public opinion that already existed. Newspaper pressure helped cause the war by keeping diplomacy unsettled in the face of mounting public opinion and ranking congressmen. Yet neither Cleveland nor McKinley assigned it first place among their woes. It is not too much to say that, had all other forces except the sensational newspapers been active in 1898, war would have come without the yellow press.[38]

This is perhaps the most reasonable statement on the role of the press in causing the war. Later work has tended to confirm this view, casting doubt on the apparent role of the yellow press as a powerful and pervasive influence for war. Conclusions about press influence are at best impressionistic, and even in this case must be viewed with scepticism.[39] Public opinion may have pushed the country into war more quickly than might otherwise have been the case; it may have helped to keep the pressure on the administration when they were tempted to equivocate or negotiate; but the problems that produced the war were there in reality and would not have gone away, press or no press. If the press was a factor, it was a minor one. The *New York Times* noted on his death that "Mr. Hearst played the loudest horn in the war clamor that heated the public frenzy to a cherry red."[40]

At the same time, the *San Francisco Chronicle* noted that, at the time of the war, "people were talking about 'Hearst's one-man war.'" It added that, although evidence to support this conclusion was questionable, "New Yorkers had begun calling the *Journal* 'The War Cry.'"[41] In view of what has been said earlier, the title would seem justified but somewhat unfair; it could equally have been applied to other war-mongering papers, such as the *World*, even though Pulitzer's view of the war differed from Hearst's.[42]

It is instructive to consider the chapter headings dealing with the war in books on Hearst. One biographer chose "Owner of the Spanish-American War."[43] Another author, in two books about Hearst, selected "Hearst Seems to Own a War" and "A Journalist Liberates a Country."[44] Since the second heading appeared in the later book, published after Hearst's death, one must assume that continued reflection on the subject led the author to the firmer conclusion expressed in this work: "Well within the span of many living Americans, one major war was brought about by a single individual, William Randolph Hearst."[45] The evidence for this, again, is dubious.

For the subsequent history of the Hearst press, however, it was important that "the Chief" himself believed he was responsible for bringing on the war. Early in May 1898 Hearst's New York paper asked, on its front page, "How do you like the *Journal's* war?" and the *Examiner* was not far behind in claiming credit for bringing on hostilities.[46] Having worked on the public, stirred up the nation and its representatives, and chronicled the progress of the country into war, Hearst clearly believed that the war with Spain was his responsibility and his creation. "The journalism that acts" had not only acted itself; it had induced decisive action in others. The first major national campaign mounted by the Hearst newspapers had, to all appearances, been a huge success.

At least partly because of this, the campaign waged by the Hearst newspapers for war with Spain, for the war itself, and for its aftermath provided a prototype for the campaigns, attitudes, and policies that William Randolph Hearst and his newspapers were to maintain for fifty years. Patterns established around the turn of the century were repeated with remarkable consistency as the twentieth century wore on. It is probable that the success that seemed to attend Hearst's advocacy at this time accounts substantially for his course from the end of the war until his death in 1951.

Whether or not Hearst believed in his crusade for war with Spain – and there is considerable evidence that he did – he was convinced that he had succeeded in getting his country into the war by intense and incessant pressure on the government, sometimes even by usurping its legitimate functions. He (and much of the nation) saw a concrete example of the power of the press, of its ability to move the people and their representatives. Although it may be too much to claim that Hearst and his newspapers enjoyed the influence ascribed to them in later years – the record of success in major campaigns of the Hearst press may say a good deal about this – it is probable that "the Chief," having conducted his war campaign up to 1898 and seen its results, believed the power of the press to be almost limitless. It may be that, having – as he thought – got the nation into the Spanish-American War, William Randolph Hearst never got over it.

2 Hearst and His Newspapers

From its beginnings with the *San Francisco Examiner* and the *New York Journal*, acquired, though rather differently, in 1887 and 1895 respectively, the Hearst chain of newspapers spread, so that by the mid-1930s, at its greatest extent, "the Chief" owned newspapers in almost every major city in the country and, according to one estimate, controlled a circulation of 5,100,000 with his daily papers and of 6,800,000 with his Sunday papers.[1] Two years later the Hearst organization gave the circulation figures as 6,889,000 for the dailies and 7,364,000 for the Sunday papers and estimated that approximately 30 million people read Hearst newspapers every day.[2] At this time financial difficulties forced consolidation, disposal, or elimination of some of the newspapers, but in 1941 seventeen Hearst dailies still accounted for a circulation of 4,475,264 and thirteen Sunday papers totalled 7,110,890.[3] These circulation figures trace the growth of the largest newspaper chain the United States has ever seen.

More remarkable, however, is that the newspapers making up the Hearst empire were controlled by a single man: William Randolph Hearst. During the preceding chapter and throughout those that follow, the phrases "Hearst press" and "Hearst newspapers" have been used interchangeably with the name of Hearst. This has been done deliberately, to indicate that these expressions are not merely synonymous but, in every important sense, the same. Throughout his life Hearst controlled the newspapers and their editorial policies. Even in the thirties, when financial control was removed from him as his empire encountered monetary problems, he retained a firm grip on the editorial policies of his papers.[4] His detailed attention to his newspapers, their content and form, continued until a few months before the end of his life.[5] In fact as well as in name, Hearst was "the Chief."

His involvement in the business of producing newspapers was amazing. He read all his papers every day and returned them to their editors with comments pencilled in the margins. He read the Hearst wire daily and thus was able to change editorials of which he did not approve before they appeared in print.[6] His control of the papers was so tight that, for example, he directed his editors to print financial tables in the style of one of his competitors and to print comic strips following the format of one of his own papers.[7] On occasion he went even further: in a letter of late 1915 he admonished an editor because, in that morning's edition, the second head on the first page referred to the battleship "Kentuck," and in another column "the Minister of Greece" was quoted as saying that the British attitude to "u.s." was infamous whereas "what he really said was that the British attitude towards us [Greece] is infamous."[8] He ordered that, in the search for accuracy and freedom from prosecution, reporters and typesetters responsible for "offensive" stories should be dismissed if their reasons for printing the stories were unacceptable and that notices of dismissals and the reasons for them should be posted in the city rooms of the newspapers concerned.[9] He instructed that no attacks on individuals or policies should be made in editorial columns before being cleared with a responsible editor, [10] and he ensured that editorials by Arthur Brisbane (an editor and writer who enjoyed particular independence during his career at the Hearst papers) were not omitted by any of his papers.[11] He set policy on the relationship between editorial and cartoon comment in his newspapers,[12] on the character of the news headlines,[13] and on where important editorials should appear.[14] In addition to such oversight, he frequently wrote editorials himself. For it was the editorial that Hearst regarded as of paramount importance. He believed that newspapers existed to provide their readers with news and information rather than comment or entertainment.[15] He also saw them as organs of enlightenment and felt that newspapers should act as "the attorney for the public."[16] Out of these convictions came the methods he pursued, with little variation, throughout his long career as a newspaperman.

One of his more prominent editors has described Hearst's editorial methods at length. James T. Williams, Jr worked for Hearst from 1925 to 1937, and his reminiscences provide a detailed account of Hearst's editorial methods and the way he treated those who wrote for him. Williams held that "probably one of the biggest things [Hearst] did" was to direct "his whole effort to get the mass of the people to read the editorial page."[17] Williams comments:

His type was designed for that purpose. I always thought he overused the capital letters of certain words. He would underscore the words he wished in caps ... He was also extremely careful about the use of words.

Good Anglo-Saxon words and short sentences, and sequence, were the things he emphasized. He had made a great study of editorial writing. It was for the mass. That was his target.[18]

Williams goes on to explain Hearst's theory that "the tabloid would bring into the circle of readership a vast number of people who weren't reading any newspaper. He felt that the size would make it possible for vast numbers of people to read a tabloid when they were going or coming on the bus or the subway, or for the tele operator who could carry on her work."[19]

Holding this view, Hearst set out to bring his message to the masses, and one of the methods he used was to control editorial policy. Not only did he send out, directly or through his secretaries, a continuous stream of instructions on the editorials he wished to see or the campaigns he wanted to mount in his newspapers, but he wrote himself or had written regular editorials on topics of importance to him. Once this had been done, these editorials were followed, where necessary, by others on the same subject.[20] Williams notes that "Mr. Hearst did not send out a central editorial daily. It varied. Sometimes there was an editorial every day, but he wouldn't release it every day. He didn't want them to get too piled up. Sometimes he would release them three times a week. Then, of course, he would write his own editorials."[21]

The signed editorials and statements by Hearst were printed in all Hearst papers, usually on the front page. These overtly set the editorial policies of the papers as a group, and his editorial writers were expected to follow them. One of the exceptions was Arthur Brisbane, who in effect became a partner in the Hearst enterprise of bringing newspapers to the masses. No other writer or editor held Brisbane's authority during his career with the Hearst papers,[22] although there were others to whom Hearst accorded the privilege of writing as they wished.[23]

Generally, however, editorial policy was the province of Hearst or one of his few trusted advisers. Williams indicates that he himself wrote three types of editorial. First, he wrote in response to instructions from Hearst; such editorials, one must assume, made up the bulk of the editorials in all Hearst papers. Second, Williams submitted memoranda on topics of interest, which might be accepted, rejected, or changed as Hearst saw fit. Third, he wrote editorials or columns of his own, which were printed under his byline – the proviso being that, if any changes were made, his name would not be used. Hearst never obliged Williams to write against his expressed views, but nevertheless, "he was the editor-in-chief of the newspapers, could kill any editorial, or revise it."[24] In other words, control of the editorial policies of the Hearst newspapers belonged to "the Chief" alone.

Yet Hearst's methods were considered reasonable by Williams, an experienced and respected newspaperman. "I don't feel," he wrote, "that your editorial integrity is impugned or betrayed if the editor or the owner orders an editorial of a certain kind, and you draft it according to your instructions, provided your name is not at the head of the paper as the editor. That is why I declined the title of editor-in-chief of the Hearst newspapers."[25] Others took a less understanding view of Hearst's practices, seeing his methods of running his papers and of setting policies as the irresponsible whims of a "modern Louis XIV."[26] But Hearst's internal working methods and policies are not the major concern of this work: what is important here is how he pursued his political ideas and mounted his campaigns.

Hearst's method of retailing the news and expounding his opinions earned him the unsavory reputation he carried with him to his grave. When he died in 1951, the *London News Chronicle* called him "a wicked old reactionary ... opposed to all that was liberal and Progressive,"[27] and the *Manchester Guardian* noted that "it is hard even now to think of him with charity," concluding that "perhaps no man ever did so much to debase the standards of journalism."[28] *The Times*, while giving him credit for ability and for serving "upon occasion as a public watchdog," noted that "in politics, indeed, as in journalism his methods were inconsequent and brazen."[29] In the United States, press reaction was scarcely more charitable. The *Christian Science Monitor* judiciously noted that "in the exploiting of news he did not invent sensationalism, but [he] introduced many devices to further dramatize the printed word for a generation becoming literate."[30] The *Washington Post*, averring that "few men have come nearer to reshaping the world in their own image than William Randolph Hearst," held that "the atmosphere of the contemporary world with its frenetic excitement, alarms, scientific grotesqueries, scandals in high places, and generally pervasive aura of violence and sex, very much resembles that of a Hearst newspaper in the palmier days of the 'yellow press.'"[31] The *Los Angeles Times* regarded him merely as an anachronism, left over from some earlier age, and suggested that judging him would be like applying the standards of the twentieth century to Charlemagne.[32]

A rather different perspective came from the one paper with more cause than any other to regard Hearst without charity. The *San Francisco Chronicle,* commenting on his "violent kind of journalism that bred violent emotional reactions," also noted that "it was never less than a colorful, rampaging kind of journalism that threw down a stimulating, if often irritating, challenge to the rest of the newspaper world." The *Chronicle* went on to say that Hearst was "not great by a definition that would require an editor always to be correct in his policies," a kind of greatness that could be achieved only by confining "forthright editorial stands to such matters as sin and the weather." But "he never faltered; you always knew where he stood, and he always stood ready to defend his position with every ounce of his wit and courage and pertinacity." An editor could be wrong as long as he was sincere; but it was "the privilege of no editor to be dull or obscure or sloppy in the production of his newspaper, and Hearst was always meticulous in avoidance of those errors." The *Chronicle* concluded that "he lived as he worked – spectacularly ... For this, as well as for the rigidly uncompromising position he took against his political and ideological foes, he won an outsize share of venomous detraction. And for this same tendency of all-outness, which he applied with equal zeal (and equal lack of restraint or discrimination) to causes he deemed right, his adulators were always in roughly the same quantity and degree of enthusiasm as his detractors."[33]

Hearst's devotion to the "gee-whiz" emotion,[34] his pandering to the baser side of human curiosity in the lurid stories of violence, sex, and scandal of all kind that his papers thrived on,[35] his perfection of methods developed by Pulitzer and others to build circulation by sensational, exaggerated, and not always accurate reporting[36] – all these aspects of Hearstian journalism (and of "yellow" journalism in general) have been discussed fully elsewhere. But along with these negative aspects of Heart's brand of journalism went its positive side: his part in exposing and curbing corruption and venality in public life; the small victories scored in political battles; the long fight against the trusts and for better public health and working conditions; the promotion of disaster relief in many parts of the world.[37] These favourable contributions are too often forgotten in the vilification and criticism that Hearst's detractors have heaped upon him.

It must be admitted, however, that Hearst's campaigns on political issues or against individuals have seldom, if ever, been equalled in American journalism. Hearst's strength lay in mounting a highly visible, concentrated, and (if necessary) extended campaign on a selected issue. The method he employed was always the same – a method perfected in the years when he and other "yellow" editors in the east were pushing the nation towards war with Spain. He combined news coverage and editorial comment to an extent never done before and perhaps never so effectively since. Banner headlines displayed his editorial message on the front and other news pages while, on the editorial pages, similar headlines, along with cartoons containing the substance of the message, preceded editorials and reiterated the essential ideas about the subject under discussion. In the Cuban situation, for example, these were the brutality, oppression, and inefficiency of the Spanish authorities on the island; the heroism of the rebels; and the vacillation of the McKinley administration. In subsequent campaigns, the same technique of preaching – succinctly and forthrightly – a core of ideas, adapted to changing circumstances but always basically the same, was followed until the editorial line of the Hearst papers on such subjects as the League of Nations, the World Court, the Communist menace, the "yellow peril", and other leading questions became entirely predictable to their readers. Perhaps it was this habituation of Hearst's readers to what he was saying that resulted in the Hearst papers' achieving what was perceived as their greatest effect.[38]

But Hearst used the same approach in his personal vendettas. In the late years of the last century and the early years of this, he pursued the publishers of the *San Francisco Chronicle*, ridiculing them and their newspaper in editorials and cartoons day after day as the two papers struggled for the city's circulation. But perhaps his longest and most persistent campaign was his pursuit of Elihu P. Root, in which he combined many of his favourite targets: the trusts and the eastern establishment, foreign entanglements, and overseas responsibilities.

Root, whose public career began well before that of Hearst, was a public servant of intelligence, ability, and probity. He held Cabinet office under McKinley and Theodore Roosevelt, and he maintained considerable influence over the affairs of the Republican Party and the nation until his death. He had, however, received his law degree in 1867 and begun his law practice in New York City by accepting work from prominent Wall Street interests. He had also, unfortunately, taken part in the Tweed case, in which New York political boss William M. Tweed was convicted of forgery and larceny after milking the city's taxpayers of millions of dollars – thus providing Hearst with what Root's biographer has called "the Big Bertha of his journalistic artillery."[39] To the *Examiner* and later the *Journal*, Root became the "defender of Tweed" and "jackal" to the "hyenas" of Wall Street.[40] When he accepted office in McKinley's and then in Roosevelt's Cabinet, he was invariably pictured as the tool of the trusts, the lackey of the big business interests against which the Hearst papers were crusading. Every cartoon picturing McKinley or Roosevelt as defenders of business interests contained a small, smiling figure labelled "Root" gleefully following the president or the puppeteers of the trusts who pulled the strings that controlled the government.

Even when this identification with Wall Street was no longer relevant and Hearst had let up in his campaign against business interests, he still pursued Root whenever an opportunity offered. In 1915, for example, when there was a solid movement to give Root the Republican presidential nomination the following year, the *American* commented that "Mr. Root has great intellect, great ability, extraordinary competence and experience in public life" but that he was still the "tool of Wall Street."[41] Years later, when Root took a leading part in the attempt to persuade the United States to join the League of Nations and the World Court, the same arguments (that he was a servant of the sinister financial interests that had inveigled the nation into the First World War) were adduced against him. Adherence to such international organizations was seen as part of a plot by these interests to involve the nation in affairs that did not concern it and would only end in further wars.[42]

Many years before this, however, Root had responded to Hearst's attacks in a way that must have given Root immense satisfaction. In 1906, when Hearst was running against Charles Evans Hughes for governor of New York, Root, then secretary of state under Roosevelt, accepted an invitation to speak on Hughes's behalf just before the election. The campaign was regarded as an important one by the administration, and Hearst as a major threat to its continued strength in the east.[43] Both Root and the president were looking for a chance to stop what they saw as the extreme menace of Hearstism. In September, Roosevelt had written: "Hearst of course appeals frankly to the spirit of unrest, and there is, I believe, nothing at which he would stop in the way of adding fuel to the fire of discontent, reasonable or unreasonable, innocent or fraught with destruction to the whole body politic."[44]

By the end of October the president and Root had planned his speech against Hearst. Roosevelt wrote: "Root is going to make a corking speech, and he is going to say that he speaks by my authority when he comes to the climax. After that speech not even the Hearst papers can have the effrontery to say that Hearst and I stand for the same policies." Such measures were necessary because "I certainly feel that neither Tweed nor Benedict Arnold began to do as much damage to this country as Hearst has done."[45]

The speech, given at Utica, New York, on 1 November, lived up to this advance billing. Beginning by defining a demagogue as "one who for selfish ends seeks to curry favor with the people or some particular portion of them by pandering to their prejudices or wishes or by playing on their ignorance or passions," Root went on to pin this label on Hearst and to accuse him of "day by day and year by year sowing the seeds of dissension and strife and hatred throughout our land." He added: "It is not the calm and lawful redress of wrongs which he seeks, it is the turmoil of inflamed passions and the terrorism of revengeful force; he spreads the spirit, he follows the methods and he is guided by the selfish motives of the revolutionist; and he would plunge our peaceful land into the turmoil and discord of perpetual conflict." Root then proceeded to give examples of the leaders on whom Hearst had heaped his vituperation: Alton B. Parker – "a cockroach, a waterbug"; Grover Cleveland – "a living, breathing crime in breeches"; Thomas B. Reed – "a toad to the public eye"; and Roosevelt, who had "sold himself to the devil and will live up to the bargain." After announcing the president's consent to what he was about to say, Root concluded by telling his audience that when Roosevelt, in his first message to Congress after his predecessor's assassination, spoke of "the reckless utterances of those who, on the stump and in the public press, appeal to the dark and evil spirits of malice and greed, envy and sullen hatred," he was thinking of Hearst, and that "what he thought of Mr. Hearst then he thinks of Mr. Hearst now."[46]

At the time many people, including the president, credited Root's speech with having a decisive influence on the outcome of the gubernatorial campaign;[47] Roosevelt exulted at its success and the defeat of Hearst in New York.[48] But the point to note here is that, ten years after he began to be known nationally, Hearst had succeeded in turning against himself two of the most powerful political figures of the day, one of whom he still affected to admire and support. He had incurred their wrath to the extent that they were prepared to forgo his support because they believed that he was dangerous to the nation's welfare. Had this reaction been confined to just two political leaders, it might be dismissed as predictable. But Hearst provoked the same hostile response from all but two of the ten presidents of his time.[49]

Later he attracted animosity from all sections of the public: such diverse men as historian Charles Beard, journalist Heywood Broun, Communist leader Earl Browder, Franklin Roosevelt's secretary of the interior, Harold Ickes, and novelist Sinclair Lewis, who would probably have agreed on little else, regarded Hearst as a dangerous fascist.[50] He brought on himself the dislike and fear of many members of the American liberal community in the twenties and thirties, even though prominent liberal and Progressive politicians like George W. Norris, William E. Borah, and Hiram Johnson used the Hearst press to get their messages across to the people.[51] He was heartily disliked by many members of his own profession, who felt he degraded American journalism and pandered to the baser instincts of readers in his brazen quest for increased circulation.[52]

Doubtless, Hearst was motivated by the quest for circulation and profit in many of his campaigns, and the line between this and his genuine concern for those on whose behalf he fought is impossible to draw. His newspapers were vulgar, prurient, and sensational; his interplay of news and comment was excessive, outrageous, and at times vicious. By using such methods, he may have squandered the opportunity to establish himself as a substantial and responsible leader; he was (as Root called him) a demagogue, and a violent, irresponsible, and changeable one at that. In spite of the views expressed in this book about Hearst's attitudes to American foreign relations, and in spite of the evidence found occasionally in his correspondence that he wished merely to be fair and informative and sometimes became concerned about excessive negativism, this conclusion is in general inescapable.[53]

But there was more to Hearst than is revealed by the surface of his papers. He may well have been all the things his detractors accused him of being – indeed, evidence for many of their charges was so liberally splashed across his newspapers for more than fifty years that they are impossible to deny. It is easy to mock his campaigns but to forget how unpopular many of them made him and how he continued whether he was unpopular or not.[54] His concern for the mass of the American people – put upon, as he saw it, by moneyed and powerful interests who sought to deprive them of their just deserts and of their government – was genuine: at least, I have discovered no evidence that it was not.[55] A demagogue he undoubtedly was, but like all effective demagogues he had a knack of putting his finger on the real resentments and grievances of the people to whom he catered and on whom he depended.[56] Over the years he fought many battles for the benefit of the mass of Americans and for better, more efficient, and more honest use of resources. Few of his fights on major issues were successful at the time, but they were often for measures that later were put into effect.

Hearst struggled for municipal ownership of public utilities, for government ownership of railroads and natural resources, for state and municipal development and control of electric light and power. He supported men like Hiram Johnson as they fought for the initiative, the referendum, and the recall, and for direct primaries in an attempt to put government back into the hands of the people. He also supported female suffrage, the eight-hour day, and a minimum wage.[57] He probably did much to make the business and moneyed interests against whom he constantly inveighed more responsive to public interest – or at least more wary in their ventures into politics.

He began his political life as a Progressive and long remained true to what he saw as Progressive principles.[58] But he was never a party man, and though some discerned in him a drift towards Republicanism as he grew older,[59] in fact he continued, as he had always done, to support administrations of both parties when he thought they were doing right. For he was too independent, too careless of political influence, and too concerned for the causes he fought for to stand squarely and loyally behind one party for long – which may say as much about the American party system as it does about Hearst. Besides, he was not fighting, in the main, for a political cause or a political group.

He was struggling to maintain his view of the United States of America. He saw it as a place in which individual initiative and enterprise could work as they had for his father and himself, in which most people could have a good, useful, and comfortable life and in which the political and institutional structure of the nation was basically sound. There were, of course, threats to this system, but these could be identified and controlled by a vigilant press – the attorney for the people – by a conscientious electorate, and by honest and watchful administrations at all levels. With these features of American life maintained as strong influences in society, the system could be made to work and to implement the aims of the Founding Fathers, to whom he constantly referred and to the virtues of whose time he wished to return.[60]

In the end, this was what Hearst sought and what his newspapers, for all their bluster, coarseness, and nonsense, were trying to keep the governments and people of the United States up to. He was, at bottom, a passionate American, believing unquestioningly in the virtues of the nation's ideals and system of government, and he never hesitated to remind his readers and the nation's leaders of them, even when loudly expressed feelings and noisy patriotism grew less fashionable as the twentieth century aged. Shortly after his death a fellow journalist spoke of this when, in attempting to assess Hearst's legacy to the United States, he noted that "his insistence upon fundamental American principles has not been the echo of a discredited past, but a constant reminder to the American people that there is a faith that transcends fashion. If Hearst's fashions were of another century, his principles of government were eternal. And he has made millions remember them. We can well ponder that fact."[61]

At the turn of the century William Randolph Hearst was thirty-seven years old. He was to remain the dominant figure of American journalism until his death in 1951. By 1900 he had taken a failing and second-rate newspaper in San Francisco and turned it into the city's leading journal; he had bought and expanded a New York paper in similar condition, fought a successful battle for the city's mass circulation with Pulitzer, and been at least partly responsible for America's entry into the war that made her a world power. He had made himself a national reputation both as a newspaperman and as a politician in the Democratic Party. He had stirred up much animosity, and many already regarded him as dangerous and disruptive. But he was, at this point and for a few years thereafter, at the peak of his authority, a power great enough in national politics to make a substantial run for the Democratic presidential nomination in 1904 – and for Woodrow Wilson, the eventual nominee in 1912, to spend as much time attacking him as Champ Clark, whom Hearst supported[62] – and in state politics to be the Democratic candidate for governor in 1906. His influence in the politics of New York City was also considerable, and it was in this period that, for the only time, he gained elective office as one of the congressmen from New York.

He was, in his own terms and those of most of his contemporaries, a success, and it was his newspapers that bought him that success. Though his influence was never again as great as in the first ten or twelve years of the century, he continued to employ the journalistic methods he had perfected as his empire expanded to cities in all parts of America. His readers were fed, again and again, the formula Hearst used with such success in his campaign for war with Spain. His mind seemed to have become set in the mould of his first, greatest, and most successful campaign, so that it was repeated, on an endless variety of subjects, until the strident excess of his methods made most of the nation's responsible leaders, politicians, and journalists forget, if they had ever noticed, the good and enduring things for which Hearst stood.

3 Hearst and Europe

When William Randolph Hearst died in 1951, most of the British newspapers that commented on his passing noted his reputation as an anglophobe.[1] This belief was widespread in England and the United States, but Hearst strongly denied it.[2] However, it is impossible to read his editorials over the years and take seriously his protestations that he entertained the "friendliest feelings" towards England – or indeed towards any of the major European powers on whose actions and affairs he commented.

As a strong proponent of Americanism and American democracy, he was offended by most of the European monarchies and by the inequality that he believed almost inevitably went with them. In 1907 he wrote about the birth of an heir to the Spanish throne:

A King was born in Spain the other day. If he lives he will succeed his weak-faced father, tail end of a worn-out line, in the task of governing and taxing Spain by "divine right" ... But no baby need envy this little "royal" creature, or the destiny that awaits him. The days of the King business on this earth are drawing to a close. Human beings have replaced the divine right of Kings both with divine right of every man to have what he produces and to consider himself other men's equal. The little Spanish king will live among flunkies, flatterers. He will be watched and controlled, over-educated in all lines EXCEPT THE ONE IMPORTANT LINE OF HUMAN LIBERTY. His rule by divine right is nothing but a jest, and no matter how stupid he may prove to be he cannot help knowing that.[3]

OLD STARS-AND-STRIPES, THE BUSINESS DETECTIVE

A THRILLING TALE OF THE CORONATION

(COPYRIGHT, 1902, BY W. R. HEARST.)

"Yes the coronation procession will be hawe - inspiring spectacle. W`en Huncle Sam sees it, 'e`ll feel like 'arf a tuppenny. An' to complete 'is humiliation, we'll 'ave William Waldorf Hastor bring hup the rear, carrying the wather pail!"

These treatening words where spoken in a loud, harsh voice by a short, fleshy person, in a red coat. He was addressing His Gracious Majesty Edouard the Seventh and Sir Michael 'Icks-Beach, who where listening attentively.

"'her's the throne we're going to use, "he continued, triumphantly. "Hit's made hof the best hold Henglish hoak. Them Yankees can't turn hout nothink like that in their bloomin' country!"

'They can't, eh!'

All eyes where turned in astonishment toward the speaker, who had entered unobserved. He was magnificient-looking individual, with striped trousers. "Now, John," continued the stranger, "just look here!" and stepping foward he lifted the seat of the throne and displayed the under side of it, which bore the words:

MADE BY THE EAGLE FURNITURE CO.

GRAND RAPIDS, MICHIGAN.

"We make everything John," pursued the stranger, "If there's any other bric-a-brac you're going to need for the coronation, now's the time to place your order!"

"Ha!" hissed the red-coated person in a tone of fury. "I'm hup against 'im once more. Hit's my himplacable hadversary, Hold Stars and Stripes, the Business Detective.   F.O.

San Francisco Examiner, 5 May 1902

Five years earlier the Hearst papers had expressed outrage at the proposal of the United States government for the observance of the coronation of Edward vii. When it was revealed that the administration wished to send a fleet to England and a prominent citizen such as Grover Cleveland to represent it at the coronation, Hearst pointedly asked: "Why should this republic concern itself about the coronation of any king? Are European monarchs given to dispatching fleets and special envoys to our capital when we inaugurate our President?"[4]

To the royalty of only one nation did Hearst give his approval. In 1907 he noted that the death of Oscar ii of Sweden had removed "the most democratic and the most beloved sovereign in Europe. If all kings were of the type of this unassuming and kindly ruler there would not be so much complaint of monarchy." The editorial also maintained that, dealing with his people like an elder brother, the Swedish monarch was "of the type of the ideal king," and advanced the rather curious notion that "doubtless the reason for all these superlative qualities in King Oscar is that his family had not been royal long enough to remove it from the people."[5]

The institution of kingship elsewhere in Europe was reviled as the instrument of oppression, the source of inequality and injustice, of pretensions and snobberies with which the United States and its people should have nothing to do. At one extreme were the fearsome despotisms of Turkey, perpetrating such enormities that the peoples of its oppressed provinces would gladly settle for the worst that the Cubans had ever endured,[6] and of Russia.[7] At the other, alongside the shining example of benign Sweden, was the crown of Norway in the gentle person of Haakon vii, who "rules not unkindly, but still he is a king."[8] In between, at various levels of darkness or enlightenment, were the other monarchies and their representatives, whose doings – births, deaths, marriages, coronations, and scandals – the Hearst press chronicled with an eagerness that belied its scorn for their position and condition. For it is probably true that, though Hearst's dislike of many Europeans and their institutions was genuine, he, like many of his countrymen, also exhibited a grudging admiration, almost a fascination, for things European. Nowhere is this more clearly seen than in his attitude towards the English.

A study of anglophobia in American politics in the last thirty-five years of the nineteenth century has shown that there was, in American society at that time, a "substructure of real sentiment," of resentment against British social customs, structures, manners, and pretensions.[9] Although this resentment was less overt after the turn of the century and not so inclined to show itself in politics or government policies, it remained, revealing itself in small patches and isolated incidents, of which the Hearst press often made the most. Along with this sensivity, however, pro-British feeling in the United States emerged, not merely in the usual protestations of common language and common heritage but as a desire to imitate and identify with the British and particularly with the ruling classes. This was an attitude Hearst lost no opportunity to decry.[10] One suspects, however, that he was not himself immune to the charms of the British.

Never perhaps has this ambivalence been better expressed than in an article written by one of Hearst's former editors in the early nineteen-thirties:

His attitude towards a certain famous jade, Mother England, that is, always seemed to me to be on the whole the standard American attitude. Since we are all properly ashamed of this attitude, naturally we seek a scapegoat to blame for it. And since it is the job of editors to be scapegoats, and since Hearst as an editor is smeared over more territory than any other American, surely he will do as well as another. He should be thanked for betraying in public, in absurd and painstaking detail, an emotion shared by all of us of the old ancestry and tradition. We all hate her and adore. We all thunder that we wouldn't accept a title from a mere king of England for anything on earth, and we'd all love to wake some fine morning and find that we had become Dukes of Buckinglamorganshire overnight.

The article continued with the fantasy that Hearst would emerge from San Simeon every summer and go to England, just dying to be accepted by the aristocracy. When he returned each fall, he would show "a mellowness toward our ancestral isle," but quite soon "he'd be lashing out at England again with redoubled fury, doubtless ashamed of his own temporary defection. Why, I remember once he actually called her 'perfidious Albion,' just like that, in plain print, unsmilingly."[11]

Hearst felt, as many Americans doubtless did, that his country had never quite shaken itself free of the mother country. Great Britain, the world's major imperial and commercial power when Hearst began his career as a newspaperman, seemed to him to be carrying its influence, ideas, and attitudes not only into its own possessions – where they presumably had some place – but into the affairs, internal and external, of the United States, where they clearly had no place. In 1895 an Australian wrote to the *San Francisco Examiner* to enquire why the West Coast of the United States spent so much time fighting the British. To this the *Examiner* replied: "We have no ill-will toward England or any other country. We have the warmest good will toward the English colonies, especially those which seem friendly toward us, such as Australia. But it happens that England is the only country that is continually treading on our toes, and continually forcing us to choose between talking plainly to her and giving up the control of our own affairs."[12]

This was, in many ways, the crux of Hearst's complaint about the British – that they seemed constantly anxious to attach the United States to their side of any dispute, never apparently giving any credence or understanding to the American position, always following their own interests at the expense of others. Thus, when a dispute between Venezuela and Great Britain over the boundary with British Guiana brought the two powers into at least potential conflict in the late 1890s, the Hearst papers greeted the outcome with relief. They maintained that the United States had finally obliged an unwilling British government to consider the United States and the Monroe Doctrine and "to take this country seriously into account in dealing with its own interests on this continent." The editorial also stated that "this is a valuable point gained, for it is a recognition either of the right of the Monroe Doctrine or of the determination and ability of the Americans to enforce it … England's friendship is better than its enmity, and if there are any Americans ready to explain it on the ground of a recognition of our power, rather than as an expression of natural sympathy, they are welcome to the choice."[13] There was little doubt which of these two choices was correct for the Hearst press, however. In the years that followed "the Chief" continued to direct his barbs at the British from time to time. In 1902, in contrast to his later calls for a union of the English-speaking world, he even asked why Rhodes scholarships had been instituted for the United States.[14]

In these and other editorials Hearst poured scorn on the British, consistently belittling them and their rulers and expressing the feeling that Americans who went so far as to live in England and to express admiration for its ways "reflect neither credit nor honor on this country."[15] Only occasionally was a favourable lesson drawn from the experience of Great Britain, and this was usually when Hearst made the distinction – as he was almost always careful to do – between the activities of the rulers of Great Britain and the people they governed.[16]

Alongside his aversion for British kings and aristocrats, Hearst conducted another campaign, for the freedom of the Irish from the oppression of their rulers. His papers usually marked St Patrick's Day with an editorial demanding the end of British rule in Ireland and vilifying the English, who continued to oppress that nation against the demonstrated will of its people. "Ireland," he wrote on that day in 1906, "drained of life blood by emigration, weakened from year to year by oppression that has driven the youngest and strongest away from home, STILL FIGHTS ON FOR LIBERTY, still refuses to admit the right of any race of power to rule in Ireland against the will of Irishmen ... In England ... THE GREAT QUESTION IS THE IRISH QUESTION, AND THE INTELLIGENT ENGLISHMAN KNOWS THAT THAT QUESTION CANNOT BE SETTLED UNTIL IT IS RIGHTED IN FAVOR OF THE IRISH, OF FREEDOM AND JUSTICE."[17] For many years annual editorials like this appeared in the Hearst press, interspersed with others lecturing the English on the iniquity of their ways.[18]

In January 1906, under the headline "English Idiots to Populate Ireland," an editorial expatiated against a plan to populate parts of Ireland with the scrapings of England, with "worthless 'wastrels,' the gin-soaked hopeless criminals and worthless vagabonds of White-chapel."[19] Such a scheme could be implemented because Ireland would be obliged to accept these people, whereas Australia, the erstwhile dumping ground for English riffraff, now refused to do so.

During the First World War, too, Hearst took the opportunity to remind the British that they were fighting for freedom, justice, and democracy and that this meant freedom, justice, and democracy for everybody – even the Irish. In 1916 the Hearst papers took up the cause of Sir Roger Casement, the Irish landowner convicted of running guns to the rebels, demanding that he be freed rather than, as he ultimately was, executed. In an editorial headed "England Should Honor, Not Kill, Casement," the writer noted that "England learned by the loss of the American colonies that she could not treat English colonies with absolute selfishness and injustice and still retain their loyalty," since when she had been more reasonable towards her remaining colonies. But "England can probably never learn that she cannot treat Ireland with brutal selfishness and injustice, even with stupid race hatred and religious prejudice, and expect loyalty there." Maintaining that "this lesson is more important to England than it is to Ireland, because the whole future of the British Empire depends on it," the editorial concluded that any man, like Casement, who was trying to teach the English this lesson should be honoured there – though this was probably a vain hope, for the English "learn like the dull boy at school, only through the application of the rod."[20]

As soon as the United States entered the war in the spring of 1917, Hearst took another, more specific tack with the Irish question. Calculating that America's position as an ally gave her some leverage with Great Britain, he began to insist that one of the features of a peace settlement should be "justice and freedom for Ireland." He continued: "We shall have a great voice in the final settlement of world affairs. That voice will have been won at a great cost," and he demanded that

Americans resolve that the voice speak out loud and clear for universal liberty, "that it shall speak as firmly for the freedom of Ireland as
for the freedom of Belgium."[21] The lives, the fortunes, and the sacred
honour of Americans should be pledged to this cause, a cause the
Hearst papers reminded their readers of from time to time as the war
continued.

But the Irish question was merely one of the sticks with which the
Hearst press chose to beat the British during and after the First World
War. In 1916, reacting angrily to British attempts to impose restrictions on American trade with Europe and in particular to deprive
American companies of their British trade, the Hearst papers, suggesting through the title of an editorial that "We Might Try an
Humble Appeal to Our Masters' Gratitude," noted that the British
government, by forbidding eighty-six American firms to trade with
the United Kingdom and the American Red Cross to send supplies to
Germany and Austria, had "taken occasion to emphasize again its
contempt of American rights and its perfect confidence that our government will do nothing to defend American rights against British
aggression."[22] At this time, too, frequent comments pointed out
the arrogant and dictatorial nature of British press censorship and
the generally scornful manner in which that nation dealt with non-
belligerents.[23]

The war, however, did improve Hearst's view of Anglo-American
relations; when it ended, the Hearst press announced that "War Has
Brought a Better Understanding Between Britons and Americans."
Wartime alliance ensured that the two nations had "come to understand one another better ... we begin to sympathize with each other's
aspirations and ideals; and surely, doing both these, we cannot help
but honor one another ... Today the hands are clasped in friendship."[24] This euphoria did not last. Within a year, responding to a
suggestion from a London newspaper that the United States and
Great Britain might conceivably have enough common interests to
unite, Hearst, under the headline, "British Press Demands Proof that
America Is Part of Empire," demanded: "What shall our America be
henceforth, countrymen – the glory of the world and the mighty mis-
tress of her own destinies, or a subordinate partner of a greedy, insa-
tiable empire, glutted with the conquest of weaker lands and littler
peoples?"[25] The old attitude of mistrust and abuse had quickly returned. An editorial dealing with the steady increase in British trade
with Latin America and headed " 'Hands Across the Sea' and a Knife
Thrust Between the Ribs" reported that the British were pursuing a
predictable policy of more trade with Latin America by decrying
America and American products. There had, of course, been no com-

plaints from the British when their backs had been to the wall and they had received help from two million American fighting men. "It is only since the armistice and more especially since the discovery that America was not keen to underwrite British imperialism that the flaws in our sails loom into killing proportions."[26]

And so it went throughout the interwar period. The brief honeymoon of the last year or so of the First World War and its immediate aftermath was replaced by almost unrelieved suspicion of the British and their designs. True, the carping and outrageous tone of the pre-war editorials in which Hearst and his writers had railed against the British monarchy and all that went with it was no longer present, and the nonsense in some of these earlier pieces was not repeated. But the general attitude remained the same: Great Britain was not to be trusted since she was concerned with her own good, her own interests, and her own advancement and could not be relied upon to understand or accomodate those of the United States.

The single exception to this view was the call for a union of the English-speaking nations that came from the Hearst press in the early thirties. In 1920 an editorial claimed that a real league of nations might be formed from the base of the British Empire. "The glory of the British Empire as a laboratory of experiment for a successful League of Nations in which [all countries] are independent, equal associates, sovereign each with respect to the other and voluntarily associated, would exceed the glory of an empire, very much expanded, which is based upon force."[27] Several years later Hearst translated this idea into a concrete proposal for the development of co-operation among the English-speaking peoples of the world. He was careful to point out that such a suggestion was not in any way contrary to his customary advocacy of avoiding "entangling alliances" and equally careful to note that he excluded such "subject peoples" as India and Egypt, a position he had presumably forgotten by the time he criticized the u.s. government for supporting colonialism after 1945. Thus, the United States, Great Britain, Ireland, Canada, Australia, New Zealand, and South Africa would join together to ensure peace among themselves and, as far as possible, in the rest of the world. "It would be an understanding, an agreement, a compact to prevent the parties to the agreement from making war among themselves, and to protect any one and all of the parties to the agreement from the warlike aggressions of others." The only barrier to the scheme seemed to be the attitude of powers like France, Germany, and Italy – but he felt that they could make no reasonable objections to the proposal, for "the English-speaking peoples could be made the greatest force for peace in the world."[28] To further this idea, Hearst directed his editors, in one of his famous and laconic directives, to "kindly make editorials from time to time in support of these proposals."[29]

Hearst clung to this idea for some years, writing occasional editorials about it. In 1930, in a statement published by British, Canadian, and Australian newspapers, he commented that, although he had "long entertained the hope that a cooperative agreement could be worked out in a practical way between the English-speaking people of the world," he was not then "very hopeful that any such understanding will ever be arrived at" because the "jealousies and antagonisms" that existed were being aggravated rather than eliminated.[30] Part of the blame for this lay with the short-sighted British: "London does not understand as yet the great opportunities of such a cooperative alliance" because "the proximity of Europe shuts out the rest of the world from London's view" and "the war-clouds of Europe settle over London like a black fog, obscuring vision."[31]

Thus, while advocating co-operation among English-speaking peoples, Hearst still played true to form in his attitude to Great Britain. His occasional protests that he bore no ill-will towards the British, his statements that he was not anti-British but pro-American, had little or no effect on the British – the British press in particular believed that such views were merely a rationalization of his bias. After his death only one British paper maintained that the prevalent feeling that he disliked and distrusted the British was exaggerated.[32] Whatever its source, the attitude of the Hearst papers and their owner to the British can hardly have been helpful to the leaders of either country in defining their relations with each other and explaining them to the people to whom they were responsible.

Towards the other major powers of Western Europe, Hearst's attitude was more variable. Early in his career he wrote that the United States had derived much good from its early association with France, "when Lafayette and his men and the money and power of France enabled us to beat the English," and might benefit again from looking at "the great French nation free from class prejudice, free from plutocracy, free from superstition, and always forging ahead."[33] Years later, commenting on a speech that had labelled the French decadent, he came to their defence: "The French nation is about as far from being decadent as anything existing on top of the earth" and anyone who so described it "would simply expose his own pitiful ignorance."[34] When Theodore Roosevelt announced to the French that they were not having enough children, Hearst invoked population control, claiming that "there is more value in a small French family producing one such boy as Pasteur, Hugo or Danton than in all three hundred millions of Asiatics that breed like mice and remain supine under the control of England."[35]

Such feelings seemed to grow out of genuine regard for the French. France was, after all, a republic and therefore, in Hearst's eyes, honourably associated with the United States. However, these feelings did not save the country from criticism. France was no more than a European power, with all the drawbacks of that condition – the tendencies to militarism and conquest that the nations of the Old World constantly evinced, the underhanded and untrustworthy methods of operating by which Europe had lived for so long and which even the example of the United States could not remove. Soon after the First World War, with conflicts again arising in Europe and the Continental nations swiftly reverting to what Hearst saw as their normal condition, he branded France the prime offender. Undertaking a quick survey of French history, he concluded: "The only considerable periods of peace in Europe since modern history began have been periods when France has been too exhausted by war, or too severely defeated in war, to disturb the peace until she had taken time to recuperate her finances and her military power." This conclusion, according to Hearst, revealed "one of the most striking and significant facts of history and is a convincing proof that the real militarist of Europe is France herself."[36]

Finally, there came the incident of 1930, when Hearst was asked to leave France. He believed the reason for this request was twofold: first (and most immediately), his publication two years before of the secret Anglo-French naval treaty, and second, his papers' opposition to American entry into the League of Nations and their advocacy, constant and strong, of full payment of French war debts to the United States.[37] The incident was clearly a storm in a teacup, and Hearst appeared to regard it as such, affecting – in his public statements if not in his private communications – to be considerably amused by the whole affair.[38] Certainly, it caused no noticeable change in his attitude towards France and her affairs.

"Problematical" might best describe Hearst's attitude towards Germany. He was accused before and during both world wars, particularly the first, of being pro-German and, if not of conducting a pro-German campaign before American entry into each war, then at least of regarding the German cause more favourably than most of his fellow countrymen. He was further accused, in the thirties and later, of supporting Hitler and Nazism. For these perceived views he and his papers attracted a great deal of hostility and criticism.[39]

Before the turn of the century he wrote that "the Germans have been among the best friends of the United States. German blood flows in the veins of a large proportion of the inhabitants of this country. The German government has shown this nation a friendship that it has not always found elsewhere. And it is important for the future progress of the world that there should be a closer agreement between Germany and the English-speaking nations, instead of division or war."[40] Hearst seldom departed from this view in the next fifty years, even though he was obliged to recognize the deficiencies of the German government at various times and to acknowledge that cooperation with such people was impossible. He drew, as he almost always did in considerations of European nations, a distinction between peoples and their rulers.

Thus, he frequently criticized the German emperor, Wilhelm II, in the early years of this century when that gentleman crossed the path of the United States or in other ways failed to please "the Chief." A good example is his treatment of the Venezuelan dispute. In 1901 Hearst reacted in typically belligerent fashion to the Kaiser's threats against Venezuela: "The Kaiser generally has his own way – in Germany. Theodore Roosevelt says that the Monroe Doctrine is still doing business in South America and, therefore, Germany must keep her hands off down there. We are inclined to believe that before the Kaiser gets through with the strenuous young hero of San Juan Hill he will know more about the real meaning of *lèse majesté* than he can find out in any German work on the subject."[41] He later wrote that the "plain people of Germany" did not share the anti-American feelings of their Junker masters and that "Germans and Americans in the mass like and respect one another." Thus Americans should not harbour hostile thoughts towards Germans except when the latter did something to deserve it, and then "so long as the Kaiser defers to the Monroe Doctrine there will not be the smallest occasion for our navy officers, or anybody else, to grow hot at the sound of *Die Wacht am Rhein*."[42]

Hearst believed that the fate of the monarchy in Germany would inevitably be the same as the fate of monarchy and aristocracy everywhere. Well might the Junkers be worried by the rise of the Social Democrats in Germany and demand that measures be taken to suppress the party; this betrayed "a perfectly well-founded fear of the rising tide of democracy" when "the rapid growth of Social Democracy in Germany is the most impressive in contemporary European politics."[43] In the future the Kaiser and his acolytes would leave the scene, while the army of which he boasted to the world "will go marching on ... as the nucleus of a greater German people, freed from Emperors, from kicking, cuffing Lieutenants, from rules, now nearly dead, which made the great number of them submissive to the few."[44]

Before the First World War, perhaps believing that what he regarded as an oppressive government in Germany would finally pass
away, Hearst worked on behalf of the German-American Alliance in
its attempts to encourage close relations between the two countries,
and used his editorial pages to further this effort. He considered the
interests of the United States and Germany virtually identical,[45] but
he also espoused the idea that, faced with a growing Oriental threat,
the white races should unite to protect common interests. One of the
best means of doing this was through a German-American alliance.[46]
After the Moroccan crisis of 1911 almost involved Germany in war
with France and Great Britain, a dispute in which the government of
William Howard Taft refused to become involved, Hearst further expressed his admiration and sympathy for the Germans. He wrote that
the United States should sympathize with German attempts "to find
standing room on the planet for their great and growing race," for
"this powerful and prolific German nation is hemmed in on every
side by densely populated military empires," which left "no possibility of peaceful German expansion in Europe." It was therefore "not
because of belligerence of temper in the German government, but because of natural necessity that the foreign policy of that government
has for forty years been directed to the securing of over-sea colonies."[47] For the next forty years, almost unmoved by two world wars
in which the United States and her allies fought Germany, the Hearst
papers maintained this sympathetic attitude towards that nation.

Hearst argued for many years that, apart from trading connections,
the only contact between the United States and Europe should be that
occasioned by necessary (though unfortunate) European interests in
the Western Hemisphere. Over the Venezuelan crisis with Great Britain, and for once almost in concert with Cleveland and Secretary of
State Richard Olney (who, supported by much of the press, pushed
the British hard), Hearst argued for a firm reassertion of the Monroe
Doctrine, maintenance of which, he believed, would preserve and
protect American interests and prevail upon Great Britain to stay out
of America's way. The best course would be to secure the agreement
of the powers to stay out of the Western Hemisphere in return for as-
surances that the United States would stay out of Europe's affairs.
Failing that, America must be constantly on guard to restrict and ultimately limit its involvement there.[48]

Hearst never wanted more to do with Europe than was necessary
for trade because he believed that substantial involvement in European politics would lead to dissipation of American resources and to
defeat and humiliation at the hands of European powers. Despite his

endlessly repeated faith in American ability and virtue, he reverted regularly to the theme of the inadequacy of American representatives when faced with the slippery, experienced, self-interested statesmen of Europe. This point of view sharpened in focus during the interwar period, as – in the view of Hearst and other prescient observers of the European situation – the nations of the Continent moved towards yet another war.

In an interview published in Manchester in the fall of 1934 Hearst argued that "there are apparently only two conditions in Europe. One is a state of war and the other is a state of preparation for the next war ... War is the suicide of civilization but all European nations are victims of this suicidal mania."[49] For publication at home, he wrote that America should never become involved in Europe's problems because European ways were different from those of the United States: "European nations do not speak the language of altruism. They do not understand the meaning of idealism. Professions of high principle are merely camouflage in European diplomacy ... We want no part or counterpart of Europe's despotic governments and no share of Europe's vicious intrigues and destructive wars."[50]

Because Europe conducted its relations through "vicious intrigues," it followed that the innocents from the New World would be hoodwinked into doing whatever the Europeans wished: "The American Government is an utter innocent in the diplomatic field, and the foreign nations know it ... They borrow money of us and do not pay it ... They make agreements and do not keep them ... To use the popular phrase, they are sharpers and we are hicks. We play their shell game and they make fools of us."[51] Referring to attempts to secure U.S. participation in international finance, Hearst asked whether, "twice betrayed," the country should "go on and on, to the greater humiliation of the United States and the greater glory of a foreign power?"[52] The answer was an unequivocal no; the European powers must not be encouraged to believe that what Hearst had termed the "European Association of 'Gimmes'" would always have its way with "our amateur statesmen." Ceaselessly, he argued for an end to all involvements with "European confidence men and holdup men."[53]

Such arguments were common in the Hearst papers in the interwar period, but nowhere were they made more strongly, consistently, and distrustfully than over the question of war debts that plagued American relations with Europe during these years. Soon after the war, when the United States was faced with requests by the major European powers for loans and by Germany for help in paying reparations, Hearst set the tone his papers adopted for two decades:

Let the governments of Europe rescue the peoples of Europe from the quagmire into which they have led those peoples ... It is hard medicine, bitter medicine, sorrowful medicine. But if it exorcises alike the abominable diplomacy and the idiotic obedience to the masters of the abominable diplomacy which has soaked Europe in blood and made its soil foul with the bones and blood of millions upon millions of poor human beings, then it is well that the medicine should take its harsh but healing course. We have no billions to pay Germany's war debts, no billions to lend to England and France, no billions to part with to anybody while we ourselves are staggering under the colossal debt piled upon our own shoulders by a wicked and abominable war, planned and brought on by less than a dozen men plotting in London, Paris, Rome, St Petersburg, Berlin and Vienna. We have had enough of foreign wars and their cost. [54]

The theme, from the First World War to the Second, was quite simple: pay! The reputation of powers often rose and fell in the Hearst press according to their real or apparent intention to pay. In 1923 Great Britain was described as following a "decent, honorable course towards this country," in contrast to France, which was trying to avoid payment.[55] The British, it seemed, were only perfidious in some things.[56] But this view altered quickly as Britain's intention to pay her debts waned. By 1926 Hearst was vilifying Winston Churchill and the British for having tried to place the blame for Europe's massive debt on the United States, whereas everybody knew that it was "the direct result of Europe's insanity in destroying her wealth by war." This led him to conclude that "we have helped these ungrateful nations until they are becoming dependents, almost parasites, upon us." This was too much, and they must now learn to help themselves.[57]

Only one European nation, Finland, emerged with credit from the long discussion of European war debts. Following the Russian invasion of that country in 1939, Hearst, in an editorial headed "Let Stalin Keep His Blood Stained Hands Off Finland," maintained that it was dangerous to toy with American sentiment thus: "Finland is the most upright and honest nation in Europe ... the one nation that has recently paid its duly contracted debts to us ... [and] the one nation whose word of honor is worth a centime or a farthing."[58] Hearst's admiration for the Finns, for their honesty and their "noble struggle for liberty," did not, however, persuade him to advocate abandoning one of his most strongly held principles by advising u.s. intervention to help them against the Russian onslaught. This was to be left to the powers of Western Europe, who by helping Finland would in fact be helping themselves.[59]

To Hearst, the failure of these nations to intervene in such causes was a logical extension of their selfish attitude to other problems. He returned repeatedly to the debt question during the twenties and thirties as the chances of payment receded and the United States made, or tried to make, agreements with the European powers. His scorn was almost equally divided between the powers that were, he felt, taking advantage of the United States and the governments that allowed themselves to be thus duped. Asked what he thought about Great Britain's suggestion that debts should be cancelled to help stabilize world trade, Hearst replied that he had "nothing to say except that this is a good example of an attempt of Great Britain and other foreign countries to use the United States to their own advantage and to the disadvantage of the United States." They expected to persuade the United States to give all and get nothing in return, and this "makes clear to the average American why we should keep our country free from all political and financial entanglements with foreign nations."[60]

Similarly, he denounced the American government for acceding to European requests for modification or abandonment of debts to the United States, putting the powers and the government side by side as agents or dupes of international bankers and other practitioners of evil. In an article published in two major British newspapers in the summer of 1931, Hearst condemned, first, the latest American proposal of a year's moratorium on debt payments, as "a plan to plunder the American people in the interests of foreign nations for which most of these international bankers are financial agents"; second, President Hoover, for making the proposal; and third, France, as the "war menace of the world, defaulting on her debts, and using money so misappropriated for building up a gigantic war machine for the subjugation of Europe."[61] This campaign was in opposition to a government trying to restore relations with Europe, but this did not, of course, deter Hearst.[62] Later in the year he began a concentrated campaign against the cancellation of war debts in general and the Hoover moratorium in particular. In addition to signed and unsigned editorials of his own, he arranged for influential figures like Bainbridge Colby (briefly Woodrow Wilson's secretary of state) and Senator Hiram Johnson of California, sponsor of the 1934 Debt Default Act, which forbade loans to governments in default to the United States, to write and broadcast against the Hoover moratorium and the question of debt cancellation.[63] Hearst turned the full force of his armory against the president for his consistent willingness to deal with the debtor nations. In October 1931 an editorial discussed Hoover's statement on the moratorium under the headline, "Weasel Words Hint

Debt Cancellation," and from this point to the end of his term of office, Hoover was the butt of a stream of editorials on the debt question.[64]

Under Hoover's successor, Franklin Delano Roosevelt, Hearst continued the same line of argument, advocating trade sanctions of various kinds against defaulting nations. For example, in November 1933, when France, in an effort to collect debts from Brazil, imposed heavy tariffs on certain Brazilian imports, he pointed out that his own country could well learn from this.[65] A little later, in January 1934, in one of the appeals to American history that frequently appeared in the Hearst papers, he wrote – under the headline, "Andrew Jackson Knew How to Deal With Defaulter France" – that Jackson's message to Congress in 1834 had begun a successful attempt to recover debts owing to the United States from France and that "perhaps we have another Andrew Jackson in the White House" who would see that "the just claims of America against defaulter France will be enforced."[66] Hearst pressed this argument unsuccessfully until war broke out again in Europe and Europe again looked to the United States for help.

4 Hearst and the Yellow Peril

Between the two world wars William Randolph Hearst published a pamphlet that brought together some of his earlier statements on American foreign relations and international affairs. In it he argued that the United States, having become unnecessarily involved in one European war and having spent thereon enormous amounts of blood and treasure, should never be drawn into another – which, after the Versailles settlement, he believed to be inevitable. However, it was unimportant which nations of Europe were dominant, on the Continent or elsewhere: what was important was that, wherever government was in question, it should be "good, sound, stable, democratic and European."

This consideration led to a more important one, "the possibility of that domination being Asiatic." Hearst then summarized his view of the Asian problem:

The only real question is the race question. The only vital question is how long will Asia, with twice the population of Europe and rapidly developing European perfection in slaughter, through European war methods which they have been taught, remain the subject power in the world? How long after they have been sufficiently drilled and armed and united will they refrain from becoming the dominant power in the world? That question really means something. It means everything to our Occidental standards of living, to our standards of morals, to our methods of government, to our racial and national and individual freedom, to our spiritual ideals, to our material comforts, to our happiness and to our very existence.[1]

In Hearst's conception of the world the United States, protagonist of freedom, justice, and democracy, was beset by enemies in her struggle not merely to bring these advantages to the world but even to retain them at home. Later, the menace of Communism became for him the overriding threat to the United States and to the world, before which all other dangers became secondary.[2] His hostility to Communism, however, came at least in part from suspicions about the Oriental element in Russia, suspicions felt by many other Americans, so that aversion to a political creed and a racial stereotype fed off each other.[3] Thus, for most of his career the "yellow peril," a term that first appeared in Germany in the 1890s during a scare about the expansion of the East Asian races, ranked with the "red menace" as a threat to all that Hearst held most precious. It was not that he regarded the "yellow races" as unrelievedly vicious and threatening: his attitude to them often appeared similar to his view of the European powers, whose peoples were oppressed and made threatening by obscurantist governments.[4] It was not even that he regarded the Chinese and the Japanese as inferior: one of their most frightening attributes was that they appeared to be precisely the reverse. The problem was that there were so many of them, that they had been so long oppressed and backward, isolated and disunited. Hearst could not believe that, once these disadvantages were overcome, as was bound to occur with the opening of China and Japan and the introduction of Western ways and technologies, the "yellow races" would not quickly become assertive, adventurous, and, ultimately, dominant in the world. This state of affairs he anticipated with horror.

Around the turn of the century the issue of Oriental immigration to the United States was kept constantly in view by Washington and by the western states. It also provided a fruitful subject for the *Examiner*. In Hawaii, where Japanese immigrants made up almost a quarter of the population by the mid-1890s, Hearst and many others found a clear example of the dangers of allowing unfettered Japanese entry. In 1895 the *Examiner* published an editorial attacking an article in the *New York Evening Post*, which had ridiculed the fears of many people on the West Coast that Japanese immigration might become as serious a problem as Chinese immigration. The *Examiner* claimed that such feelings showed little imagination and forethought on the part of the *Post*, for although the number of Japanese immigrants was still small, that situation might well change and regulation become necessary. Inevitably this would occur because "the Pacific Coast of the United States would be inhabited by just such an unmanageable conglomeration of races as makes Hawaii, in the opinion of the *Post*, unfit to be annexed, even as a Territory."[5]

At this point, however, Hearst was not inclined to take the Hawaiian question very seriously and did not join the cry for annexation that was included in the Republican platform in 1896 and became government policy with McKinley's accession to office in March 1897. In an editorial published soon after the one quoted above the *Examiner* adopted a mocking tone in reference to the revolution in Hawaii and the abdication of Queen Liliuokalani, calling it a "burlesque of a revolution" and a "harmless affair whose proper punishment would be a $5 fine or five days in jail on poi and water."[6] None the less, almost three years later the Hearst press began to reconsider the Hawaiian situation, claiming that "the commercial and military advantages of Hawaii have won its case before Congress and the people of this country."[7] The editorial maintained that if present conditions in the islands could be preserved, many might consider annexation inadvisable. But if this seemed impossible, the United States was obliged to guarantee the islands' integrity. Soon, in what must be regarded as a classic statement of the duty of superior races to lesser breeds, the *Examiner*, in an editorial headed "THE MORAL ASPECT OF ANNEXATION," declared for annexation, explaining that "the superiority of Western civilization and Western government is established by the progress that has been achieved under its direction ... Under such government, and under it alone, can the lands inhabited by inferior races be brought to the highest degree of development ... The annexation of the islands is a duty that is the highest of all duties – a duty owed in the name of humanity."[8]

Hearst's change of heart occurred because of the growing danger of Japanese expansion in the Pacific. America's duty to humanity was allied to her duty to herself, and the establishment of the Hawaiian islands as an American outpost in the Pacific against Japanese expansion became a vital question to the Hearst papers. Earlier, Hearst had written of aggressive Japanese expansion and of the equally aggressive nature of the large numbers of Japanese living and arriving in Hawaii.[9] This was adduced as a powerful reason for annexing the islands, which occurred in August 1898. But Hearst's concern over the Japanese issue did not diminish. As the years went by, he wrote repeatedly of the need to fortify the islands physically and also legally, by reducing Japanese immigration and, if possible, the actual Japanese population of the islands – largely the result of the greed and lack of foresight of major sugar interests, which had long encouraged the entry of Japanese labourers.[10]

The larger problem, however, was that of Oriental immigration to the United States. As a matter of general policy Hearst had consistently argued that immigration should be at least highly selective. In

1896, for example, he went so far as to advocate "a total prohibition of immigration for five years," which was at least the time needed "to absorb in production work the unemployed now with us."[11] In the twenties he attacked an immigration bill before Congress as "the worst and silliest measure ever devised" and argued instead for exclusion only of "unasssimilable races, and unassimilable people, generally."[12] The Hoover administration tried unsuccessfully to enlist Hearst's help in 1930, when it proposed new immigration regulations; [13] a few years later Hearst expressed the hope that the country would never close its doors against immigrants whose "courage and idealism and progressivism" had "marked them for persecution" under reactionary governments and from among whom had come "some of our most devoted and most valuable citizens." [14]

While arguing for restricted immigration in general, it was on the question of Oriental immigration that the Hearst papers concentrated their attention. This was, of course, particularly true on the West Coast, where the "problem" was most acute. In the last years of the nineteenth century the Hearst papers directed their wrath against all who contemplated the relaxation of restrictions on Oriental immigration. Late in 1897 a strongly worded editorial opposed a proposal, recently introduced into the House of Representatives, to permit naturalization of Americanized Chinese. It proclaimed: "The experience of the American people teaches them that any such letting down of the bars against the Chinese as this measure contemplates means nothing less than the opening of this country to the naturalization of all the Chinese who are here and of all who under the favoring Providence of complaisant or stupid American officials, and conniving Canadian officials, are destined to come here."[15]

By 1900 Hearst saw Japanese immigration, previously regarded as only a potential threat, as a real and growing problem. The *Examiner* called upon the federal government to investigate the situation, with a view to imposing restrictions similar to those controlling Chinese entry. In an April editorial the newspaper laid out its objections to the Japanese, which, it said, were the same as those against the Chinese: "The Japs can live on wages that will not support the white laborer. In the struggle for existence they can beat us. That is good reason for keeping them out. Our civilization is good enough for us, and we like our country. We will not be driven from one or the other, by peaceful competition or armed force, while we have the power by law or arms to maintain our place."[16]

Later the same year Hearst broadened his view of the threat posed by Oriental immigration. Hitherto he had described it as a threat to the American, and particularly the Californian, labourer. Now, as the expiration of the Chinese Exclusion Act of 1892 came closer, he declared that "it is not alone the laborers that are threatened by the Chinese influx. The Chinese are able to compete with white employers and white merchants as well as white laborers."[17] In this editorial, headed "Keep Up the Dikes Against the Yellow Flood," and others during the next two years, Hearst campaigned vigorously for renewal of the exclusion bill and against those who opposed renewal, "the most powerful lobby that ever disgraced the national capitol."[18] He raised the spectre of the Chinese allied to evil forces in American life. "The Chinese," the *Examiner* stated, "works hard, asks for little money, eats rice, doesn't want to vote, and keeps for a thousand years on the same plane. He is satisfied merely to be alive. He is even fairly well satisfied when someone of his superiors decides to cut off his head." Such a threat to the American working man was doubly dangerous because "your Chinese gentleman is the kind of workman that the American trusts would like to employ. One or two million Chinese coolies in the United States would give the trusts just the hold they want over labor unions and wages."[19]

Even after the renewal of the exclusion bill in 1902, the campaign continued. The question of Oriental immigration required constant vigilance to overcome the devious ways of the Chinese and the foolishness of those who failed to see the danger of allowing them unrestricted entry. In 1904 the *Los Angeles Examiner* noted that the Chinese, wherever they went, failed to assimilate themselves into the society around them. A Chinese man remained "at best ... an industrious barbarian, [whose] very industry renders him dangerous, since he can exist on next to nothing." Thus, "economically, ... as well as morally and socially, the Chinaman is a pest," and "this nation never did a more judicious act than when in self-defence it put up the bars against the Chinese."[20]

The Hearst papers never varied in their hostility to any change in the policy of Chinese exclusion and in their view of the danger to the United States presented by any relaxation of the official attitude towards the Chinese. They attacked a proposal to use Chinese labour to dig the Panama Canal on the grounds that, since American taxpayers were paying for the canal, the money and benefits should go to American merchants and labourers and that, since the canal area was American territory, the Chinese should be forbidden entry for the same reasons they were forbidden to enter the West Coast of the United States proper.[21] They opposed a suggestion that Chinese should be allowed to intermarry with white Americans because "we think the American race, made up of an assortment of European races of types admirably chosen, because each one was brought over here by enterprise and courage, is far superior to the Chinese race."[22] Thus, if Chinese men had to stay in the United States, they should import Chinese women to marry. Theodore Roosevelt, by suggesting that some revisions might be made to the exclusion act, brought down on himself the strictures of the Hearst papers, which charged him with breaking the law and threatening the country with another, unnecessary and avoidable, race problem.[23] He had raised the spectre of illegal Chinese immigration on a large scale, either directly or through Mexico.[24] On the issue of Chinese immigration Hearst's attitude remained firm, as it was on immigration in general.[25]

Soon, however, the question of Japanese exclusion assumed equal importance. In October 1906 the San Francisco school board segregated almost one hundred Japanese children in a separate school, a move that was merely the latest in a series of anti-Japanese incidents. In February 1907 the mayor of San Francisco, the governor of California, and the president of the United States moved to secure the defeat of the school board. The *Examiner*, however, proclaimed that "Californians do not want their growing daughters to be intimate in daily school contact with Japanese young men. Is that remarkable? Would YOU like your daughter to be subjected to this contact? And if you objected how would you enjoy being denounced as a blackguard on fire with degraded race hatreds?" There followed all the familiar arguments against Oriental immigration, against allowing the admission of "a people who cannot be made into Americans nor their children after them." The conclusion was that "common sense and patriotism are with the reviled Californians," a view that seemed to coincide with that of at least a substantial minority of Californians, who continued to support severe restriction on Oriental immigration.[26]

The local, state, and national governments did not, however, see it quite that way. As the question remained on the front pages during the following years, they came under attack as insensitive and bullying autocrats too foolish to see the best course for the state. In 1909 the *Examiner* noted, on its front page, that "the work of the President's big stick and the Governor's club was apparent when men who originally proclaimed themselves anti-Japanese, dropped away from the bill when the test came." An editorial on the same day, headed "PRESIDENT ONLY MAKES JAPANESE ISSUE WORSE," noted that "the course of Mr Roosevelt is better calculated to provoke than avert what he professes to fear" and responded to the threat of war with Japan by saying that "if Japan wants war because Americans run America upon American lines, then war she shall surely have. Better fight forty Japanese wars than conduct the business of a State upon undigested orders from Washington or the affairs of the nation along plans made in Tokyo."[27]

At this point the connection that clearly existed in Hearst's mind between Japanese expansionism and emigration began to come into sharper focus. He saw – though not perhaps always explicitly – the movement of Japanese to Hawaii and the United States and the expansionism of Japanese governments as part of the same problem. With the comment just quoted he began to make this connection clearer to his readers. America should not be taken in by politicians who told them that the threat from across the Pacific was not serious.

Along with his virulent opposition to the president on the Japanese school question, Hearst now began criticizing his policy towards Japan, particularly the question of allowing Japanese immigration. "Peace with Japan ... is not to be had by the President's policy of truckling and turning pale at the thought of her strength, but by giving her plainly to understand NOW that her coolies will not be received, and that California, in common with every other American state, is sovereign in state concerns."[28] Hearst maintained this position long after Roosevelt had effectively passed from the scene. In 1919, for example, when the question of Japanese exclusion arose again, the *Examiner* stated its position unequivocally that "courteously, consistently, and as firmly as the necessities of the occasion demand, we shall adopt a policy of self-protection. The Japanese is not wanted as a laborer in the United States. On that platform, without bargain or compromise, we must stand."[29] And that, on the question of Oriental immigration, was that.

It would be unjust, however, to leave the impression that Hearst's attitude towards Oriental immigrants was one of unrelieved opposition or that his views of the problem were unusual. He argued for fair treatment of those Oriental immigrants who had been admitted. Reiterating that "there is no possible doubt as to California's attitude toward unchecked Asian immigration," he also maintained that "at the same time we must act with fairness and justice towards the Asiatics who come here under our regulations. It would be the part of a bully to annoy and insult Chinese who land here just because China is not in a position to resent by force, annoyances and insults offered to her citizens."[30] Both justice and material interest dictated that unnecessary hardships not be inflicted on the resident Chinese.

Nor should it be imagined that, in his campaign against Oriental immigration, Hearst was out of line with major sections of American opinion in the early years of this century. As with many of his campaigns, Hearst's continual and often extreme references to the yellow peril drew criticism from many quarters,[31] but there was still widespread support for Oriental exclusion. As so often happened, Hearst went his own way, regardless of criticism, apparently convinced of his own rectitude and stating his views in the loud and forthright way that his readers and critics had come to expect. What Hearst did was to crystallize and state directly and unabashedly the views and prejudices that many others held and expressed more circumspectly.

His attitude towards the Oriental reflected that of his father, Senator George Hearst, who like many of his contemporaries maintained that the Chinese did white California much harm.[32] They were industrious and frugal, making and saving a great deal of money, most of which went back to China. They had been useful as labourers, particularly on the railroads, but this usefulness had passed and further immigration ought to be prohibited, for they were unlikely to be assimilated into the white population, thus forming a separate and homogeneous group out of sympathy with a majority of the people of the state. Such a situation could only produce continual strife. This attitude, commonly held in the California of Hearst's father's day and his own, selected the more beneficent of what may be seen as two strands of American nativism: first, a xenophobic dislike of foreigners, especially those who looked or talked different from white, English-speaking Americans; and second, a thoughtful concern that the nation might not be successful in absorbing groups that were racially and culturally different from the majority. Hearst – and many of his fellow Progressives – were expressing this latter concern.[33]

Despite attempts by the Roosevelt and Taft administrations to restore and maintain friendly relations with Japan, American governments in the early years of the twentieth century perceived the existence of a Japanese threat they felt they could not ignore.[34] After the Russo-Japanese War the administration moved to safeguard American interests in the Far East against Japanese encroachment.[35] Though the aggressive activities of such officials as Willard Straight, American consul-general at Mukden (Shenyang) in Manchuria up to June 1909, went beyond the cautious approach of Roosevelt and Root, even these two probably felt the need to support and consolidate American interests in the Pacific. When Roosevelt was succeeded by William Howard Taft, the policy of the United States became more explicitly supportive of American commercial expansion in the Far East, particularly in China, and opposed to the extension of Japanese influence in that area.[36]

Hearst had long advocated this position. In his early years, however, he had looked almost with favour on Japanese growth in the East, apparently feeling that Asia had been exploited by Europeans for long enough and should be left alone. Commenting in April 1895 on a Japanese scheme to form an alliance with China, he noted the strength that a combination of "Chinese numbers and resources with Japanese science, official integrity and organizing skill" would give; doubtless it would "put an end to Christian larceny and leave Asia free to develop in her own way."[37] In the following month he regretted that the French and Russians were pressuring Japan, that "plucky Japan must be involved in the complications of European politics," and that "the policy of the United States does not permit us to offer more than moral support to Japan." This could not be, however, because "the price we pay for complete supremacy in the New World is abstention from forcible interference in the affairs of the Old."[38]

By the end of the century, however, this tone of mild approval and support became one of opposition, increasing and growing more strident as time went on. Perhaps the only surprising thing about Hearst's "yellow peril" campaign in the first forty years of this century is that, on 8 December 1941, there appeared no editorial headed "What Did We Tell You?" The expansion of American interests in the Pacific and the growing feeling of Hearst and others that the Western ocean represented a fruitful field for future American commerce produced growing concern about Pacific affairs and Japan's role in them. In 1899 the *Examiner* responded delightedly to a statement from Lord Charles Beresford, who had expressed his pleasure that "America is recognizing that the Pacific Ocean is her ocean." Hearst felt this to be an apt description: "The Pacific Ocean is our ocean, and the fruits of its commerce belong to us. The United States are the greatest power that fronts on the greatest of oceans, and if they seize the advantages of their opportunities, THERE IS NO POWER THAT CAN TAKE FROM THEM THE COMMAND OF THAT SEA." He then discussed the developing powers in the Pacific region and allowed that they had great contributions to make as they developed. But the editorial finally returned to its opening theme: "The primacy among all these lands belongs to the United States. This country is first in wealth, first in energy, first in capacity … The Pacific Ocean is our ocean. We will take our share in its commerce and government."[39]

Alongside this belligerent-sounding attitude towards the affairs of the East, however, Hearst preserved his European policy of advising that America keep hands off – at least to the extent of fighting. In the spring of 1900, after he wrote the editorial just quoted, he noted that its recently achieved possession of the Philippines put the United States in a favourable position to expand the China trade but that, equally clearly, European machinations seemed likely to prevent this. The favourable treaties between the United States and China would be violated if the European powers obtained special privileges, and the nation would obviously be justified in protesting against this. The only question was whether it would pay to get into such quarrels; he concluded that "the United States neither can [n]or will fight Europe in order to get these advantages. Whatever is got must be had by peaceful diplomatic negotiation."[40] If this could be achieved, American "enterprise and skill will give them their fair share of the trade." This view led him, the following year, to applaud the rather hollow conclusion of negotiations over access to the China trade. This he hailed as "an important success" and an excellent example of the value of temporary alliances in which nations bound themselves to achieve limited goals – in this case, trading concessions in China – but not to united action in a vague future. "The United States wish to be on friendly footing with all nations, but our friends may as well understand that the nation is playing its own hand and will be guided solely by what it considers best for its own interests."[41]

In line with this view, the Hearst papers supported limited intervention in China as, in June 1900, the Boxer rising brought the imprisonment of the American legation (as well as other foreign legations) in Beijing. "The Chief" recognized that it was "war – bloody, desperate war – that confronts us in China," that it was "no affair of chasing Filipino sprinters through a jungle or potting a few dozen half-starved Spaniards on Kettle Hill" but a "death struggle with innumerable murderous fanatics, who have learned how to stand up and fight, and who may yet prove themselves a match for the entire civilized world."[42] Half measures were not enough to deal with the situation, and American troops must be allowed to protect American property in China.[43] No more than this was permissible, however, for Chinese independence must be maintained. In this Hearst was in accord with the McKinley administration.

The Russo-Japanese War brought the phenomenon of the yellow peril clearly into focus for Hearst and his readers. In the autumn of 1904 an editorial headed "Is There a Yellow Peril?" discussed the recent advances of the Japanese and the possibility of alliance with the Chinese. "Fighting harder, eating less, caring nothing for death, indifferent to fatigue and danger those brown men and their philosophic, fatalistic Chinese cousins might give us earnest thinking and trouble very suddenly. Perhaps we ought to think seriously about their possibilities, before the actual time of trouble shall come."[44] When the Treaty of Portsmouth, which, partly through the president's mediation, ended the war, was signed in 1905, Hearst believed that the Japanese, who had gained "the respect and admiration of the civilized world" by their efforts, were nevertheless disappointed with the treaty. He further suspected that, partly because of Roosevelt's insistence on the terms of the treaty, hostility growing from this disappointment might be directed against the United States.[45]

From this time on the Hearst papers discussed the yellow peril as a substantial and growing threat to the United States – and ultimately to white civilization – that the nation could not afford to ignore. Early in 1906 Hearst wrote that "the awakening of the East is likely to prove a tragedy for the United States." Japan had been opened to civilization and in half a century had almost caught up with America; the same was about to happen to China. "What will happen," he asked, "if the Japanese, being of kindred race to the Chinese, take charge of the awakened China, as they are now taking charge of Korea, and make it a grand industrial nation with tremendous military and naval power?" Concluding that "the Asiatic peril was never more real than to-day," he commented, in the wounded tone he customarily employed in such situations: "It is curious that the nation most threatened is the one which has done the most to bring Japan to its present point of development, and which in China has scrupulously observed every principle of international honor, neither seeking to seize territory nor joining in any international piratical expeditions."[46]

The Japanese now began what the Hearst press saw as a concerted effort to gain commercial and then physical control of the Pacific, and the press lost no chance to point out their iniquities to readers. In May 1906 it noted that "the little yellow men" were trying to buy American merchant ships for use in the Pacific.[47] In August a front-page article quoted Captain Richmond P. Hobson, a Spanish War hero and congressman whom Hearst seems to have employed to lend authenticity to warnings of this kind, as believing that "Japan is the power in the Orient that the United States must reckon with," for "the Japanese have taken up the cry of Asia for the Asiatics and are now drilling the Chinese in warlike methods."[48] Concluding that "the commerce of the world of the future is to be controlled by the power that controls the Pacific," Hobson made a strong call for American attention to the economic, military, and strategic problems of the Pacific – particularly those relating to the adequate defence of the Philippines and Hawaii. A November story, headed "JAPAN GETTING READY TO WHIP THE UNITED STATES," quoted "absolutely reliable" figures of the Japanese build-up in her army and navy and Japanese officers as saying that there was "not the slightest doubt that Japan's next victories were to be won in and around the Philippines."[49] In December the press noted the growing concern in government circles about the danger from Japan,[50] remarked on the Japanese threat to Hawaii,[51] and bemoaned the president's unfortunate lack of concern about the little brown men.[52]

Largely because of the Russo-Japanese War, Hearst now regarded the Japanese as a major military power. "It is idle," he wrote, "longer to regard Japan as a Lilliputian land ... in the path of her destiny lies Manchuria, a fertile and coveted domain with an area of 35,000 square miles. From every point of view Japan occupies a leading place among the fighting powers."[53] Notwithstanding this, however, Hearst believed that the United States was ultimately the only power against whom Japanese aggression could be directed. He thus welcomed the occasional shows of strength that the Roosevelt administration mounted in the Pacific. For example, Roosevelt, in an attempt to resolve the crisis brought on by worsening Japanese-American relations resulting from continuing problems in California, sent the American battle fleet on a Pacific cruise, beginning in December 1907. Hearst noted with approval – but scarcely surprise – that "the battleships in the Pacific have instantly softened the attitude of the Japanese Government toward our own, but enough has been learned on these earlier interchanges to make absolutely plain the racial and commercial animus which makes it impossible for America to trust Japan in the Pacific or to let down a single bar in that splendid naval preparedness which is at once our guarantee of peace and our protection in case of war." It was incumbent on the American government to continue such protection and to let the Japanese know that the United States was determined to defend her interests. This, he hoped, would be enough to preserve the peace in the Pacific. The Japanese, "badly spoiled and unduly puffed up by the thoughtless and almost maudlin praise of other nations," were nevertheless "discreet enough to know that behind that American battle fleet in the Pacific stands not only the valor of an unconquerable republic, but the riches of a nation whose almost inconceivable resources would scarcely be touched when her own depleted war chest was utterly exhausted."[54] Both the president and other American newspapers expressed similar sentiments.

During and after the First World War, as he felt the Oriental menace becoming stronger, Hearst returned to his theme of the yellow peril. The real enemy was not Germany or Russia, he proclaimed, but the Eastern races: "All the world is threatened by the advancing empire of Japan." If this threat became translated into successful action, it would mean an end to the white man's civilization, for "in the yellow man's scheme of things independence is not a merit; equality is not a benefit; morality is not a virtue, humanity is a weakness and Socialism a madness."[55] The result would be the substitution of despotism for republicanism and tyranny for democracy. This was the one great menace against which the white races had to guard themselves, and they must ensure that their own quarrels did not weaken them and lead them to ignore the real enemy.[56]

This campaign continued. On successive days in May 1919 the *Examiner* published editorials headed "How Japan Is Spreading Out Upon the Mainland of Asia" and "Constant Preparedness Is America's Only Guarantee Against Japanese Danger."[57] Three years later the Japanese government was characterized as "an unscrupulous, treacherous, faithless and cruel autocracy and militarism, working day and night to secure domination of all Asia, and looking forward to the conquest and subjugation of the White race by the Yellow race."[58] But Hearst's worst scorn was reserved for the short-sightedness of his own government in such matters as the Washington Naval Conference of 1921–22. The Five Power Treaty, signed in early February 1922, provided for a ten-year holiday in capital ship construction, for scrapping some British, American, and Japanese ships, for size limits on capital ships, cruisers, and aircraft carriers and their armaments, and for a ratio of 5:5:3 in capital ships and aircraft carriers for the United Kingdom, the United States, and Japan. In a signed editorial Hearst noted that the United States, "the one first-class Power of the world, in wealth, in potential strength, in strategic position and condition," had been changed into a second-class power by accepting a position subordinate to the United Kingdom and Japan. This was not, however, the worst feature of the agreement. Hearst thundered that "Japan, by the recognition formally accorded it in this Conference, has been made the dominant nation among the yellow nations of the world, the militaristic leader of a thousand million racial enemies of the white peoples." He concluded that "not only the people of the United States but the peoples of Europe, of the white race throughout the world, will pay dearly for this act of criminal folly in times to come."[59]

Hearst's view of the Japanese, and to a lesser extent the Chinese, was quite unequivocal. He never maintained, as he did about the British, that he entertained the "friendliest feelings" towards Japan – though, as the thirties advanced and he saw the Japanese threat of which he had spoken for so long taking shape, he did moderate his tone, holding that there was no reason for enmity between Japan and the United States and pleading, belatedly, for a more moderate policy towards Japan.[60] Events later proved him right about the Japanese threat to the United States, but Hearst himself contributed to the decline of Japanese-American relations in the twentieth century. At the time of the San Francisco school crisis Theodore Roosevelt had expressed anxiety about the effect of California hysteria on these relations. At the same time Elihu Root stated publicly his hope that extreme expressions of anti-Japanese views would not damage the friendship between the two nations.[61] The pleas of the late thirties for reason and caution in dealing with the Japanese came too late to erase the impression, doubtless alive in Japanese minds as well as American, of William Randolph Hearst as the foremost exponent of anti-Japanese sentiment in the United States. In any case, by the time the threat of Japan was transformed into actual conflict, another force was replacing the Japanese in Hearst's mind as the greatest menace to the tranquillity of the United States.

5 Hearst, the Czar, and the Bolsheviks

In July 1902 a Hearst editorial commented that the government of Czar Nicholas II "should be made to understand that while it refuses human rights to human beings it is looked upon as a pirate among nations." Warming to this theme, the editorial continued that Russia "should be made to feel that no nation wants it for a friend. Especially should this be so in America. As well sympathize and make treaties with a cannibal chief in the South Seas as with a Russian that kills liberty. The cannibal chief simply eats a few men ... The Russian government destroys men's minds – which is worse than destroying their bodies. It typifies the most hideous social organization, a union of church and State – the State based on tyranny; the church based on idolatrous superstition, and manhood degraded equally by both."[1] During more than sixty years in which Hearst commented on Russian affairs, nothing (with a few short-lived exceptions) changed beyond the characters, the words, and some of the rhetoric. The charges against the Russian government, the objections to its conduct, were virtually the same.

In the late nineteenth and early twentieth centuries the government of Russia was ranked alongside that of Turkey as the most oppressive, barbarous, and corrupt in Europe. As the Hearst papers had cried for action to stop the Armenian massacres and prevent their recurrence, so they called for American government action when similar atrocities occurred in Russia. In 1903, after the massacre of the Jews at Kishinef promoted by Minister of the Interior Vyacheslav Plehve, the *Examiner* proclaimed that "the American public has a right to cry out against the persecution of the Jews in Russia and it will be false to its spirit and duty if it shall not do so."[2] Later the same year Hearst pointed out the anomaly in the proposal that Russia be asked to join in European intervention against Turkish actions in Macedonia. "How can Russia," he queried, "be asked to join in intervention for the prevention of further massacre and outrage in Macedonia? How can she be expected to feel horror at the revolting crimes which continue to shock Christendom?" These questions were firmly answered by saying that "Russia equals Turkey in her barbarities ... The atrocities reported from Gomel parallel those of Kishineff [sic] ... Russia, notwithstanding that she is received as a member of the family of civilized powers, is still a barbarous nation, true sister of Turkey."[3]

The Hearst papers, seeing that this barbarism was not directed only against the Jews, regarded the Russian government as uniformly oppressive. Perhaps the most succinct statement of their view of the Russian government appeared in the editorial headline of early 1904: "They Sing 'God Save the Czar' – But God Help the People."[4] With Russia as with most European powers, Hearst drew a clear distinction between the government and the people. In the summer of 1904, discussing the Russo-Japanese War, in which Roosevelt sympathized though did not side with Japan, he noted that "the war between Russia and Japan is merely a war of a class in Russia against the whole nation of Japan ... The Russians, as a people, have little to do with the war; they were not consulted. If they had had their way, there is no doubt that the war would never have begun. They did not GO to war; they were DRIVEN to war." It is at this point that the phrase "red peril" entered the Hearstian vocabulary. The Russian government, "a corrupt organization of autocrats who rule the Czar himself," knowing that the people opposed their war, sent recruits to the front and kept their best troops at home because they were afraid of revolt. The government was secretly executing at night hundreds of agitators who demanded just government, but it was still afraid of the "red peril," which resulted from "their disgracefully tyrannical system of slavery."[5]

The only member of the government for whom the Hearst papers ever expressed sympathy was the czar himself, "the most perplexed and wearied man to-day in Russia ... who must choose between chaos or a constitution."[6] But this sympathy quickly dissipated as Nicholas demonstrated that he did not have even the courage of the greatest Russian tyrants: "Russia's power came from her despots who were brave, and her internal convulsions have always gone apace with her rulers who were cowards ... Cowardice is the cause of the

USEFUL LITTLE BROWN UNDERTAKERS

THEY ARE DOING A GOOD THING WITHOUT KNOWING IT
Called the Yellow Peril, But in Reality They Are Burying the European Peril, the Bloodthirsty, Aristocratic, Red Peril-of Russian Misgovernment.

San Francisco Examiner, 11 December 1904

supremest contempt, and the Czar now has the contempt that his own people and all the people of the world have for a bigoted weakling."[7] The ills of Russia, both internal and external, found their source in its feeble and ineffectual ruler, and Russia was soon to learn the lesson that the Romans had been taught by the barbarians, the Persians by Alexander, the English under George iii by the Americans, and the French under Napoleon iii by the Germans.[8] The result was that Russia would be "hopeless till revolution comes."[9]

As the Russo-Japanese War ended in Russian ignominy, the Hearst press recorded the process by which Russian autocracy became further degraded. Echoing its treatment of Evangelina Cisneros, the *Examiner* told its readers "WHAT THEY DID TO PRETTY MARIA," recounting, on its front page, "The Inhuman Horrors of the Treatment of the Young Girl Who Shot General Lugenovsky, the Cossack Leader Who Flogged to Death Maria's Poor Old Father."[10] But soon after this – and at the same time that other horror stories were being recorded – hope for relief came as the czar called the Duma, the national parliament, which Hearst wrongly saw as a representative assembly on the Western model. He greeted this event with the rather extravagant notion that "there was something distinctly awe-inspiring about the day, with visions of the chains falling from another branch of the human race, and the Russian people taking up the march of modern civilization."[11] The same editorial did, however, modify its euphoria by noting that "the great jarring note on this occasion" was the distrust between government and people, a distrust impossible to conceal.

This hope died when the czar dissolved the Duma and pushed his government back towards autocracy. In the summer, weakened by military defeat and by the czar's abandonment of even limited democracy, the country lurched towards revolution. Hearst recorded that "the Russian navy is permeated with disloyalty, the army is not much better, and at last the peasants are up, burning the mansions of the nobles, killing the masters and appropriating their lands." He referred to "the hideous Russian situation – which presages such a cataclysm as modern mankind has never witnessed."[12] As the revolution of 1906 was put down, the Hearst press noted that "the Czar has had his opportunity ... Had he been anything but a weak, cowardly little aristocrat, he could have accorded his people a measure of liberty that would have made Russia a great nation." But this was not to be: the czar had thrown away his chance, and "all that is lacking now to revolution is organization. That will come in time. Leaders will rise who will unite the oppressed people and direct them intelligently in their war on their oppressors." Eagerly anticipated, the time would come when the people would overthrow their czar and "the revenge that they will take will be a lesson for all tyrants in all times."[13]

Until the collapse of the czarist regime in the revolution of 1917, the Hearst press kept up its attacks on the Russian government, losing no opportunity to indicate its distaste for the czar and his cohorts by returning to the subject of their oppressive rule, by lampooning them, or by blaming them in large part for the outbreak of the First World War.[14] The Russian Revolution in March 1917 allowed Wilson to claim in his war message on 2 April that now all the major Allied powers were democratic, and Hearst's first reaction was to welcome it, not only as signalling the end of autocracy in Russia itself but also as the harbinger of similar changes throughout Europe. On 21 March he wrote: "I do not know how complete the Russian revolution is – whether it is merely a change from one autocrat to another or whether it is in reality a step toward popular government ... I imagine, however, that every disturbance of this kind makes more or less for popular government and that the Russian Revolution is significant in that way ... The revolutions are not going to be confined to

Russia ... there is going to be a new freedom coming for Germany as well."[15]

On the following day, however, Hearst allowed himself to deliver extravagant praise for the events in Russia and those who had made them. "The whole world," the *Examiner* cried, "owes a debt of gratitude to the courageous men who have overthrown autocracy and bureaucracy in Russia." This was because, "as the Hearst papers have pointed out time after time, the victory of the Allies is Russia's victory, the victory of Slavism over the Teutonic and Magyar peoples; the domination of both Asia and continental Europe by this Asiatic nation – for the true Russian is an Asiatic by origin and by habit and in his morals and ways of thought." This being so, "it will be of infinite benefit if Europe is to be subdued to the domination of these Asiatics, that they shall at least have adopted a form of government in harmony with the ideals of modern Europe, and that they shall have adopted institutions and laws that are European and not Asiatic."[16] Hearst also sounded this note of warning about the international consequences of the revolution in discussing its domestic consequences. Two days later he wrote that the only matter so far certain was that the revolution had shown that it could take power. In this, however, he saw "the sure hope and confident prediction of Russia's ultimate deliverance, freedom and regeneration." This would probably, however, be a long time coming, for "the road may be long and desperately beset with hardship, suffering, bloodshed and that hope deferred which makes sick the weary heart."[17]

Nevertheless, Hearst applauded the revolution and rejoiced that the people of Russia had apparently thrown off their oppression. In May 1917 he wrote: "The more we hear of that wondrous Russian revolution the more it impresses the people of liberty-loving America. And as the days stretch into weeks it begins to seem that the Russian people really intend to make their suddenly acquired liberty of permanent value, as they are overcoming the disorders and animosities that naturally follow the overturning of an established regime." The editorial ended with the fervent hope that they would achieve this objective and that the Russian people, like the French, would gain peace, freedom, and republican government.[18]

At this point there seems to have been very little, if any, difference between the views of Hearst and those of many American liberals and progressives on the revolution.[19] The change came later in the summer and, finally, after the Bolsheviks seized power in October.

In October, Hearst made his first suggestion that closer relations with the new Russian government should be established: he wrote an editorial supporting a suggestion from Professor Leo Wiener of

Harvard that exchanges between American and Russian students should be encouraged.[20] But the October Revolution itself was greeted with editorial silence, even though developments within Russia were reported on the news pages of the Hearst papers. Not until the following January, asking, "Just what ARE conditions in Russia today?" and concluding that there were "grave difficulties in the way of our getting the right notions," did the *Examiner* enjoin Americans to withhold judgment, for "criticism of them may be criticism of our teachers." Sympathy was in order at this point: "the wide-visioned sympathy of our own great leader, Woodrow Wilson – even though it may not amount to endorsement of all their inner, economic aims for Russia's reconstruction – should be our guiding cue." There was a chance that the country might yet enlighten the world, for "Great Russia is in the melting pot of political development. Hers may yet be a great message."[21]

Soon this guarded optimism became outright enthusiasm. Less than a week after the appearance of this first expression of cautious sympathy, the Hearst papers announced firmly that "the Great War for Human Freedom is Won." Like many such Hearstian pronouncements, this was a trifle premature. The editorial went on to proclaim that "the old order is not changing. It HAS changed. It awaits only exterior peace to vanish away completely in swift revolutionary uprisings in every country in Europe."

Admitting that this was not a common view, and certainly not that of the chancelleries of Europe, the editorial claimed it to be "the just view, the really statesmanlike view, the foreseeing view – and the view that will be finally approved and ratified by the progress of events and the final verdict of time."[22] Little more than a month later, in a signed editorial dealing specifically with the Bolsheviks, Hearst called the Russian government the "truest democracy in Europe, the truest democracy in the world today," and the Bolsheviks the representatives of that government. Having established this, he went on to ask why the United States was fighting the war, answering his question by saying, "We are in it for democracy." This being the case, "For heaven's sake, why not recognize a democratic Government? We recognized the IMPERIAL Government of Russia, but when Russia secures a DEMOCRATIC Government we have so far not recognized it." Failure to recognize the new Bolshevik government would discredit professions of a war for democracy, whereas recognition would enable the nation to carry on "an inspiring fight for democracy with some truth, some sincerity and some conviction."[23] The United States government, however, refused to recognize the Bolshevik government or even to reply to its peace proposals, sent to the Allied governments early in December 1917. Moreover, Wilson's Fourteen Points, setting out American war aims and presented to Congress on 8 January 1918, had no effect on the Soviets' determination to leave the war, which they achieved in the Treaty of Brest-Litovsk in early March.

Ten days later Hearst attacked those who criticized Lenin and the Bolsheviks for making peace with Germany at Brest-Litovsk. They had been obliged to do this "because of apathy abroad and treachery at home." The United States, for example, had not recognized the Russian government "because the aristocracies of Europe did not want the proletariat of Russia established in power."[24] But this did not diminish his conviction that the "modern revolution" would come in Russia, even though "the autocracies, the aristocracies and the privileged classes of the world in this war for 'democracy' would rather see Russia defeated, dismembered, destroyed and lost to democracy than see the proletariat of Russia survive and the new revolution succeed."[25] At this time, too, not yet having arrived at the point where he considered that President Wilson could do nothing right, Hearst praised the government's policy towards Russia. Under the headline "President Again Shows Wisdom in Message to Russian Soviets," he supported Wilson's promise to stand by the Russians and to aid them as "the right policy beyond any doubt or shadow of doubt." Even though this promise may have come too late to achieve the desired results, it was nevertheless "a wise move and an inspiring message, and an evidence of more farseeing statesmanship and more sincere sympathy with the people of Russia than any of the leaders of the Allies have shown."[26]

As 1918 wore on, Hearst, once charged with being pro-German, saw this charge renewed – with the addition that he was now seen as pro-Bolshevik.[27] However, in June he argued, as he had done in January, that the American people and government should inform themselves fully of the Russian situation before judging it and that they should look sympathetically on the Russian experiment: "It is the part of statesmanship, wisdom and justice for the American people to inform themselves concerning the real character of the Bolsheviki and to understand that the Bolsheviki have committed no act of treason or disloyalty to their allies; that they have done nothing that we in their circumstances would not have done; that they are today working out the problems of democracy as they can never be worked out by war in Russia." He called for rejection of the denunciations of the Bolsheviks by "men who pretend THEY are for this war for the sake of democracy, but who hate the Bolsheviki because the Bolsheviki are real democrats."[28] During the following month Hearst's enthusiasm seemed to be waning somewhat; he maintained that "the Bolsheviki party may or may not be worthy to direct the great destinies of Russia in her most critical hour," while still holding that those in America who were speaking loudly about conditions in Russia could not know the real situation and that therefore the president must show the country which way it should proceed in this difficult situation.[29]

It was this view, wavering between almost unqualified support for the Bolsheviks and rather careful uncommittedness, that the Hearst papers maintained through the summer and fall of 1918, while the American government and people, largely preoccupied with the progress of the war, refused to make any commitment to the Soviet government. In this Hearst differed from many of his political allies, whose views of Soviet Russia already seemed to be hardening. As one scholar described the situation, "the Bolshevik revolution burst upon the outside world with staggering force,"[30] and it produced a much greater effect than had the March Revolution. "Conservative and capitalistic America" was swiftly repelled by seizure of the means of production and distribution, by repudiation of debts, by the overthrow of the churches, and by other examples of the emerging extremism of the new rulers of Russia.[31]

His papers also differed from most of the press – especially influential eastern newspapers like the *New York Times*, which declared its hostility to the latest revolution, writing of a "nightmare in a lunatic asylum."[32] But, at least initially, the Hearst press had powerful support from other quarters. Most progressives and liberals adopted their attitude during 1917. The "peace progressives" tolerated the revolution until Brest-Litovsk ended Russian participation in the war.[33] Even then, however, they tended to see the problem as one of what institutions Russia would produce. This was also the view of many American liberals, who, though they regarded Germany as the prime enemy and thus were angered by the Bolshevik eagerness to leave the war, did not adopt the "blind outrage" with which many sections of the press and public reacted to the Bolshevik revolution.[34] Much like Hearst, they vociferously deplored the hostility of their own countrymen to Soviet Russia; they believed not only that the establishment of democracy would benefit the Russians themselves but that "in the long run German imperialism and militarism could be met by no more deadly menace than the permanent establishment of democracy in Russia."[35] Thus, among liberals and progressives there was at least qualified approval for the revolution.[36]

Soon after the war ended, the attitude of the Hearst papers towards the Russian government began to cool. In an editorial headed "Civilization Faces a New Struggle Even More Portentous Than the One Just

Ended," Hearst discussed the response of the Soviet government to a Swiss protest against Soviet terrorism. The Soviet response was labelled, "An appeal of the Soviet Government to the working classes in all countries to unite in the forcible overthrow of existing political and social conditions and the substitution of Internationalism and Socialism." Hearst suggested that, because the Russians "want to turn existing society upside down," the world will now see "a new conflict of principles of human government and human social relations, and this conflict will eventually be fought out in every nation under the sun."[37]

From this perceptive view of the socialist revolution in Russia and its international implications, the editorial proceeded to analyse the situation. It stated that the *internationalists* in Russia regarded the outcome of the war as a victory not for democracy but for capitalism, abhorring "the victory and the victors almost as thoroughly as they abhorred the autocracies and aristocracies overthrown by the war." The Soviet declaration made plain that the Soviets "mean to use violence and terror to the limit ... it is, indeed, another declaration of universal war, and it must be met with serious conception of its gravity, and with heroic effort to stay its terrors." There were two ways of meeting the threat: "to attempt to put it down with fleets and armies and court-martials – with violence," or to "acknowledge all that is rightful in the demands of the European socialists and, above all, to make haste to feed the European masses – of whatever nations – and relieve them of their miseries." The second course was clearly more desirable, for if the attempt was made to destroy by force the government in Russia and socialism elsewhere in Europe, "the Socialist extremists of all countries will unite and Europe will go smash and the white man's civilization be again drowned in blood and tears." The editorial ended with a plea for moderation, so that Europe could secure "necessary reforms and progressions by constructive methods instead of by a desperate appeal to fire and sword and all the appalling accompaniments of the Red Terror."[38]

Thus, almost exactly a year after the October Revolution there began the distrust of Soviet Russia and its methods that Hearst was to carry with him for the rest of his life. True to form, he had greeted with pleasure the beginning of revolution in Russia. Drawing a sharp distinction between the Russian people and their rulers, he believed he had detected, in 1906 and again in 1917, the beginnings of genuine popular government in a country cursed by benighted and autocratic rule. He had therefore been prepared to see what the revolutionaries of March and their successors of October could do to right the wrongs of Russia, and he had advised his readers and their government to do the same. But by November 1918 it was obvious to him that the brave experiment of October 1917 was not what it had seemed and that a small group of ruthless, organized, and determined men whose principles and methods he regarded as abhorrent had grasped power in Russia. The honeymoon, if such it was, was over.

The problem of relations with the Bolshevik government now settled into three distinct questions, one of short-run importance and the other two occupying the United States and the Hearst press for the rest of Hearst's life and beyond. The immediate question, of American intervention in Russia, was one to which Hearst was and remained unequivocally opposed. Early in 1919 he compared the White Russians to the Tories of the American and French revolutions, for they were "willing to bring the foreign soldier into their country to shed the blood of their fellow citizens in order that they may repossess themselves of their lost property and position." The question of whether the United States should become involved was easily resolved – "We don't care whether these people get their property in Russia or not" – and the idea of shedding American blood to help them do so was outrageous.[39] When, in April 1918, Japan became the first country to move towards intervention, the Hearst papers expressed grave suspicion of Japanese motives, muttering the usual imprecations against the yellow peril. [40] But this was not sufficient to persuade "the Chief" that American troops should be committed to Russia. In this he was supported by many leading progressives, whereas the war liberals, who regarded the revolution as a menace to civilization and the successful prosecution of the German war, supported or at least acquiesced in intervention. [41]

Wilson insisted that Russia must be allowed to settle its own fate and accepted that Russia should participate in some peace discussions. On the first question, however, he agreed, albeit reluctantly, to send limited numbers of troops to support the British and French interventions, bowing to the French prime minister, Georges Clemenceau, while on the second he bowed to American public opinion.[42] Hearst, by now antagonistic to Wilson's foreign policy in any case, opposed the move into Russia vehemently. In spite of growing misgivings about the new Russian regime, he felt that it should be left alone to resolve the problems of Russia and that the Russian people should be allowed to sort out their own form of government – even though, as he wrote to one of his editors, there would be a reaction in Russia and excesses would doubtless be the result, for "it is probably necessary for a nation, after throwing off the grip of such a despotism, to go through this period of travail and violence before it settles down to a sound and stable democracy."[43] The government that failed to recognize this was attacked with all the scorn at the command of "the Chief" and his papers. "Behold, we liberty-loving Americans, whose watchwords were humanity and democracy, are now fighting in Asia hand in hand with these cruel Cossacks, hand in hand with the imperialistic Japanese, to crush the developing democracy of Russia and to restore the vicious despotism of the Czars and the military government of the Cossack hordes."[44] All the principles of national and international action that the Hearst papers espoused cried out against the iniquity of such an action.

The two long-term questions that presented themselves in viewing American relations with Russia were rather more complex. The first of them – recognition of the revolutionary government of Russia – the Hearst papers had advocated from the beginning. In the enthusiastic days of 1917 the United States government was asked to stretch out its hand in friendship to a sister republic whose founders had, like those of the United States itself, risen up to throw off oppression. From this position the Hearst press never varied – though, as will be seen, it did waver.

In late 1920 and early 1921, as the Wilson administration staggered to its close under a president who, within a few months, had changed – in the Hearst press – from a leader of overpowering statesmanship to a blundering fool whose foreign policy was fit only for abuse,[45] the question of Russian recognition was used to criticize the government further. In an editorial headed "Our Studied Insults to Russia the Worst Policy That Can Be Imagined," the *Examiner* claimed: "The whole policy of the administration for the past six years has been to strengthen our probable enemies and to alienate and weaken our only probable friends."[46] This was later followed by a purely economic argument in which, asking "Why Waste Good Patrons?" the paper advocated opening trade and communication with Russia at once.[47] Having supported famine relief for Russia late in the summer of 1921, and condemning fiercely those who would use the famine as a weapon to destroy the Bolshevik government, Hearst returned in the spring of 1922 to recognition for the sake of economic advantage.[48] He held up the example of Great Britain, which had begun trading extensively with Russia, and decried the short-sightedness of France and the United States in refusing to take advantage of this vast potential market.[49]

Throughout the twenties the Soviets gained more international acceptance and the United States government continued to sit on the sidelines, refusing even formal recognition of the Soviet regime. In this it was supported by influential groups in the u.s., including, among the newspapers, the *New York Times* and *Chicago Tribune*.[50] The Hearst press, however, allied itself to those who advocated both trade and recognition. In 1923 an editorial written on the occasion of Japanese recognition of the USSR referred to the beginnings of the Russian regime. They reminded readers that – unlike many American newspapers – the Hearst papers had warned that the Russian regime was rooted firmly in "the soil of the Russian peasants' character, sturdiness and aspirations, and that it would not be conquered by any of the forces from without that were being hurled at it," and had called for recognition. Now that the world knew the Hearst papers had been right, they still called for recognition because the United States was being left behind by other nations in trading, communicating, and establishing formal relations with the Soviet Union.[51]

Hearst occasionally speculated about the reasons for American slowness to deal with the Soviet Union, concluding that it was largely the result of the incompetence, corruption, and foolishness of the government and of the trusts and business interests that propped it up. Writing in 1924, he noted: "Revelations in Washington make it perfectly clear to the intelligent citizen why Russia has not been recognized by the United States. The scandal in oil is only typical of the condition to which our government and our politicians have fallen. It is the curse of the political control by organized, rapacious Big Business." It was this corruption and the consequent fear of being shown up by the Russians that prevented recognition.[52]

Only as the prospect of recognition of Soviet Russia became a reality after FDR's inauguration, however, did Hearst begin to express doubts. He had never really approved of the system that the Russians were erecting, but he had advocated that they be given a chance to become equal members of the international community, that the United States and other nations trade with Russia for their own advantage and to help the Russians overcome the problems remaining from the old regime. Nevertheless, as the American government came round to their view, as the possibility and then the reality of negotiations came about, the Hearst editorial writers began to feel that the Russians were no better than other European nations who, having got themselves into a terrible mess, came to the United States, not for advice or co-operation but to be bailed out. Thus, while the Hearst papers greeted with pleasure the arrival in Washington of Maxim Litvinov, Soviet commissar for foreign affairs, to open the negotiations that ultimately led to recognition of the Soviet Union in November 1933, they also sounded a warning.

An article by Julius G. Berens, the financial editor of the *New York American*, noted this. "The Hearst newspapers," he wrote, "favor recognition of Russia. These papers, however, do NOT BELIEVE in recognition AT ANY PRICE." The Hearst press saw that the Soviets wanted money from the United States but argued that it must be made perfectly clear that money would come only in the form of loans. Further, neither loans nor recognition would come unless the Russian government gave satisfactory answers to questions about the possibilities of repayment and whether the money so acquired would be spent in the United States.[53] Nevertheless, when recognition finally was given by the United States government, the Hearst papers expressed pleasure and looked forward to new and profitable relations between the two powers.[54]

The second long-term question – the implications for the United States and for Americans of Soviet Communism – will be dealt with in the next chapter. At this point it remains to examine Hearst's initial attitude towards Russian Communism, in the twenties and early thirties, before he began the violent and extreme campaign against Communism that occupied the remainder of his life. Such an examination forms an essential part of this study, since it is in his view of Communism and, later, in his view of the machinations, both internal and external, of Soviet Russia, that the clearest evidence can be found of a close correlation between Hearst's views of American domestic affairs and the nation's conduct in the world.

Hearst was a Progressive; he even occasionally described himself as a radical. In internal American matters he fought long and hard for most things the Progressives wanted: he fiercely and constantly opposed the trusts and the overweening influence of big business in the United States; he espoused regulation of child labour and of working conditions, women's suffrage, direct election of senators, and greater justice and better conditions in general for the mass of Americans. In this he allied himself with the Progressives of the early years of the twentieth century, in particular Theodore Roosevelt, Albert Beveridge, Robert La Follette, William E. Borah, and Hiram Johnson, who represented the Republican wing of the party.[55] For in spite of his Progressivism, even his radicalism, Hearst was fundamentally a conservative.

In 1918, writing of the need for reform in the United States, Hearst developed a theme that was familiar in his thinking: that radicalism, violence, and class hatred were all caused by resistance to legitimate demands for reform that, by being ignored or suppressed, became more extreme and ultimately less controllable. The worst menace in any society was not radicalism, which was controllable, but that "selfish, self-satisfied class which stands stolidly and stupidly in the way of all reforms." He called for a brand of "enlightened capitalism" that would reform without disturbing society and without injuring established interests, a capitalism "capable of adapting itself to new conditions and so able to protect itself in all situations."[56] Speaking of his political beliefs in a later statement, Hearst noted that for his "political inspiration" he went back to "the days of Lincoln and his declaration for a government 'of the people, by the people and for the people,' and further back yet to the days of Jefferson and his declaration in favor of a government 'for the greatest good of the greatest number,' and still further back to the time of Washington and his appeal for a government free to serve the best interests of our own people without foreign 'entanglements' or alliances of any kind." He declared, "I am in some things an utter conservative, determined to conserve, as far as I possibly can, those principles and policies of the Fathers which for so many years have made our country the freest and happiest, the most prosperous and most powerful nation upon the face of the earth."[57]

In this he was no different from the majority of his fellow Progressives. Most of them were members of the prosperous middle, often upper-middle, classes; many – Roosevelt, for example – were part of the established eastern aristocracy. Clearly, they liked it that way – their Progressivism, their great and undeniable interest in bringing more freedom, more justice, more prosperity, and more comfort to the lives of the mass of Americans was also self-interest. The Progressives, particularly that group in the party with which Hearst is most clearly identifiable, had no desire to change the structure of American society, to turn it upside-down. On the contrary, they wished to preserve it substantially as it was. Despite much of its rhetoric and the appearance of many of its actions, Progressivism was essentially a conservative movement.

Like all intelligent conservatives, Progressives understood that the way to preserve the status quo was not by oppression or by denying the working and lower-middle classes redress of legitimate grievances. They understood – like the British ruling class, which, over the last five centuries, has demonstrated a firmer grasp of the essentials of the *ancien régime* than the ruling class of any other European nation – that the way to retain power is not to deny it absolutely to those who desire it but to surrender part of it from time to time, to remove the conditions that make for discontent with the existing order. They acted, in other words, like Tom Stoppard's Henry Carr, who, finding that his butler has depleted his champagne supply but realizing the value of a good and contented butler, suggests that he be given more champagne.

In addition, as noted elsewhere in this study, Hearst was passionately American, believing that his country's ideals of freedom and justice would benefit other nations if they could only be brought to understand and accept them. In this he was entirely in tune with many influential groups and individuals among his contemporaries as the spread of American ideas, practices, and industry continued through the years with which this study is concerned.[58] The growth of Bolshevism in the twenties and later confronted those who believed as Hearst did with a proselytizing force as strong and determined, and at least as ruthless and subversive, as the one they represented. The trouble with the Bolsheviks was that they wanted precisely what the American Progressives were anxious to avoid – they wanted on a universal scale what they had already achieved in Russia: to reverse the existing order. This was clear in their response to the Swiss message, and to this danger Hearst, with his undoubted knack of stating his views and prejudices more directly and clearly than most, addressed himself. In an open letter to Senator James A. Reed of Missouri, a member of the Senate Foreign Relations Committee, published in the Hearst papers early in 1919, he wrote: "It is very clear in my mind that what we call Bolshevism is merely the extreme of radicalism, which is the result of reactionary conditions equally extreme and equally indefensible; that it is merely the violent and inflamed protest of the masses against the selfishness, arbitrariness, injustice and corruption of the classes ... Surely, that is what it is in Russia, and as far as Bolshevism exists in America, that is what it is in America." Happily, the extreme autocracy that had produced Bolshevism in Russia did not exist in the United States, but this did not mean that the danger of it or something like it did not exist. "We have a certain development of lawless and violent radicalism in America, and that is surely the result of a certain lawlessness and violence and brutal disregard for the rights of others which characterize the only autocracy we have in this country – the autocracy of wealth and privilege."[59]

The conclusion to be drawn was obvious to Hearst, and it represents the core of his Progressivism, the heart of his concern for reform in the United States: "Bolshevism in this enlightened country can only be serious when backed by just and legitimate cause of popular complaint. Deprived of that proper cause of complaint Bolshevism will be limited to the naturally lazy and the constitutionally lawless ... Moderate progressive measures now will avoid the necessity for immoderate and excessive measures later ... A few hard blows at the real root of the evil and the rank growth of Bolshevism will be forever destroyed."[60] The heading under which this message appeared in the Hearst papers was "Bolshevism Must Be Eradicated at Root by Eliminating Creative Cause, says Mr Hearst."

More editorials on the same theme followed this letter. Six weeks later a piece headed "If There Is No Bourbonism, There Will Be No Bolshevism" was printed in the Hearst papers,[61] followed in April by one headed "The World Is Confronted by Two Ways of Fighting Bolshevism."[62] In the meantime, pleading that world peace would be secured only by obeying the Golden Rule, Hearst had commented: "There is only one way to arrest the march of revolution, and that is to make conditions so much better that no considerable number will want to revolt," and concluded that the United States should "do unto each of these as we would that they do unto us."[63]

Already, even while advocating that the United States give Soviet Russia a chance to prove that she could develop into a liberal democracy and that, to further that purpose, maintain some control over Russia, and help herself by increasing her overseas trade, the nation should recognize the new government, Hearst had turned against Bolshevism. It may be doubted that he had ever been in real sympathy with its philosophy of cataclysmic change, and certainly, by the middle of 1919, he was perceived as being anti-Bolshevik by some branches of the government. In June the suggestion was made by the assistant chief of staff of the American Expeditionary Force in Europe to the Military Intelligence Division in Washington that an anti-Bolshevik campaign in the American press would assist their work in Germany and that the logical arena for such a campaign would be the Hearst papers. This suggestion, never put into effect, was made on the twin assumptions that Hearst was both anxious to atone for his pro-German activities before 1917 and to stop the spread of Bolshevism in Europe and elsewhere.[64]

Although the proposed campaign was never carried out, its objectives were probably achieved anyway. Hearst lost no opportunity to point out the wrongs being perpetrated by Communism and the dangers inherent in giving in to it. By 1923, concluding an editorial with the statement that "the Russian experiment has developed into the most terrible national tragedy of history," he emphasized that the Soviets, "hard at work on their theory that what ails the world is the accumulation of capital, ... are trying to abolish capitalism," adding that the real danger to the United States was that the country was "shot through with Sovietism which thinks that industrial genius that accumulates capital should be penalized and not encouraged."[65] While recognizing that such thinking was a growing danger, Hearst continued to maintain that extreme measures were unnecessary to combat it. In 1930, although the capitalist world had been shaken by the Depression, he applauded the work of a group of San Francisco businessmen who had helped to alleviate conditions in their city by placing a substantial ship-building contract with a local firm. This, he said, was "answering Communism the RIGHT way": "Communism can't be answered by talk, for it is itself the world's champion loud-speaker. But it COULD be answered by deeds – economic acts of faith, political acts of intelligence." Pursuing this line of argument, the editorial concluded that "investigating Communism does no harm. But investigating Capitalism, revealing its possibilities if led by statesmen of vision and courage, could do more good."[66]

Thus, in the twenties and early thirties Hearst dealt with the Soviet Union and Communism as two separate and distinct questions. The first was an issue purely for the external affairs of the United States, and although there were hints of discontent and disillusion during this period, Hearst was prepared to allow the Russians to settle their own affairs in their own way. Thus, he argued vehemently against American intervention in Russia when this was proposed and carried through by the Wilson administration, and he also contended that the Russian government should be brought into the community of nations, recognized, traded with, and treated by other nations as an equal, for such a course would help both the Russians and the rest of the world.

At the same time he saw, within little more than a year of the October Revolution, the dangers that Bolshevism posed for the rest of the world, for the capitalist system, and for the United States. His progressivism and his innate conservatism again led him to advocate vigilance against this menace and implementation of measures to remove it. With his deep-seated belief in America and the American Way, he was convinced that, contrary to appearances and much evidence, the capitalist system in America was healthy and unchallenged. Led by enlightened and intelligent governments, it could meet this provocation by the sort of peaceful means that he advocated. This situation was, however, to change.

6 Hearst and the Red Menace

The change occurred in the mid-thirties as Hearst came to grips with the implications of Soviet rule in Russia. In November 1933 the United States government, strongly supported by the Hearst papers, recognized the Soviet Union. Less than eighteen months later the same newspapers suggested that this recognition should be withdrawn. Thereafter the Hearst press rarely had a good word to say for the Soviet Union and its ruling party. This chapter will attempt to explain the reversal of policy shown by these two positions.

Up to the time when the United States recognized the Soviet Union, Hearst had separated the issue of recognition of and intercourse with the Soviets from that of Communism and its spread throughout the non-Russian world.[1] During the thirties, as Hearst saw the extension of Soviet activities in Europe and the United States aided by politicians too foolish or too conniving to stop them, and as he saw democratic rule retreating before the onset of Communist totalitarianism, such a separation was no longer possible. Russia and Communism he increasingly identified as a single issue and the greatest menace to the principles and ideals for which the United States stood.[2]

Hearst's change of mind occurred when he was losing confidence, not in the principles for which America and its capitalist system stood but in the ability of the government he had supported to set matters right. At the same time, he believed – or affected to – that Communism was poisoning American life at all levels. Short on specifics but long on innuendo, he attacked not merely the small Communist Party but liberal-leaning academics and trade unionists. As the thirties wore on the word "Communism" came almost to serve as a code-word for everything Hearst decried in the United States. Seeing himself and his beloved country assailed from within and without by this alien creed, he lashed out against it in all its manifestations.

This growing conviction was reflected in a stream of editorials in the Hearst papers from early 1934 onwards. In the spring of that year Hearst called upon Congress to take note of the increase in Communist subversion and activity in the country. Having exposed in his papers "the spread and increasing boldness of Communist propaganda in our midst," he expressed surprise that Congress had taken no notice. He used the occasion of a speech in April by a former justice of the Michigan Supreme Court, George N. Clark, who had declared that 90 per cent of American professors were teaching Communism, to proclaim that "this is appalling! It cannot be ignored!"[3] By the fall of the same year he was telling his editor-in-chief that "we must make a powerful crusade against Communism and against revolution of all kinds if we want to retain our liberties."[4]

The crusade opened that winter, when a letter of instruction by Hearst to his editors was published in the Hearst press. Writing on the dual menace of Fascism and Communism, he noted that "Communism as actually in operation is government by a class, for a class," while Fascism "is government by an opposing class." Both forms of government were contrary to the principles of American democracy, which "is government by all the people, expressed through the will of the majority." Thus both systems were equally unacceptable because both deprived the people of the right to govern themselves, the most precious of American freedoms. He expressed his view that "the Communistic Party today is largely composed of agitators with the greed of power, position and property, but without the competence to acquire them except by criminal violence and certainly without the ability or the will to exercise them for the general benefit ... The Communist policy is to substitute plunder for labor." Fascism, by contrast, did not really exist in the United States, for "the menace of Communism is what developed Fascism in Europe," so that "there will never be a genuine Fascist movement in this country until COMMUNISM COMPELS IT."[5] Two weeks later, in a signed editorial, he vigorously continued the attack:

We recognized Russia.
Now it is just as well to recognize what we recognized.
It is the same old Russia as under the Czars.
It is the same old tyranny under another name.

There is the same old protest by assassination against cruelty and tyranny.
There is the same old wholesale indiscriminate slaughter of opponents of the
despotism.
There is the same old injustice and oppression and the same old implacable
hatred by the people of rule by blood and iron.

Not only this, but the threat was now being brazenly pushed beyond
the Soviet Union into the United States. Hearst asked, "Is it not time
for us to realize that those who are attempting to transform this
American Republic into a Communistic tyranny of class against class
are, above all others, the Number 1 Public Enemies of our country
and our people? They are the most flagrantly seditious and traitorous
element in our community."[6]

Thus began a campaign that was to be continued with all the considerable force and vehemence at the command of the Hearst press
for the rest of its owner's life. It was carried forward on a number of
fronts simultaneously, emphasizing one aspect or another of the
struggle against Russia and Communism but always returning to the
theme of the threat posed to democratic societies by the vicious, untrustworthy regime in Russia and its subversive tool, international
Communism. Hearst naturally devoted his major attention to the
threat to his own country, and here he set out to expose Communism
in all its frightening aspects.

Three weeks after the editorial quoted above he began that part of
his anti-Communist campaign that was to bring down on him and his
papers the greatest condemnation of this period. In a telegram to
Hearst editors his secretary, Colonel John Willicombe, instructed that
"names, pictures and activities of disloyal professors and others
should be printed continually and commented upon."[7] This attack
had already begun, but now it was stepped up to such an extent that
it brought quick replies from those against whom it was directed and
from their defenders. Early in February 1935 a meeting of American
educators, led by Charles A. Beard, one of the most distinguished and
widely known historians in the country, called for a Senate investigation into the "spurious anti-Red campaign now current in the Hearst
press."[8]

While his papers attacked Communist subversion in the nation's
colleges and universities, Hearst reminded his readers of the situation
in Russia, taking a position that, it should be noted, was closer to the
truth about the Soviet Union than that taken, at least in the thirties, by
many American intellectuals and journalists. Early in January 1935 he
delivered a radio broadcast entitled "Government by the Proletariat"
over the NBC network; the text was published the following morning

in the Hearst papers. He noted that "the truth is slowly leaking out of Russia. And the truth is that revolution is rife, starvation stalks starkly across the land, executions are commonplace, murder a routine of government; and that the national colors of Communism are daily dipped in the blood of subject classes to keep them bright." All this was the direct result of an "optimistic adventure in government by the least executive element of the community," the proletariat, which had produced "the rule of the LEAST capable, the LEAST successful and apparently the LEAST humanitarian element of the community." He concluded that, since 1917, when he had asked for forbearance, understanding, and the reservation of American judgment on the new Soviet government, Russia had become subject to "government by the mob, government by ignorance, limited by nothing, by no kind of law and absolutely no rule" and was now "the fearful failure that it needs must be and definitely deserves to be." This condemnation was joined to an attack on those who, at that point, advocated grain sales to the Soviet Union to alleviate conditions there. Why, he asked, should America "rescue this vile and vicious system of robbery and murder, so that these Communists can in return proselyte [sic] in our country to the end that we be robbed and murdered too?"[9]

He advanced a similar argument when the Russian government attempted to sell gold bonds in the United States. In mid-April 1935, Colonel Willicombe sent Coblentz a number of Hearst's comments on this action. He maintained that, since the Soviets had repudiated every other debt, there was reason to believe that they would repudiate this one, too: "The Soviet cannot even pay them [the gold bonds] and would not if it could." Stories put about in the United States of the success of the Communist regime were "merely an imaginative tale to sell Soviet bonds to gullible Americans," for in reality the "5-year plan has been a 5-year disaster."[10]

The Hearst papers came to the meat of their anti-Communist campaign in July, when a trade agreement was signed between the United States and Russia. This was greeted with an editorial headed "ROOSEVELT ADMINISTRATION SURRENDERS TO SOVIET." Characterizing the agreement as, "in dollars and cents, ... an ironic jest," the editorial noted that, "in order to secure a negligible number of dollars in export business, we ignore the question which we previously raised of settlement of the Russian debt to the United States, involving SEVEN HUNDRED MILLION DOLLARS." The Roosevelt administration "shows a tender willingness to forgive foreigners, whether they are defaulters, propagandists, or what not," and the "exclusive wrath of this bizarre New Deal Administration is reserved for high grade American citizens, who as business executives and investors laid the economic basis for our superior living standards." This kind of behaviour, the editorial concluded, "justifies the question which has arisen in the minds of many: 'Is the Roosevelt Administration Communistic?' "[11]

A few days before this editorial Hearst had telegraphed Coblentz to "dwell on Russian treaty until whole country understands outrage of it."[12] This instruction was duly carried out: first the treaty was condemned, then the administration that had signed it. In August an editorial demanded, "Sever Relations with Russia and Outlaw Communism." Commenting on the Comintern meetings in Moscow, it noted that, on the eve of this event, the United States government had chosen to conclude a trade agreement "with the one AVOWED AND ACTIVE ENEMY of our democratic-capitalistic system that must notch, in view of what is being revealed in Moscow, the high-water mark of stupidity on the part of Secretary Hull and Ambassador Bullitt."[13]

From this time on the Hearst press continually played up the twin topics of Communist subversion in the United States and the supposed connection of the Roosevelt administration with this activity. Early in September the *Examiner* commented that, "no matter what our future relations with the Government of Czar Stalin are, the biggest of all problems is, what are we going to do with the Reds on our soil who are working day and night to destroy all that has been built up since 1787?" This editorial concluded, in a significant departure from Hearst's earlier view of the best way to combat Communism, that "anti-Communist legislation should be the FIRST WORK of the next session of Congress."[14] Advocacy of this sort of action was soon combined with proposals for ridding the country entirely of subversives, particularly those who were immigrants. Late in 1935 Coblentz told Hearst editors: "Chief instructs that he wishes all his papers to make a vigorous and aggressive fight against 'criminals, cranks, and communists.' "[15] This attack opened early in 1936.

The group under fire quickly came to include those who opposed policies advocated by the Hearst papers, particularly policies concerned with national security, at home and abroad. One of the few Roosevelt programs the Hearst papers still supported was that for national defence.[16] Opposition to this program was quickly branded either Communist-inspired or the product of a lack of understanding, for "every Communist and every deluded pacifist who opposes the patriotic preparedness program of the American Government is an actual ally of militaristic Red Russia."[17] The film industry came into range as Hearst attacked the spreading of Communist propaganda through newsreels,[18] and the national radio systems were accused of permitting the dissemination of Communist news and opinions.[19]

But perhaps more important than the fight against subversive elements was the second line of attack now pursued by the Hearst papers: to link the Roosevelt administration with the spread of Communism in the United States. The summer of 1935 saw the first suggestion of Communist sympathies in the government. By the spring of 1936 the attack became direct and specific, as a Hearst headline proclaimed "Communism Here!" There was no difference, the following editorial claimed, between Earl Browder, the general secretary of the American Communist Party, and Rexford Tugwell, whom Hearst portrayed as FDR's spokesman: "We have, in all its essentials, a Communistic administration at Washington ... WE HAVE COMMUNISM IN EVERYTHING BUT THE NAME."[20] The Hearst press soon identified the real danger – that, under the guise of democracy and the New Deal, the means proposed to pull the country out of the greatest depression in its history, the United States was being sold not recovery but Communism, an alien and subversive creed bent on overthrowing all that was most precious in the American way of life.

The attacks on Communism in Russia also continued, but the real target now became the machinations of the Comintern in attempting to foment international revolution. In early July the *Examiner* warned that "what happened in France can happen – IS HAPPENING – here." The editorial went on to claim: "While we fatuously do nothing to stop them, the Communists here in America are boring into our ARMY, our NAVY, our FACTORIES, our POLITICAL INSTITUTIONS, and are, as they did in France, gradually worming their way – MASKED – into HIGH PLACES IN THE GOVERNMENT."[21] A week later, under the headline "The Red Advance," the *Examiner* cautioned that "the Communists, fresh from their triumphs in France, are now crossing the Channel to England."[22] Further editorials on the world-wide advance of the Communist menace followed, until, in August, the *Examiner* brought the lesson home again to the United States in an editorial headed "The 'Leftist' Mask": "From behind the innocent-appearing screen of the 'Radical-Socialist' party in France and the 'Popular Front' party in Spain now appears the face of the RED TERROR, just as from behind the innocent-sounding word of 'Bolshevism' in 1917 appeared the Lenin-Trotzky reign of terror." The Spanish and French voters had been fooled into voting for a "Leftist NEW DEAL," and "no sooner was this Leftist New Deal in power in Spain than its ruthless disregard for individual rights and deep-rooted traditions lit the fuse of one of the most terrible civil wars of modern times." The editorial ended with the ominous warning that the same thing could happen in the United States.[23]

During the presidential campaign of 1936 the Hearst papers continued to attack the Roosevelt administration and the president himself. By now Hearst's disillusionment with FDR was complete, and his campaign against the president's attempt to secure re-election was virulent. Having been partly instrumental in securing the nomination of Alfred M. Landon by the Republican Party, Hearst did all he could to ensure his election.[24] This effort now included an attempt to tie Roosevelt directly to the Communist Party. In September the Hearst papers published information that Moscow had issued orders to American Communists, enjoining them to support FDR. This claim was followed – despite denials from both the president and Communist leader Earl Browder – by other news items and editorials purporting to show that the former was accepting Communist support. A news story revealing that two members of the Democratic ticket in New York were "Red supporters" was followed on the same page by a reprint of a signed article by Upton Sinclair in the *Daily Worker*, stating that Browder was supporting the president, and by a statement to the same effect from Norman Thomas, the Socialist candidate for president. A subsequent published article informed readers that the American Labor Party contained Communist groups and that the president had publicly and gladly accepted the support of this party. All this added up to "the sensation of the campaign," which, it was claimed, "has done more to swing voters away from Roosevelt than anything that has been done yet in the campaign."[25]

In spite of the singular lack of success of all such attempts to reduce FDR's vote, the Hearst papers continued to brand both the president and members of his administration Communists or Communist sympathizers. The attacks on the USSR, the Soviet government, and its activities in Europe and elsewhere continued unabated, as did those on Communist subversion in the United States itself. Hearst wrote to Coblentz in April 1937 expressing amazement that Italy and Great Britain could possibly have believed that Stalin would keep his word about not intervening in Spain, and relegated the USSR to the same international category as France as "repudiators of pledges and debts."[26] At the same time the *Examiner* discussed a Soviet request for a loan to build up her navy and concluded that "Uncle Sam would be UNCLE SIMP ... if he should build a navy for a possible and his MOST PROBABLE enemy."[27]

Similarly, attempts to expose the iniquities of Stalin's regime inside the USSR went on. In February 1938 an editorial headed "Butenko Lifts the Last Veil on Soviet Russia" quoted the revelations of Feodor Butenko, the Soviet chargé d'affaires at Bucharest who had recently defected. "Butenko says that Russia under the Czars was freer than Stalin's Russia today; genius flourished and living and wages were on a higher level." Other opinions along the same lines followed until the editorial summed them up thus: "This is the horror-land that Robespierre Stalin asks the workers of America to sacrifice their lives for in case Soviet Russia is invaded!" The conclusion was that "Communist Russia is beyond the pale of ALL people" and that the United States should break off relations with it.[28]

Meanwhile, the attack continued on Communist and other forms of subversion inside the United States. Hearst spared no effort to expose Communist activities in the press or the film industry.[29] He maintained the campaign against those branded enemies of the United States. These people should be deported or imprisoned, for "we have too long harbored the scheming hordes of Red anarchists and other imported or domestic DESTRUCTIONISTS who plot against us in the guise of harmless liberalists and crackpot idealists." Hearst noted that "America is a great and hospitable country, but it has no room for conspirators, traitors, ingrates – and fools."[30]

These campaigns came together, however, in a bid to outlaw the Communist Party in the United States. In 1938 Hearst applauded the work of the House Committee on Un-American Activities under its chairman, Rep. Martin Dies of Texas, one of the most prominent red-baiters in Congress, saying that it was time for patriotic Americans to wake up. Asking who the red–baiters were, the editorial proclaimed that they were "not only the Dies Committee, but every really PATRIOTIC and ALERT citizen and organization in the United States." "The time has now come," Hearst concluded, "to WEAR THE BADGE OF RED BAITING PROUDLY."[31] Two years later, in 1940, the Hearst papers enthusiastically endorsed the first state initiatives to outlaw Communism. Praising the action of the Arizona legislature in making it impossible for Communists to vote or hold public office in the state, the *Examiner* advised that "the Communist Party should be outlawed, preferably by sweeping Federal action if Congress can be persuaded to be sufficiently American to do so; but certainly by the individual States, as Arizona has done."[32] Other states were congratulated for their patriotic actions in outlawing Communism until the campaign reached its logical conclusion, in an editorial on a Wisconsin law outlawing Communism, by claiming that outlawry was insufficient and that justice could only really be served by making adherence to Communism high treason.[33]

But what he saw as the Communist tendencies of the Roosevelt administration concerned Hearst most. He had supported the candidacy of FDR in 1932, having abandoned Hoover because the president had failed to live up to his promises, both domestic and foreign, and believing that Roosevelt, with his avowed opposition to the League of Nations and his progressive domestic program, was the more progressive of the two.[34] Thus, he supported FDR throughout his post-convention campaign and applauded his early pronouncements on domestic and foreign affairs. The Hearst press also supported most of the new president's Cabinet appointments, and though it spoke against such men as Cordell Hull, secretary of state, Harold Ickes, secretary of the interior, and Rexford Tugwell, undersecretary of agriculture, for a variety of reasons, they were not seen as seriously threatening.[35] For most of 1934 Hearst continued to support the new administration as it introduced its program to combat the Depression, even expressing enthusiasm for the beginning of the National Recovery Act (NRA). Although it began to comment on errors by the administration and to point out a growing tendency towards presidential dictatorship, the Hearst press placed its weight behind Democratic candidates in the 1934 election.[36] Hearst maintained good personal relations with the White House and was invited to stay there by the president in the fall of 1934.[37]

But the warning signs were out. Hearst was now beginning his campaign against foreign and domestic Communism, and the progress of the New Deal gave him growing cause for alarm. He was troubled by the government's inability to deal convincingly with the nation's economic troubles and by the commitment of the Roosevelt Cabinet to government intervention in the economy and to deficit spending. Such actions, he felt, could lead in one of two directions: either the nation, having reached the limit of the effectiveness of such a course, would pull back and revert to old-style progressivism, or it would – to the peril of American institutions – undergo a period of Communist protest.[38] It was clear which way Hearst thought the country should go. Like many of those whom he supported in Congress – men like his fellow Californian Hiram Johnson, or William E. Borah – he could not accept the direction in which the federal government seemed to be moving; above all, he feared the imposition of Communist-style government in the United States.[39]

Thus, in the winter of 1934–35, oppressed by the growing power of Communism abroad, its evident and unabashed espousal of revolution on an international scale, and also by the continuing depression at home and the government's apparent inability to cure it other than by means employed in the USSR, Hearst turned against the Roosevelt administration and included it and its members in his increasingly violent denunciations of government policy. In a pamphlet on Communism and Fascism published in 1935 Hearst wrote that the president had grown up under the aegis of Woodrow Wilson and that he and his mentor shared, along with their colleagues in government, "the same abiding faith in their own inspired intelligence and divine authority; the same mania to remodel everything according to their own ideas and prejudices; the same desire to control and reconstruct not only their own country but all the rest of the world; the same readiness to discard the wisdom of their fathers, and to consider all the great men of the past, all the patriots who preceded them 'back numbers,' whose principles and policies are out of date."[40]

At the same time, Hearst instructed Coblentz on the attitude of the Hearst papers towards the president and the administration. In the spring of 1935 he wrote his editor-in-chief: "I think we will have to settle down to a consistent policy of opposition to this administration." There was no point in criticizing Hull or Tugwell or Henry Wallace (secretary of agriculture and later vice-president) while excusing or apologizing for the president, for they were all part of the same devious operation: "He [FDR] is not frank, he is not sincere, he is not truthful. He is in office under false pretenses. The things he is doing were not in the platform, and not even hinted at in the platform. If he had submitted his policies to the American people, he would never have been elected."[41]

By fall 1936, as he moved into his aggressive campaign to defeat Roosevelt, Hearst was openly accusing the president of abrogating the program on which he had been elected and adopting the "platform of the Karl Marx Socialists in almost every word and letter." FDR had, he charged, "sent Secretary Tugwell to preach Bolshevik doctrines throughout the country, to array class against class and to urge that the farmers and workers 'surge forward' ... to establish a class government." Roosevelt had compelled the recognition of the Soviet Union, "a dictatorship born in riot and revolution, and sustained by murder and plunder." The president, whom Hearst thought did not have "a great deal of knowledge," must nevertheless have known that Stalin was continually plotting the overthrow of "all established forms of government in other nations, including the overthrow of the Republic of the United States founded in liberty by our fathers."[42]

The anti-government editorials went on until the United States entered the war. No member of the government was safe from censure. Rexford Tugwell was a favourite target; another was Harold L. Ickes, whom Hearst repeatedly accused of Communist sympathies in the late thirties (for his part, Ickes – at least in private – condemned Hearst as either a crook or a fool).[43] But he reserved his greatest venom for the president, whose initial election Hearst had supported and who had disappointed his hopes, like almost every other national leader. As the dictatorships of Europe gained in power and confidence, Hearst saw the same threat overhanging his beloved

United States: now the greatest danger was "the growth of executive power." Too cautious to accuse the president outright of a design to set up a dictatorship, he wrote that "the New Deal has created the all-pervasive air of a coming dictatorship," so that "the one hopeful fact is that the great tradition of the American people is against all forms of one-man power."[44] After the outbreak of war in Europe, Hearst went further and linked this tendency towards dictatorship with an attempt by the administration "to DELIBERATELY project us into COMMUNISM." The danger of war and the move of the government towards building up American defences – a move that the Hearst papers otherwise applauded – was being used as a pretext for communizing the country. "Are we now," the *Examiner* asked, "in the hands of the FOUNDERING FATHERS of a Russianized United States?"[45]

Throughout his campaign against the New Deal and its progenitors, Hearst maintained his attacks on the Soviet Union and its international policies. Although his flirtation with Nazism and Fascism in Europe has been exaggerated into support for Hitler and Mussolini and their methods, he did, in fact, regard them as a bulwark against Soviet Russia and Communism, the primary enemy of the United States and of Europe. Writing early in 1940, he indicated that "the present war in Europe is essentially between natural allies," because all the nations then involved had a common-enemy in Russia. The powers of Western Europe should heal the breaches between them; "otherwise they may soon find themselves under the yoke of the Russian conqueror, instead of as an independent power."[46] The same consideration applied to the United States, since "in the mind of the ruler of red Russia the United States of America is as plainly 'staked out' for conquest as is China, as was [sic] Finland and Poland and as the rest of Europe will be when the grand collapse comes." Other enemies were now becoming secondary, and differences between other powers should be resolved, for "Red Russia is the universal enemy of civilization – and, above all, of those free institutions and civil blessings that have put the United States in the van of democratic states."[47]

This was, after all, what William Randolph Hearst sought to preserve. He had once believed that radicalism and socialism, both dangerous to the American society he wished to safeguard, could to some extent be combatted by stealing their thunder – by adopting, carefully and judiciously, those parts of their programs that could justifiably be said to improve the lot of the lower classes and to remove the just grievances under which they laboured. He had once thought – though not for long – that if the Bolshevik revolution were to burst upon a country not blessed like his own with an open and democratic system of government under which genuine differences could be composed and grievances redressed, it would achieve the same objects through somewhat more precipitate means. But like his fellow progressives, Hearst was not a revolutionary. He wanted to give the working class, the mass of the people, their just deserts; but he also wanted to keep the system substantially as it was.

As the thirties progressed, Hearst saw what he had once thought of as a hopeful experiment in mass rule in Russia degenerate into a bloody and oppressive dictatorship, ruled by ideologues who sought to spread their pernicious doctrines outside their own country, by persuasion if possible and by subversion or force if not. At the same time he watched the Roosevelt administration – which he, along with so many others, had greeted in late 1932 and early 1933 with such hope – take what he had regarded as its progressivism in a direction he could not accept, down a path he saw leading to a socialist state tied to the same pernicious ideals, the same repressive system, that existed in the Soviet Union. To Hearst the two phenomena were inextricably entwined, the one sustained by the other. Communism in the USSR, strengthened by the failure or refusal of the other powers to recognize it for what it was, made itself more secure; Communism outside the USSR, assisted by the knowing collusion or the unwitting blindness of those who parroted its doctrines, spread its menace into the democratic processes of the nations of Western Europe and of the United States, states whose political systems were perhaps too delicately balanced to resist such a determined attack.

It is easy to dismiss Hearst's anti-Communist campaign of the thirties as just another publicity stunt by a master of media manipulation or as the ranting of a disgruntled old man who looked out from his San Simeon hilltop on a world of which he no longer approved. A full accounting must surely go deeper. The heart of the campaign lay in Hearst's almost desperate attachment to his vision of the United States of America, a country where – with occasional setbacks and with considerable vigilance from the press – the democratic and capitalist system really worked. The system could overcome even the threats and debilitating effects of the Depression because within it lay the sources of American greatness, which had raised the nation to a pre-eminent position in the world and brought unrivalled prosperity. Hearst never varied in this view of his country: as the twenties and thirties progressed and he saw the apparent, or at least threatened, breakdown of the system to which he was devoted, he railed against the architects of this collapse and increasingly demanded that they and their doctrines be expunged from

American life (and, incidentally, from that of other countries). It was a narrow view and a simple one, but so compelling that Hearst spent his life upholding it.

7 Hearst and Peace

The search for international peace preoccupied Hearst as it did all other practitioners and observers of international relations of his time. He believed, or affected to believe, that war would eventually disappear from the earth. Early in 1911, commenting on a statement by a Hungarian statesman that wars could be reduced in size and destructiveness but never abolished, the *Examiner* argued that this was simply not true, that "the modern world has inherited war as it has inherited the white plague," and that "both are marked for total abolishment." It was naïve to believe that this could be done "by resolutions or prayer meetings." However, "if the greatest of industrial nations can get rid of privilege and monopoly it will achieve an unparalleled economic power, and will be formidable as an enemy and so indispensable as an ally that it can compel the peace of the world."[1]

Though the means of achieving it varied from time to time, Hearst never wavered from this view. In 1927, in his *Original Proposal for Anglo-American Understanding,* he wrote: "If war violates the principles of sound business, if it shows no profit to either party to the conflict, if it brings nothing but disaster to the individual nations concerned and demoralization to the business world, it is doomed to die." The only remaining question was, how could the United States "approach the abolition of war or, as we have lately decided to state the proposition, the establishment of universal peace?" His proposal was to build understandings among groups of nations for "peaceful and protective purposes," the first and most important group being the English-speaking nations of the world.[2]

Hearst's proposals always carried some means of enforcement. He had no faith in peace conferences or the power of simple persuasion in international affairs – even though he occasionally allowed himself to be drawn into applauding advances in these directions, and he did consistently support the principle of international arbitration. In 1899, for example, he glowed with national pride as u.s. representatives at the first Hague Peace Conference, called by the czar to discuss disarmament and the prevention of war, secured recognition for the principle of international arbitration. The United States attended the conference with the new status conferred by victory in the Spanish-American War, and Hearst forecast a great and beneficent future for his country as a world power.[3]

But a few years later, just before another Hague conference, he wrote that, for all their "fine resolutions," Andrew Carnegie and his friends would do well to spend some money on balloons and other kinds of airships, since "the tsar, for example, wouldn't be so keen on war if he knew that it would mean an airship or two destroying each of his palaces," and "nothing causes a fighting spirit to cool down so much as a certainty that it is going to get thrashed."[4] Again, Hearst applauded the establishment of a permanent international court of justice: it would have "an incalculable moral influence" and be "a constant reminder that arbitration, rather than bloodshed, is the true method of settling international differences."[5] Soon, however, he came back to the question of enforcement, supporting Carnegie's idea that, at some point in the future, the United States would assert herself firmly and give Europe the word that peace would occur. "The late Buck Fanshawe, immortalized by Mark Twain, had a similar idea of the preservation of peace. He was so fond of peace that he was wont to sally forth and thrash the entire neighborhood in order to assure it ... There is nothing to indicate that Providence is not still on the side of the heaviest battalion, whatever the Peace Society or Congress may argue to the contrary."[6] This should be the role of the United States, Hearst felt – much, perhaps, like Oliver Cromwell, who was prepared to use force to make his countrymen tolerant.

The other problem with international arbitration was that it tended to infringe on American sovereignty – sometimes American problems and interests had to be submitted to the judgment of foreigners. Thus, favourably as he viewed the establishment of the Hague tribunal, Hearst's attitude changed when practical questions were at issue. In 1912, responding to a proposal that the question of foreign rights in the Panama Canal should be submitted to the international court, he emphatically rejected such a notion. The court was characterized as a "foreign court," composed of Europeans and "Asiatics" whose ideas of government and whose interests were "diametrically opposed to those of the United States." The Canal Zone was as much American property as the District of Columbia, "a domestic possession of the United States" to which "our property rights ... are fully established by purchase," and issues that were "intimately and peculiarly American" could not safely be submitted to the court.[7]

After the First World War, with the establishment of the Permanent Court of International Justice, or World Court, these problems remained. From the immediate post-war period, when the question of American participation was first seriously considered, until January 1935, when the possibility was finally killed, the Hearst papers heaped on the court and its protagonists all the considerable scorn and venom at their command. Each time participation looked like becoming an issue again – and from time to time when it did not – the Hearst papers printed editorial after editorial, news story after news story, condemning it and all those associated with it. The court was an organization that would "settle problems affecting the welfare, fortune, and, in case of war, the physical safety of everybody in the United States." "One solitary American judge" would look on, "absolutely unable to affect any decision, while eight, ten or more EUROPEAN judges decided the world's important questions." The American would naturally be outvoted on all important questions, and further, "the European judges representing countries that owe billions to the United States would naturally feel inclined to let the United States pay the bills."[8]

In the spring and summer of 1923, as the Harding administration flirted with the idea of entry, the Hearst papers, assisted in the Senate by powerful opponents of American entry like Borah and Johnson, bombarded the president and his colleagues with this and similar attacks.[9] In July, for example, the *Examiner* printed an anti-court editorial headed "The Lesson Is: To Keep Out!" along with a cartoon showing Johnson speaking into Uncle Sam's ear and entitled "Hearkening to Hiram."[10] In November, when the new president dropped the plan to enter the court, the Hearst papers applauded; even so, they remained prepared to return to the attack whenever the proposal reappeared. Early in 1926 the issue was raised again, and Hearst accused the Coolidge administration and the Republican Party of dishonesty in their espousal of American participation.[11] In March, however, the Senate voted for entry, but with reservations – notably the so-called (and additional) fifth reservation, that the court should not consider a request for an advisory opinion on a dispute in which the U.S. had an interest without its consent. Hearst now wrote that the Senate and the House should act to prevent entry under any terms,[12] and two days later the *Examiner* threatened that it would not consider the court issue settled "until it's settled right."[13] Less than a week later, in an editorial headed "Must There Be a New Party for Americans?" the paper noted that the "outstanding fact" of current politics was the threat to found a new party to save the United States from the menace of internationalism and to keep the country out of the court and, ultimately, the League of Nations.[14] The campaign continued unabated through the spring and summer as the Hearst papers drummed four points into their readers' heads: the duplicity of the court's supporters in the United States; the equal duplicity of the European powers and international bankers who wished to inveigle the nation into the court; the ever-present danger of entering (and worse, of submitting to) such an organization; and the determination of the American people not to allow themselves to be bamboozled into agreeing to such a proposal.[15]

Finally, as the British vetoed the conditions attached to American adherence to the court, and the court's members agreed to all reservations but the fifth, the *Examiner* proclaimed that "America Is Again Free to Uphold World Justice." Under this headline an editorial called the British refusal to agree "the greatest favor imaginable" for the United States and "the triumph of historic American independence over false internationalism."[16] The idea of participation was not yet dead, however. In 1929 the Hoover administration revived it, and the Hearst press returned to attack a president who had been elected to keep the nation away from such foreign entanglements, thus going back on his word. Hearst's assault on the proposal drew added vigour from its basis in the "Root formula," negotiated in Geneva by the eighty-four-year-old target of his attacks.[17] Hearst now tied participation in the court to the question of American entry into the League of Nations, the court becoming variously the trapdoor, the back door, the side door, and the anteroom of the League through which sinister and un-American influences were trying to persuade the country to go, against its true interests.[18] Reminding the nation that eternal vigilance was still the price of liberty, an *Examiner* headline blared: "International Bankers Aided by Elihu Root Conspire to Crowd America Into World Court."[19] But Hoover, distracted by more pressing matters, delayed submitting the question to the Senate until December 1930, when Senate isolationists managed to delay consideration for four years.

By the beginning of the Roosevelt administration the League question was temporarily off the front pages, but the court question had taken its place. Soon after FDR's inauguration in 1933, Hearst ordered his papers to "make an everyday fight against the United States entering the world court or in any way entangling itself in foreign affairs."[20] Through 1934 he continued the struggle as entry to the court was once again debated in the Senate, following a positive recommendation from the Foreign Relations Committee and the administration and as his favourites, Borah, Johnson, and the other irreconcilables, led yet another fight to stop American adherence.[21] Early in 1935, as the court question finally came to a head, Hearst maintained that it was dishonest and misleading to try to persuade the people that past objections and conditions for entry had been met by the set of protocols now presented for discussion.[22] The campaign heated up as the Senate once again came to grips with the issue. Senators were under severe pressure from the president and the secretary of state, who were deaf to Hearst's call that, having accomplished much in domestic affairs and received a formidable endorsement at the polls the previous November, they should use their influence to ensure that the court issue stayed dead.[23] Hearst papers outside the capital and Hearst lobbyists inside whipped up opposition to the plan during January.[24] By the end of the month the Senate – seven votes short of the required two-thirds majority – had failed to ensure American entry into the court. The struggle was over.

The same considerations that impelled Hearst to oppose American entry into the World Court produced his opposition to the League of Nations, the organization established by the Treaty of Versailles in 1919 largely through the urging of President Wilson. In the interwar years Hearst argued concurrently against American participation in the League, but here his campaign against American participation was even more vehement. He was convinced that the attempt to persuade the United States to participate in the court was largely a cover to induce the nation to join the League later. He opposed the League as a restrictive and obtrusive organization, and he was sure that the peace treaty that had produced it was full of sinister implications for the United States.

The Treaty of Versailles was designed to settle a war that the United States had "won ... after it had been lost by the Allies," and won "with all the sacrifice, with all the envy and enmity, with all the weight of debt and woe of death which Washington foresaw as a consequence of our participation in European conflicts and complications." But it had brought no advantage to the United States. Rather, it had given Great Britain "the material advantage of immense increases in territory, of the complete control of the seas, and of a very much enlarged position of power and importance among the nations of the world."[25] The treaty was "a dishonor to America and a flat and treacherous repudiation of the most solemn pledges to the defeated peoples." Beyond this, the provisions of the treaty were dangerous, for they made "permanent peace – or even peace for any length of time – an impossibility."[26] From the time the president signed the treaty Hearst maintained that the gains made by some powers and the shameful treatment meted out to Germany would soon result in another war.[27]

In 1922, following a visit to Europe, he wrote, for a London newspaper: "It is probable there will be no great amelioration of conditions in any European country, no permanent solutions of difficulties under which various countries labor until the essential ideas and objects of the Treaty of Versailles are materially modified. That treaty was made immediately after the war, when hatred was at its height and when victors found it impossible and unnatural even to consider from a broad viewpoint the general good of Europe."[28] A dozen years later Hearst still regarded the treaty as "one of the most vicious instruments that was ever framed." It was "quite as much of a cause of the confusion and demoralization which prevails in Europe today as the war itself was. Furthermore, the perverted provisions of that treaty make another war almost inevitable unless some peaceful method can be found of remedying its iniquities." He labelled the settlement "a treaty of evil and injustice," at the same time pleading that, to "avoid the greater evil of war," the powers should "remedy its injustice in reason and in peace."[29]

But for the League of Nations, a part of this iniquitous treaty and a product of the machinations of the untrustworthy Woodrow Wilson, Hearst reserved his special fury during the twenties and thirties. He saw in the League not only a continuation of the disreputable methods of proceeding commonly adopted by the European powers but also a means by which other powers could gain a hold over the policies of the United States and – if need arose – force the nation into courses of action that suited European rather than American interests. Until the League collapsed at the beginning of the Second World War, Hearst maintained unswerving opposition to it. As with the World Court, his papers published editorials expressing this opposition every time American adherence became an issue and frequently when it was not, and he never ceased to remind the American people of their – and his – wisdom in refusing to have anything to do with such a pernicious organization.

Early in 1919, even before the peace treaty was signed, the *New York American* carried a letter Hearst had written to the editor (as usual, the letter also appeared in the other Hearst papers), commenting on a speech on the League by Senator James A. Reed of Missouri, who later became one of the irreconcilables in opposition to the League.

Hearst noted: "[Reed] said what we have said – that this country has prospered and grown to be the greatest country in the world under a policy of no entangling alliances with European nations, and that not only Washington, but Jefferson, Madison, Monroe and Jackson and Calhoun and Clay and Webster and Lincoln and Cleveland had advocated a policy of no alliance with Europe, and had guided the country successfully under that policy." Now seconded by Hearst, Reed wanted to preserve this policy and to know clearly where the League would take the nation before he agreed to support entry.[30] A few days later an editorial pleaded for some hard thinking about the League, concluding "LET US BE SURE" before agreeing to entry that it would not cost more than it would be worth to the United States.[31]

In March 1919 the Hearst papers began simply to condemn the League outright as a plan that, if acceded to, would violate the traditions of the United States, promote rather than prevent war, and make the nation forever a party to European conflicts. In a private letter Hearst wrote, "I do not consider it a league to keep us out of war but a league to get us into war." He went on: "A man does not keep himself free from the smallpox by going to bed with four other people who have it; and we cannot keep free from war by tying ourselves up with nations like England, France, Italy and Japan, which have the war disease in its worst form."[32] As spring moved into summer Hearst cranked up the campaign against the League, pressing his anti-League sentiments on his publishing friends and making sure that all his newspapers, particularly some that, unusually, he suspected of independent thought on the question, were with him.[33] His own editorials and those of his writers became more frequent and more violently opposed to American entry into the League until, during the fall of 1919, when the treaty was debated in the Senate, they excoriated it almost daily and urged senators to do their patriotic duty. The accomplishment of this objective came late in November. The defeat of the treaty was greeted with an exuberant editorial headed "Thanks Be to God, This Nation Has Indeed Had a New Birth of Freedom."[34]

However, the Hearst press did not relax its vigilance. In the presidential election of 1920 the Democratic candidate, James M. Cox, loaded down with the albatross of American entrance into the League by the president's and his party's insistence on including it in their platform, could make no headway against the sugary promises of the Republicans. Hearst greeted the result of the election with enthusiasm. In November he wrote: "Mr. Wilson wanted a referendum on his League of Nations and he has had it." The result was, as Hearst saw it, an unequivocal condemnation of the president's policy: "He now knows, and certain other foolish politicians now know, that the American people prefer to follow the patriotic precepts of Washington, Jefferson, Madison, Monroe, Jackson, Lincoln and Cleveland rather than the selfish ambition and visionary theories of Mr. Wilson, who, as he himself has said, 'Gets his news and views of the world from the weekly edition of the London *Times.'*" The editorial went on to claim that "this historic election is purely and simply a repudiation by sterling American citizens of the Wilson party and that party's pro-British, un-American policies" and that "our country is no longer a crown colony. It is our dear, independent United States – the Land of the Free."[35]

In September 1923, when a conflict flared up between Greece and Italy, his papers noted that, had the United States entered the League, it would now be obliged to send troops to Europe. "That," he pointed out, "is what we have escaped."[36] Two weeks later, the League having been unable to solve this problem, an editorial headed "The Failure of the League" indicated that the American people "should be proud that they are not a party to such international hypocrisy."[37] In the following year, when a new protocol was proposed to provide for enforcement of World Court decisions by force if necessary, he claimed that the League had now become specifically a plot against the United States.[38] A few weeks later, after the Democratic presidential candidate, John W. Davis, suffered a crushing defeat by Calvin Coolidge, Hearst asked whether the small vote he had received was not attributable to his support for the League of Nations.[39]

Later, in his proposal for Anglo-American understanding, Hearst wrote that the proposal was designed in part to get over difficulties presented by the League of Nations and inherent weaknesses that it could not be expected to overcome: "The League of Nations has shown that an organization of heterogeneous elements is impracticable and ineffective." The League had been unable to present a united front on any issue or to intervene effectively to secure peace on any occasion; it had confined itself "to copybook maxims that no one of its members lives up to," so that "the League of Nations is a phantom, with form but no substance." The inclusion of nations with different traditions, languages, and objectives could only ruin such an international organization.[40]

Increasingly, as the twenties went on, the Hearst papers linked the League with the World Court. In 1926 Hearst wrote that "word has been passed to World Court advocates at Washington to soft-pedal on the League of Nations until the Senate has voted the United States into the World Court." When this had been achieved, "as every League advocate knows and every intelligent citizen should know, we shall be urged to join the League of Nations also, 'for our own protection.'"[41] The two were now frequently characterized as twin plots of sinister foreign diplomatic and financial interests, designed to fool the United States into abandoning her traditional policies. Increased vigilance was necessary, since the apparently innocent movement to persuade the nation into the court was merely part of a larger and more dangerous scheme.[42]

As he saw Europe moving again towards war, Hearst stepped up his campaign against the League. In a 1927 editorial he quoted British statesman Austen Chamberlain as saying that even Great Britain could not "pierce the fog of Europe's diplomatic intrigue and be sure that her armed forces will be employed on the side of justice." If this was so for Great Britain, Hearst asked, how much more true was it for the United States? Thus, the nation should stay away from the League and require the government "to look to our defenses and mind its own business."[43] This was, in fact, what the Coolidge and Hoover administrations did during the late twenties and thirties as – despite pressure from influential people both inside and outside Congress who wished to join – the League became a dead issue politically.

There is considerable evidence to suggest that FDR repudiated the League early in 1932 because he felt that, if he did not, his chances of gaining the Democratic nomination and the presidency would be damaged. How much the opposition of the Hearst papers had to do with this decision is questionable, but it is clear that many people, probably including Hearst himself, felt that he had been instrumental in producing the candidate's perhaps insincere change of mind.[44] Thus, when in April 1932 Roosevelt condemned the League because "its major function has not been the broad overwhelming purpose of world peace, but rather a mere meeting place for the political discussion of strictly European political national difficulties," the Hearst papers saluted him for his conclusion that, "in these, the United States should have no part."[45]

Hearst never let the Roosevelt administration forget these statements, and went on printing his customary anti-League editorials. By the end of 1933 he was writing that, "of its complete failure, there can be no question" and that recent blows to the League's prestige "were merely confirmatory evidence of what had before been clearly apparent, that the League had long ceased to be an effective, or even a responsive, instrumentality for the accomplishment of any of its expressed aims." Such news was, however, merely "mildly entertaining, but not of agitating interest to A REMOTE ON-LOOKER – which THE PEOPLE OF THE UNITED STATES are resolutely DETERMINED THE COUNTRY SHALL CONTINUE TO BE."[46] In the following year, when adherence to the World Court and hence the League was again proposed, the Hearst papers conducted a strong campaign against it.[47]

In 1936, when a conference of Western Hemisphere nations was scheduled to be held in Buenos Aires, Hearst was informed by Coblentz that this was simply an attempt to secure American participation in a hemispheric league, a move that Latin American diplomats hoped would eventually bring about American membership in the League of Nations.[48] But this stratagem also failed, and the Hearst papers recorded their satisfaction as the League became less effective and more of a burden to the world whose troubles it had been founded to ease. In the summer of 1937, Hearst characterized it as "an international sewing circle for prying into world troubles, and thus ... a potential WAR-MAKER." Its undeniable failure meant that "American judgment in rejecting the League at the outset has been vindicated by the experience of other nations."[49] Later, as war loomed in Europe, Hearst smugly recorded a statement of the British prime minister, Neville Chamberlain, that the League could not provide the security that many had hoped it would. The United States had, of course, known this all along. "The League has been exactly the instrument of European political intrigue and INSTIGATION TO WAR which the Hearst newspapers predicted it would be." It had never produced peace and security and had "kept alive the elements of hate, passion and greed which caused the World War, and is responsible as much as anything in the world today for the war clouds now hovering ominously over Europe and England."[50]

This was the judgment of William Randolph Hearst on the League of Nations. For him such an organization, made up of members of diverse and conflicting traditions and interests, could never succeed, and it was foolish for the people of the United States to imagine that there lay their security and peace. Ultimately, the only way to security and peace lay in constant preparedness for war.

The campaign for preparedness was the longest and most consistent the Hearst papers ever pursued. The perceived means of preparing for war changed from reliance on naval strength alone to the need for a strong army and navy, thence to building the air force as well as the other two arms of the services, but the basic message was always the same: peace could only be assured through strength, a strength based entirely on American resources.

In 1895 the *Examiner* noted that "we are not likely to have any fighting to do in the near future. Nevertheless the constant recurrence of excursions and alarums teaches us that peace has not yet settled upon the world with the clinging comprehensiveness of a bay fog, and that a nation that would be secure must still keep its powder dry." This was followed by a plea for reform of the army and navy.[51] This plea was not, of course, based on the needs of the European powers but on the unique situation of the United States. Shortly before the Spanish-American War, Hearst commented that the nation did not need a great navy like that of Great Britain, for it was "not dependent on its command of the sea for its national life." American needs were *defensive:* "a navy that is capable of defending its coasts against any force that can be brought against them ... a force that will protect this continent from aggression, and give us the assurance of safety ... and enable us to make good our declaration that no European power can acquire further territory on this continent without our consent."[52]

This view was confirmed by the outbreak of war a few months later. Writing in June 1898, Hearst commended the speed with which the country had prepared to fight – at the same time noting that the readiness for war of the European powers had been far greater. He concluded, "While there is no necessity for the immense armaments of Europe, the appropriation for the naval forces must be more liberal in the future."[53]

Between the Spanish-American War and the outbreak of the First World War, Hearst constantly repeated this message, which was apparently ignored by the administrations in Washington, none of whose efforts met the demands of the Hearst press. "Our policy," he stated in 1901 in an editorial comparing German and American naval building programs, "is entirely defensive. We simply draw a line around the two Americas and say that within that line there is no more land open to pre-emption ... The best way to convince all the world of the impossibility of upsetting the Monroe Doctrine is to guard it by a mighty navy." In pursuit of this policy the country had been doing well up to that year, but faced with a greatly increased German building program, the Congress had authorized no ships at all for the current year. This situation could not be allowed to continue.[54] Six months later the *Examiner* called on the president to add action to a brave speech in which he called for the American navy and merchant marine to be strengthened and placed in a pre-eminent position on the oceans of the world.[55] The following year Hearst used the Venezuelan crisis to point up the same message. The affair was teaching the United States that "a concert of European powers to assault a South American republic too feeble to resist any one of them that possesses a navy, is not a very difficult thing to arrange." At the same time, the powers were finding out that the United States would "not interfere with such an assault, even if it goes to the length of seizing and sinking the Republic's warships and bombarding her forts." The American people could never, he said, be too sensitive to the demands of the Monroe Doctrine, and the time to make this point was whenever the European powers started to encroach anew on the Western Hemisphere. The time to *prepare* to make the point, however, was in peacetime – by building a navy strong enough to keep the Europeans out.[56]

This was the lesson that the Hearst papers drew from every warlike incident. When the Japanese defeated the Russian fleet in 1905, Hearst latched on to the significance of the event for the United States – that "the battle and its results demonstrate that a nation with two long coasts and with widely separated colonies, such as ours, cannot exist without a navy equal to that of any other on the face of the earth."[57] A series of editorials and news stories followed, emphasizing the need to strengthen the Pacific Coast defences and the fleet in that ocean. Hearst pointed out that San Francisco was practically defenceless and that, in a Pacific war, Hawaii and the Philippines would have to be abandoned to their fate so that the meagre fleet stationed there could withdraw to defend the mainland.[58] Better defences in the Pacific became a recurrent call as American weakness and increasing Japanese strength there grew more obvious.[59]

In the early years of the century, as the powers of Europe prepared for war, building up their land and sea forces to unprecedented levels, Hearst continued to call for a stronger American navy. "I am opposed to war," he wrote in 1908, "… and opposed to the maintenance of large military and naval establishments by the civilized nations of the world, but inasmuch as the citizens of America cannot control the actions of other powers, and inasmuch as this country, despite its desire for peace, may be forced into foreign war, I am earnestly in favor of a navy sufficiently powerful to protect the coasts of the United States of America."[60] "Preparedness," he stated a month later, "is a logical and insistible argument for peace," and he called on the Congress to do its duty and authorize larger naval expenditures.[61]

Heast also supported sending the American battle fleet on manoeuvres in the Pacific. The fleet had won for the nation "in superior measure the respect and goodwill of our South American neighbors [and] ... demonstrated to the world ... the fiber and endurance of our ships and the skill and discipline of our men."[62] Some months later, as the fleet reached China, he recorded its earlier cordial reception in Japan with satisfaction. This cordiality was "of the same sort evinced by a small fox terrier when a large bulldog drops in to visit him; but it is cordiality nevertheless, and as long as it shall endure there will be no danger of a war with the little yellow nation over the Pacific."[63]

Once again, the lesson of all this was clear: "to maintain peace in the future it is necessary to be prepared for war."[64]

A year before the outbreak of the First World War, discussing the American navy's current standing as the fourth largest in the world, Hearst summed up his message on preparedness thus: "We want no little Americans, no little navy, no bullying enemies, no threatened wars, no peace with shame. We want big Americans, in a big America, guarded by a big navy, fearing nobody, bullying nobody, insulted by nobody and sitting in peace and honor, ringed with her hundred ships of battle, ready and able to face the world in arms in a just struggle."[65] With war in Europe a fact, however, his emphasis – though not his basic message – changed. Now there was a concrete danger, not only from Europe but also from Mexico, where, with the continuing civil war, the United States might be drawn into extensive operations. The need for a strong navy remained; now, however, the Hearst papers increasingly emphasized other forms of preparedness. A great standing army was becoming a necessity, but Hearst fought shy of following this conclusion through. Even though he wanted the nation to be ready with land forces if need be, there were dangers in establishing such a force. "A great standing army makes for despotism, absolutism," and this was, of course, to be avoided at all costs.

But in the same editorial in which he described these dangers Hearst began a campaign of advocating, strongly and persistently, a measure that earlier had merited only occasional mention: formation of a trained citizen army. He announced himself in favour of universal military training, for "a citizenry trained in arms makes for democracy and equality," and "it provides the means for the Nation's protection and democracy's defense."[66] Officers for such a force could easily be obtained through "the establishment of government universities where students can receive a general education combined with a military education." If this provision were enacted, there would be no need for a more rigorous system than the one the Swiss operated, "which provided a formidable and efficient military force without interfering with the civil life of the citizens."[67] Hearst maintained these views while conducting his vigorous campaign to keep the United States out of the war, but once it entered, he did not fail to point out that "NOW it would be hard to find in all the United States a dunce so stupid that he does not perceive that we were right."[68]

The end of the war brought no change in the line taken by the Hearst papers, though it produced, at least for the first half of the interwar period, no more noticeable effect than it had before 1914. Late in 1919 a Hearst editorial supported the call of the American Legion for national preparedness and universal military service.[69] His news-

THE VOICE OF EXPERIENCE

J APAN does not want to discuss anything that will threaten its "special position" in the far East.
   Japan's "special position" is that of land grabber, trade grabber, terrorizer of weaker peoples.
   Disarmed China Knows now what premature disarmament means. The United States ought not to overlook
the sad example.

San Francisco Examiner, 18 August 1921

papers continued to advocate building a navy second to none, an issue that was brought sharply into focus by the Washington Naval
Conference of 1921–22.[70] As the discussions began, the *Examiner*
noted that they would not result in disarmament; the best that could
be hoped for was a temporary settlement in the Pacific. Great Britain,
the paper claimed, had already decided that she was to be the arbiter
of the Pacific region, had already sent her fleet there, and had defeated or disarmed her enemies one by one. "Our only possible safeguard against being the next on the list is to use our vast resources to
maintain a navy so powerful that no Power will be willing to attack

us."[71] A campaign to keep the United States out of subsequent talks and agreements was mounted, but it failed when, at the urging of the administration, the Senate ratified the Washington Treaty. The *Examiner* lamented the abandonment of the old American policy of independence and the Senate's adherence to "an alliance not with all the nations of the earth like the League of Nations, but an exclusive alliance to guarantee the possessions and indefinable rights of the three aggressive imperialisms of the earth, Britain, France and Japan."[72]

Suspicious of the Washington Treaty, Hearst was even more suspicious of subsequent events in the Pacific, where he saw the British in particular trying to reinterpret the treaty to their own advantage. He called for the administration not to be fooled and to watch British actions closely.[73] "War is the greatest misfortune that can overtake a nation," he claimed; "the only way to hold war afar off is to have the ships, the guns and the men to hold it afar off,"[74] a startling echo of the British music-hall song, popular in the war scare of 1878, that had added the word "jingoism" to the English language:

We don't want to fight, yet by Jingo! if we do,
We've got the ships, we've got the men, and got the money too.

He attacked the "weeping willows" and "parlor pinks" who would scrap the army and navy, reminding his readers that "peace is a sensitive plant which must be surrounded by a strong barbed-wire fence."[75]

In 1929, as the powers prepared to reconvene the naval conference in London, Hearst once again moved to oppose any attempt to surrender American interests to the schemes of other powers. He promised support to the Hoover administration in its attempt to secure naval parity in London and told his editors to do everything they could to help this cause.[76] As the American delegation left for London, he addressed an editorial to them, reminding them that the American people expected them to protect the nation's rights as a first-class sea power and that "yours is a first-class country, deserving and needing a first-class defense." It was, he said, better to achieve "no agreement at London at all than one falling short of complete and unrestricted parity with any sea power in the world."[77] Hoover, however, convinced (as he had noted in his inaugural adddress) that disarmament was the way to peace, had a somewhat different view of the purpose of the conference that began in late January 1930. Thus, within a few months, the conference unsurprisingly proved to be another disappointment. According to Hearst, the Americans were being "jockeyed into a position of either being responsible for the failure of the Conference, or agreeing to join the League of Nations system under another name." The delegation should come home.[78]

When it did, however, it was with a treaty that the Hearst press could not accept. The treaty, agreed on 22 April, provided for a 10:10:7 ratio for British, American, and Japanese cruisers, extended the moratorium on capital ships for five years, limited tonnage for other types of ships, and set rules for submarine warfare. A final clause allowed a signatory to exceed the limits if it believed that naval building by an outside power endangered it. In June and July of 1930, as the Senate debated ratification, Hearst took up the fight against this new betrayal of the American people, this new surrender of all the precepts of American naval policy "from George Washington to Calvin Coolidge," and fiercely attacked the president "for crippling the ability of the American Navy to perform" its job.[79] But once again the fight was lost when, after some delay, the Senate passed the measure with only nine votes dissenting.[80]

His support for a powerful American navy firmly established, Hearst took a new tack in his campaign for preparedness during the twenties and thirties. In the spring of 1925 an *Examiner* editorial proclaimed "Forget Past; Build Planes!" Hearst wrote in reaction to a statement by General William Mitchell that President Harding had called on the Washington Conference to tell the other powers about the test-bombing of an old German battleship in 1921. The United States "did not think it fair to stop building obsolete ships and let our rivals go on wasting their money on ships that couldn't hurt us if they tried." The nation should have started to build planes then, when its rivals had, but now, irrespective of the truth of this report, "the national defense requires that we quit idling and build planes!"[81] From this point on the Hearst papers became a persistent advocate of increasing the air force, maintaining that it was folly to ignore the important role of air power in any future war and drawing lessons from the events of the thirties to demonstrate this.[82]

As that decade progressed and the possibility of another war in Europe grew, the Hearst papers returned vehemently to the issue of American neutrality and the view that they had maintained from before American entry into the First World War. Once again arguing that the correct American posture was one of strict neutrality, Hearst now also noted that "the looker-on, though he may see most of the diplomatic game, may get into trouble from both sides if not properly prepared to defend himself." Holding that the European powers did not confine their hostility to their own kind but despised the United States "with all the hatred of a debtor who can get no more out of his creditor," Hearst concluded that the nation "need lose no sleep over

their hatred if we are not to lose any by being inadequately prepared," for "preparedness is the only pillow on which a patriot can
sleep."[83]

With the election of FDR in 1932 Hearst had for the first time found
an administration he could support on this issue, and the policies of
the administration did much to enable him to sleep soundly. The
United States had slipped behind the other powers, but in 1933 FDR
allocated $250 million from the National Recovery Act towards in-
creasing ship-building. Further, in the following year Congress approved the Vinson-Trammel Bill, which authorized construction up to
the limits set by the London Treaty. In January 1936 Hearst noted that
"Mr. Roosevelt, with commendable vision, has rendered a superb service to the country by submitting to Congress, for its consideration,
what is, perhaps, the most completely rounded and adequate program for the national defense by land that any President has proposed since the close of the World War."[84] The following year he gave
the same kind of praise to the President's naval program, greeting
Navy Day by saying that "four years of alert attention to the importance of naval defense, for which the Roosevelt Administration
cannot be too highly praised, will make Wednesday's observance of
Navy Day a satisfying occasion."[85]

The only real reservation that the Hearst papers expressed about-
FDR's military policies was his persistent refusal to build enough airplanes to secure the United States from attack. In 1938 Hearst noted
that the National Aeronautical Planning Conference had been told by
"a competent aviation authority that the United States is NOT PRE-
PARED TO WIN a war of defense in the air." The editorial called for a
speedy remedy for this unfortunate situation while there was still
time.[86] This plea continued up to the entry of the United States into
the Second World War, as the Hearst papers strove to ensure that the
nation was sufficiently prepared for an air war and to prevent it from
being too generous to nations already engaged in the conflict.[87]

By the late thirties, however, few people were paying attention to
Hearst's long-running campaign to see that, in the event of war, the
country was prepared to meet whatever challenge might be presented. Almost alone Hearst fought for this objective, and a partici-
pant in the events of these years has commented: "As I think back
over the years 1937, 1938, 1939 and 1940, I realize what a tremendous
effort the Hearst newspapers made to awaken this country to a real-
ization of its defenseless condition." Bernard Baruch went on to say,
"Yours [Hearst's] was one of the few voices raised in an effort to get
our country prepared. How different things would have been if your
efforts and those of men like myself had not been so futile."[88] Once

again, spurred on by his belief that the United States had ultimately only herself to rely on, that international alliances, law, and organizations were no defence against the machinations of the other nations – "nations make international law in time of peace, and break all law in time of war"[89] – and that the only real defence was the nation's own strength, Hearst had fought a largely ineffective campaign because his countrymen were, on the whole, taking no notice.

8 Hearst and War

Apart from the Spanish-American War, which Hearst did everything in his power to encourage, the United States fought in two conflicts of far greater importance during the period covered by this study. During the approach to u.s. involvement in both cases, between summer 1914 and spring 1917 and between fall 1939 and December 1941, Hearst marshalled all his forces to prevent his country's participation. In doing so, he presented a picture of extraordinary certainty as the nation and its government wrestled with dilemmas presented by war in Europe. On 5 August 1914, the day after war broke out in Europe, the *San Francisco Examiner* made its first editorial comment on the First World War. "The President of the United States," it indicated, "will receive the full approval and hearty co-operation of all right-thinking people in his counsel to the nation of calmness and impartiality and consideration during the European war ... Under all circumstances, we support the President's appeal to the press and the people to be calm, and to rise superior to the madness that has inflamed Europe."[1]

The major thrust of this comment came in the last phrase, intimating that the United States should rise above the European conflict and show herself superior to the squalid and violent wranglings of that continent by remaining outside them – and, by implication, gaining all possible advantage from them. The latter purpose came first to the minds of Hearst editorial writers. Under the heading "The Mighty Prize War Brings to Us," an editorial published early in August noted: "The conclusion is irresistible that this hideous and frightful convulsion of Europe will be the rapid rise of this nation to a height of riches, power, might and commercial dominion such as no nation has ever attained since great Rome fell." The United States had only to remain aloof and to ring herself about with a navy strong enough to insulate her from the war "to insure a century of peace and the continuance through generations of the domination of the trade and finances of the world." The editorial concluded that "such is the magnificent prospect ahead; such is the high destiny which beckons to the Republic beyond that curtain of dreadful war which hides, for the time, the embattled peoples of Europe."[2]

Less than a month later Hearst explained his primary attitude towards the European war in an editorial entitled "The Cost of Kings." He called the conflict "that most dreadful of all wars – a civil war" between states that were natural allies and ought to be living in peace and serenity and even forming a United States of Europe. All the nations, he maintained, were equally blameworthy in starting the war: it "is attributable to the survival in Europe of medieval institutions long outgrown by modern society, to the prosecution of imperial policies in the selfish interest of greedy hereditary dynasties." It was not a modern war but "a war of the Middle Ages, caused by those conditions of the Middle Ages, monarchic and aristocratic, which still persist in Europe and which as long as they persist will repress popular development and dominate popular sentiment ... This is a war of kings, brought on by the assassination of the king's nephew, who is of no more actual importance to modern society than the nephew of any other individual, citizen or subject, in all Europe." Everybody deplored anarchy, Hearst concluded, and denounced the anarchist who killed a king, so "let us equally denounce the royal anarchists who in cold blood and in snug safety murder a million fellow men entrusted to their protecting care."[3]

This was not the only matter that Hearst found reprehensible in the developing conflict. It was bad enough if the nations of Europe wished, by their own crass and short-sighted behaviour, to destroy one another and to weaken, perhaps irreparably, their internal systems and their external influence. But the disaster of this war was not merely local and European; it was world-wide, "a destruction of the heritage of civilization of which we Americans are part possessors." The war would mean "a diminution of the numbers, and a weakening of the power in the world of the white nations – of the Occidental nations of which we are one." Further, it would result in "an assault upon the standards, the ideals, the conditions of life which have been the contribution of those Occidental nations to the civilization of the world – which indeed have constituted the civilization of the modern world." Thus, the war might also mean a strengthening of Oriental ambitions and even their eventual triumph.[4]

Hearst was clearly terrified that the war, by bringing about the mutual slaughter of the white races, would advance the triumph of the yellow peril. Just a week later, in a cable to two major British newspaper editors, he warned of the consequences to white civilization of long continuance of the war – that that civilization might "again be submerged in an overwhelming inundation of barbarism." Once again, he cried, the Hun was at the gate, "but the Hun comes not, nor ever has come, from Germany, nor from any part of Europe, but will come, as he has come in the past, in successive, almost irresistible tides of invasion from the interior of Asia."[5]

Hearst was determined that the United States, while remaining aloof from the conflict, should pursue the twin objectives of engineering her own commercial advantage and of helping to secure a swift and just peace in Europe, a difficult task under any circumstances but an essential one in these. Until American entry into the war brought his argument on these questions to an end, this was the position he firmly maintained.

In this Hearst was not – at least in the early stages – far from Woodrow Wilson and the majority of his Cabinet. The president was pro-British, though he did his best to behave impartially. Secretary of State William Jennings Bryan, the only important foreign policy adviser who was not pro-British, resigned rather than send the government's second *Lusitania* note, demanding that the German government disown their submarine commander's action,[6] pay reparations, and stop attacking passenger ships. He was replaced by the counsellor for the Department of State, Robert M. Lansing, who was also pro-British, though not as overtly as the United States ambassador to the United Kingdom, Walter Hines Page.

Early in the war Hearst began an ambitious campaign for peace, a campaign that, though well organized and widespread, had little success and was in fact often ridiculed by other papers.[7] Writing in the fall of 1915, Hearst, under the banner headline, "LET US HAVE PEACE," proclaimed: "We Americans are neutral. But are we not interested? Are we not involved in this fearful struggle? Are we not involved in it as part of the human family, as members of the white race, as participants in the Western civilization, all of which is threatened by a prolongation of this dreadful carnage?" It was the duty of the United States to be interested. Although America alone could probably stop the war, "America at the head of the neutral nations of the world could stop it easily. The belligerents understand perfectly that a union of neutral nations would have an overwhelming balance of power." The nation must use this power to stop the war and, with the other neutrals, "enroll as SOLDIERS OF PEACE, with the high purpose of restoring peace throughout the world and protecting our country from the horrors of hostile invasion."[8]

On one of very few occasions during Wilson's two terms as president, Hearst supported him in his efforts to bring American mediation to the combatants, constantly urging the president to greater efforts in this area. In the spring and summer of 1916, as some prospect of beginning negotiations appeared, Hearst wrote of "President Wilson's Wonderful Opportunity" as, "with the acceptance of Germany's reply to his note on the submarine question, the path of honorable and effective mediation between the warring Powers opens before Mr. Wilson." In this situation "we are bound to believe that the President is as anxious as any other sensible and humane American to see the dreadful devastation and slaughter in Europe speedily ended."[9] This pressure on the president continued through the year until just before Christmas, when the *Examiner*'s front page for 21 December announced, "Mr. Wilson sends peace notes to war nations," and the day's editorial was headed, "In the Name of the American People, Mr. President, We Salute and Thank You."[10]

While constantly supporting the search for peace in Europe, however, the Hearst papers did not neglect other aspects of the struggle. Their attitude towards preparedness for war has already been discussed, but such preparedness was always seen as precautionary – against the day when belligerents might turn their hostility towards the United States, or the country might be obliged to enter the conflict to defend its own legitimate interests.[11] Until shortly before the latter possibility became a reality, it remained for Hearst an unthinkable eventuality.

Early in 1915 he proposed that a league of neutral nations be formed, for reasons beyond securing an early end to the war: "The position of Great Britain is that she must stop our trade with Germany in order to have any chance of beating Germany. Were Germany stronger on the seas she would contend that she must stop our trade with Great Britain and France in order to beat them sooner. In other words, we suffer no matter who wins." In this situation the United States' position was clear: "as a neutral nation we do not care whether the allies beat Germany or Germany beats the allies, but ... we do care whether either of them beats us." Thus, he advocated a league of neutrals "denouncing the doctrine of contraband and affirming the future right and the future determination to send its trading ships to any nation desiring trade, no matter whether that nation is at war with another or not."[12]

At the same time Hearst insisted that the American press and government give demonstrably fair treatment to both sides in the war. He maintained: "It would be much more complimentary to our national intelligence and information if American publications and American citizens would drop sentimental talk about 'martyred little peoples,' 'Huns at the gates,' 'scraps of paper' and all that sort of manufactured excuse, and recognize the truth that Europe's struggle is simply a scramble of Europe's financiers, military and naval aristocracies and throned rulers to rob one another of trade, profit and territory." If the American people could keep this point firmly in mind, said the *Examiner*, Americans might then be able to avoid taking sides, to preserve a real neutrality, and to "go about our own business until these war-mad lunatics get enough of their folly and quit."[13]

But the specific question of neutral rights, particularly as it affected American trade with the belligerents, dominated American discussions of United States relations with Europe. The horror stories in the American press, the clear leaning of perhaps a majority of the government and the people towards the Allies, the question of war loans – all were academic beside the concrete, damaging, and unavoidable question of freedom of the seas. In March 1915, when the British prime minister announced to the House of Commons that the government did not propose to allow any goods to be carried to Germany, the *Examiner* commended him for his frankness: "The allies did not purpose 'TO ALLOW THEIR EFFORTS TO BE STRANGLED IN A NETWORK OF JUDICIAL NICETIES.'" It was now important, Hearst felt, for the United States and other neutrals to realize that the major belligerents had abandoned all pretence of observing international law, and "the only force to be considered is that of giant howitzers, super dreadnoughts, Zeppelins, mines and submarines – and the fact that war is war." Protests would, of course, be made, but they were useless when made by nations that were neither in the position nor had the desire to meet force with force, and against "maddened peoples fighting for mere rage quite so much as for national existence and wholly indifferent to any force save that of arms."[14]

Through the rest of 1915 and 1916 blow after blow was struck at the already fragile American neutrality. Both the Allies and the Germans stepped up their campaigns to deny neutral trade to their enemies, and though each side tried, until early 1917, not to provoke the United States so much that she would declare war, the U.S. government gave up any serious attempt to make either adhere to the 1909 Declaration of London, which had been the most recent attempt to codify the law of the sea. Incidents like the sinking of the liner *Lusitania* off the coast of Ireland in May 1914, with the loss of 128 American lives, and of the French steamer *Sussex* in March 1916 helped to stir up anti-German feeling, while the increase of German submarine activity in general served to push the Americans further from neutrality. The Hearst papers, however, still held staunchly to their position of fairness to all belligerents, and strict neutrality along with preparedness as the only way of keeping the country safely out of the conflict.[15] In the spring of 1916, for example, the *Examiner* wrote that "the truest and most patriotic American is the American who is really and truly neutral in speech and act." It was just as unpatriotic to be pro-British as to be pro-German, just as foolish to publish British propaganda as to disseminate German propaganda: "Our clear duty to our own country and to mankind is to be absolutely and most scrupulously neutral."[16] The nation should resist both British and German aggression, Hearst wrote six months later, and demand "strict respect for the rights of every other nation and strict respect from every other nation for the rights of America and American citizens."[17]

Even as 1917 began and war came closer, the cry of the Hearst papers was still the same. At the beginning of February, Hearst wrote: "We are profoundly hopeful that our own peace can be maintained and that Mr. Wilson will find a way to do so with honor." But it was becoming increasingly obvious that this would not occur and that the prospect of peace was more and more an illusion. Eventually, Hearst promised that, as his papers had never been, "in all these troublous times, either pro-Teuton or pro-Ally, but always earnestly and loyally and with a whole heart American, so it will continue to be if it is written in the books of fate and destiny that our battle-flags must again be unfurled."[18]

For the next two months, as the nation edged closer to war, he continued to take this line, consistently opposing any thought that the interests of others – even potential or actual allies – should be placed ahead of those of the United States. When the Congress was presented with a request for $3 billion to make "good the more or less shaky notes and bonds of foreign nations," he advised caution. The job of the government was to see that no expense was spared in preparing the United States for war, but care should be taken "about stripping our treasury for OTHER nations' benefit."[19] Later he coined the slogan that eventually appeared on the masthead of all the Hearst papers – "America First Should Be Every American's Motto" – as he declared: "We will do our duty to our allies, our full duty to our allies, but we should not be expected to sacrifice our whole interest for the benefit of our allies and leave ourselves naked to the enemy invader."[20]

Thus, reluctantly, the Hearst newspapers watched the entry of the United States into the First World War. Their attitude between the outbreak of war and the spring of 1917 had earned them enormous hostility throughout the United States. In New York, Hearst's newspapers were hardly allowed on the streets; he himself was generally regarded as being pro-German and anti-Ally – even, in fact, as going a good deal further in his leanings towards those who would later become the enemy.[21] He was watched by agents of the Military Intelligence Division of the War Department [22] and was connected (after the war) with an investigation into pro-German activities in certain parts of the country.[23] As even one of his strongest supporters noted, Hearst was for many years widely criticized for his supposedly pro-German position.[24]

What, however, was the truth of these allegations, suspicions, biases against Hearst and his newspapers? What evidence exists that Hearst was really pro-German or even went so far as to consort with the enemy? Is there reason to hold to the belief (as many did, during the war) that Hearst actually worked for the Germans? This chapter will attempt to demonstrate that there is no substance to the allegations, no evidence of collaboration, let alone employment. Hearst was guilty, rather, of tactical errors, unfortunate associations, and a stubborn determination to stick to his guns however the fighting went. In this situation he was his own worst enemy. He criticized the Allies (perhaps more than he need have done);[25] he was careless about his contacts with such men as the German ambassador Count Johann von Bernstorff and the shady and disreputable Paul Bolo Pasha, later executed in France as a German spy;[26] he opposed almost every pro-Allied measure proposed in the United States, especially those designed to help the British;[27] he fought bitterly against the president; and even after America had entered the war and helped Britain to defeat the Germans, he wrote that, without its unfortunate autocracy, Germany would be perfectly all right, and declared "a plague on both your houses."[28] By the end, when the press, the Congress, and the public were calling for war against Germany and the nation was moving with awful certainty towards it, Hearst stood almost alone in opposition – and he did nothing to modify his stand.[29]

One of Hearst's biographers maintains that reading his newspapers between 1914 and 1918 reveals that they fluctuated wildly but that the "clearer light of present perspective ... indicates that Hearst was playing a part, adroitly, plausibly, resourcefully. Under the camouflage, amid the inconsistencies, the publisher had one aim: to keep America's men, munitions, and money out of the war."[30] One may be permitted to disagree with all but the last part of this statement. The contents of the Hearst papers scarcely fluctuated – in fact, they were remarkably consistent. Nor could his role be characterized by any of the adverbs used above. Hearst's campaign during those five years was so clumsy, careless, and implausible that it convinced almost no one – indeed, it made large numbers of people believe that he really was pro-German and even connected, in some sinister way, with the German war effort.

It has been noted earlier that Hearst's first major foreign policy campaign set the course that the rest of his career followed,[31] and the campaign to keep the United States out of the First World War is probably the best example of this. The methods he used were almost identical with those he had employed earlier: the massive headlines, the scare and atrocity stories, the violent and outspoken editorials. But their effect was different this time, perhaps because this time he was fighting a battle in which most of his countrymen did not believe, perhaps because these tactics were no longer as effective. Hearst succeeded only in attracting odium far greater than before and in making a reputation for being pro-German that he was never entirely able to shake off and that came back to haunt him as the Second World War began. One is obliged to conclude, however, that, though Hearst's tactics may have been wrong and his pronouncements extreme and inflammatory, though he may have been careless in some of his associations, this was the extent of his errors. He clung to his dictum that it was better to be right than popular (or consistent), a show of tenacity that took great courage or great stubbornness – or both.

Hearst's dissatisfaction with the Versailles peace treaty and with the president who negotiated it on behalf of the United States has already been discussed.[32] While the war was still on – indeed, very soon after the United States entered the conflict – Hearst had begun to argue that the nation was in a position virtually to dictate the terms on which peace should be made. In September 1917, for example, he wrote that the American government had the "right to dictate" and the "power to enforce" terms of peace and that it should do so.[33] At the very least, he felt, the United States had a duty to see that the peace to be concluded had no provision "which is or can be now or hereafter at any time or in any way a menace to the peace and prosperity of the people of the United States."[34] Usually, however, his editorials were pitched at a far different level. More typical was his stance that "the United States entered this war to make the world safe for democracy. The President of the United States has said it, the people of the United States have acclaimed it and fought to make it a living fact." He therefore called on the nation "to make peace on the high plane on which we have made our war." He wished to "make the world safe for democracy ... [and] this generation and future generations safe for peace and prosperity, for life and liberty by insisting on the democratization of the nations we have beaten in this war, by destroying the autocracy which is a perpetual threat to peace, a continual menace to liberty."[35]

But this was not to be, and as soon as the terms of the peace treaty were published and Wilson returned home to try to win acceptance from the American people and, more important, from the Senate, Hearst came out against both the president and the treaty. He saw no evidence that the war (devastating and exhausting as it had been for the European powers) had changed anything, that the powers were prepared to run their affairs on lines other than those that governed them before 1914. True, the autocracies of Russia, Germany, and Austria had been destroyed, but it was still too early to say how the governments that had replaced these despotisms would develop. Further, the two powers of whom Hearst was now most suspicious – Great Britain and Japan – had come out of the war greatly strengthened and in no mood to submit to the demands of the United States in international affairs. Finally, there now existed the League of Nations, the brainchild of an American president whom he despised and distrusted, the instrument of an apparent curtailment of American sovereignty, and soon the plaything of those nations whose ways appalled him. There was only one way to meet this situation. After its expensive, misguided, and unsuccessful venture into world affairs, the United States must revert to its traditional foreign policy, mind its own business, and unequivocally place America first.

It was this theme to which the Hearst papers returned constantly throughout the interwar period and which, when war again threatened, they used to persuade the public to avoid another European conflict. By 1929 Hearst was writing that "the realignment of Europe after the Great War meant nothing except another great war to resettle the boundaries of European nations according to the principles of nationalism and elemental justice." The pledges given in 1919 had been consistently and brazenly violated by most of the nations of Europe, so that there would clearly be "another war to right wrongs and to establish liberty and justice."[36] But this, he wrote some time later, would not be the result of renewed conflict. The United States had, "for no sufficient reason," entered the Great War, which had been "precipitated and conducted by European nations for European purposes of aggression and aggrandizement," and thus violated the precepts of George Washington. "Another World War would universally

and overwhelmingly end [the capitalist system], and would Russian-
ize Europe and America, too, unless America had intelligence enough
this time to keep out of the war." The capitalist nations had to take
care not to permit another war, for then Bolshevism, "not now a danger to the world ... merely an annoyance," would surely triumph and
sweep the existing system aside.[37]

The only solution to this problem was for the United States to stay
clear of the machinations of other nations, trade with them as much
as possible, collect its debts from them, and make itself strong enough
to withstand any external threat. During the twenties and thirties
Hearst saw these threats coming from a number of sources. The ever-
present yellow peril remained as the Japanese, growing in strength
and confidence, posed an increasing threat to American interests in
the Pacific, where Hearst prophesied that the threat of a new war
would most likely become a reality. In 1925 Hearst assured the Japanese of American friendliness despite their suspicion of the United
States. Japanese alarm at impending American naval manoeuvres in
the Pacific, he wrote, was based "on an assumption that the United
States is unfriendly to Japan and that these manoeuvres constitute a
direct menace." But this was clearly not the case, for "the fleet of the
United States is its best protective arm, and it is therefore the plain
duty, as well as the obvious right, of the United States to maintain its
fleet and to familiarize it with the manoeuvres necessary to protect
this country and this country's possessions." Nevertheless, he felt
that the "disposition of Japan to interfere with the right of the United
States to determine what kind of immigration it shall have, and what
kind of citizenship it shall have, is significant, and so also is the aston-
ishing attempt of Japan to monopolize the Pacific and to prevent the
United States to exercise its obvious right to maneuver its own fleet
around its own possessions on an ocean which is an open highway to
all nations."[38]

Having hinted at the causes of potentially strained relations between the two nations, Hearst continued to point out the dangers of
treating Japanese ambitions and activities in the Pacific region lightly.
In 1931 the *Examiner* commented on a new best-selling book in Japan,
a work by a Japanese general entitled *Our Imperial Nation's Crisis – the
Coming Japanese-American War*. This volume listed the many insults
that Japan had endured from the United States and that the Japanese
people were waiting to avenge. The *Examiner* editorial reminded
readers that the Japanese were consistently building more ships than
they were allowed under the naval treaty, whereas "the United States,
under the leadership of its eminent Quaker-pacifist President," was
cutting down its navy.[39] A few months later, when the Japanese in-

vaded Manchuria, Hearst warned his readers of the dangers of taking
the Japanese too lightly, cautioning that this grave situation called
"for sober approach and clear thinking," since it was again "evident
to the world that all the prating about an organized world peace is little more than folderol": Japan had signed the League Covenant, the
Nine-Power Treaty of 1922, guaranteeing China's independence, and
the Kellogg Pact of 1925, pledging the signatories to renounce war
and settle disputes by peaceful means, but all this had clearly made
no difference to her behaviour. Further, "we have a dangerous man in
the White House" who "insists upon getting into complications with
foreign nations, and at the same time reducing our army and navy to
a point of impotence." Both these tendencies should be curbed by
Congress, who should lead the nation in refusing to meddle in foreign problems.[40]

By summer 1933 Hearst was accusing the Japanese of intending to
absorb both the Philippines and Hawaii in addition to their other
conquests. "When Japan occupied Manchuria as a preliminary step
toward her eventual absorption of China, that was lamentable but
nevertheless none of our American business." Now, however, the situation was different: "When Japan takes strategic steps, preliminary
to occupation of the Philippines and Hawaii, and the prosecution of
her long contemplated war upon the United States, that is our American business; and this Newspaper advises our Government to take
heed and prepare."[41] A similar tune was played a few days later,
when the *Examiner* noted a Japanese challenge to German and French
possessions in the Pacific. This again was merely a preliminary to a
move on the Philippines and Hawaii, and possession of all these islands would give Japan "a grip on the continent of Asia no single
power could break." In such a situation, war with the United States
would be inevitable.[42]

Nevertheless, Hearst still maintained that he was well disposed towards Japan. In a New Year's message to one of the Tokyo papers in
1934 he indicated that "there are no two countries in the world which
have better reason to maintain friendly relations ... than Japan and
the United States of America. All that is necessary is for both nations
to carry on friendly commercial, financial and diplomatic relations
with each other, and apart from that for each nation to mind its own
business."[43] This was a position he maintained almost until Pearl
Harbor, especially in 1939 and 1940, as he began to use the government's Japanese policy, which he called provocative and needlessly
hostile, as yet another means to attack the Roosevelt administration.[44]

At the same time he continued to warn against Japanese aggression, obviously feeling that the Japanese were simply not about to

mind their own business. In 1936 the five-power naval conference in London, a follow-up of those of 1921–22 and 1930, broke down when the Japanese delegation withdrew and the Italians would not agree to the proposed terms. This permitted only a limited three-power agreement among the British, French, and Americans. The nominal issue on which the breakdown occurred was, he said, that of parity among the leading naval powers, but the real reason was "Japan's imperialist program."[45] In the following year, when the Japanese invaded the Chinese mainland, the *Examiner* quoted a column by David Lloyd George from a week earlier. The former British prime minister, who during the thirties wrote a regular column for the Hearst papers, had noted that, if Japan succeeded, there would be "in this militant empire a collection of virile, intelligent races numbering in aggregate three hundred millions." In this case the "conquering 'yellow peril' may become a dread reality to the white races of the world." Whichever nation won, it would be too much to hope that they would be content with such a victory; the United States had therefore to "build its defenses for the future to cope defensively with whatever military power arises in the Orient."[46]

Beyond the growing evidence of the reality of the yellow peril, Hearst was preoccupied with the danger arising from the Fascist dictatorships and Stalin's Russia. At the beginning he was inclined to treat Hitler and Mussolini indulgently, particularly as he regarded them as a bulwark against Communism. When Mussolini came to power in Italy, seeming to bring order to the nation and efficiency to the government, Hearst pictured him as the saviour of Italy and established cordial relations with him. Il Duce was, of course, a dictator, and this was distasteful to Hearst's American soul. But in a May 1934 editorial comparing Hitler, who "had a strong desire to become a Herr Mussolini," with Sir Oswald Mosley, who was trying to play Mussolini in England, he pointed out that in time all dictators failed anyway, so there was really nothing to worry about.[47]

A decade before, Hearst had shown sympathy for the emerging Nazi movement. In April 1924 he had written that it was "rather natural that the Germans in Munich should stage a popular demonstration in favor of Ludendorff and Hitler, heroes of the unsuccessful 'revolution' to re-establish the monarchy in Germany." After all, he asked, "what has the republic done for the people of Germany? Not one thing they were promised." This editorial concluded that "liberal-minded men throughout the world will hope that the German people will continue to hold to their ideal that sometime, somewhere, the German republic will yet mean for Germans freedom and opportunity to live."[48] But at this time the precise nature of Hitler's movement was unclear to most foreigners; the editorial can be taken merely as an expression of understanding for what Hearst saw as the natural frustration of many Germans.

It was not until 1934 that Hearst came to grips with the question of Hitler and Nazism. At the end of that summer he made a much-publicized visit to Germany, interviewed Hitler, and entered into a news contract with the German government. As a result, all the old charges of being pro-German were dragged out again and applied with greater fervour because he was now accused of supporting a dictator whose style and methods were increasingly odious. Of his meeting with Hitler on 16 September, one of his biographers noted: "Apparently he was impressed by the Fuehrer's fanatic power, and visualized him as a bulwark against Communism in Europe, a view not uncommon then in some influential quarters in America and even commoner now. In any event, Hearst came home with a lucrative news contract in his pocket, and a conviction that Hitler was on the right track. He had seen nothing of the black side of Germany, of course, and although he must certainly have known about it, as usual he believed what he wanted to believe."[49] But this version of the situation, like the others that branded Hearst a supporter of Nazism and of Fascism in general, is somewhat wide of the truth.

In August 1934 he cabled from Europe to Coblentz that he did not see how the Hearst papers could support Hitler and his revolution. It was, he believed, "a lesson in despotism. The German democracy has been destroyed and now instead of having peaceful democratic methods to decide differences of political opinion the Germans must resort to revolution with all its violence and bloodshed and with the cruel execution of defeated leaders." The United States should, he said, take note of this situation and absorb its lessons so that it might be led to guard more jealously its own democratic institutions.[50] This letter, like several anti-Hitler editorials that appeared in the Hearst papers, was written before his meeting with Hitler. One such editorial, recording the death of Hindenburg, claimed that he had lived in vain, since nothing remained of what he stood for: "Today the swastika is supreme in Germany and Europe is filled with rumors of war."[51] A few days later the *Examiner* printed a cartoon showing Hitler, waving a sword and a swastika flag, overlooked by Germans such as Hindenburg, Bismarck, Luther, Wagner, and Beethoven. The caption underneath noted that "when Germany encouraged art and literature, there were giants ... now all German power, might, culture is dominated by one little man."[52]

Coblentz's work on Hearst quotes the latter's memorandum on his interview with Hitler, during which he informed Hitler that Americans objected to his treatment of subject people. On this question he was assured that "all discrimination is disappearing and will soon entirely disappear." Like Neville Chamberlain later, underestimating Hitler and overestimating his ability to reason with the Führer, Hearst left the interview convinced that he had been "able to accomplish some good."[53] Later, he wrote to Willicombe that "Hitler is an extraordinary man. We estimate him too lightly in America. He has enormous energy, intense enthusiasm, a marvellous faculty for dramatic oratory, and great organizing ability." These qualities could, of course, be misdirected: "I only hope that he and the Germans may have sense enough to keep out of another war." Hearst concluded that Fascism was an anti-Communist movement, that if Communism could be avoided, then so could Fascism, and that "both are despotisms and deprive people of the liberties which democracy assures."[54]

A little later, again while still in Germany, Hearst made a private statement that summarizes his attitude towards the German question at this time:

I believe, that anything benefitting Germany will eventually benefit the entire world. Therefore anything that is beneficial to Germany meets with my hearty approval. If Mr. Hitler will give his country peace, order and opportunity for civilized development which the great war largely destroyed everywhere he will benefit not only his own people but the people of the whole world. The struggle of Germany for liberation from the iniquities of the Versailles Treaty and for freedom from the malignant oppression and compression of nations which are selfishly but shortsightedly hostile to her progress is a struggle which should be watched with sympathetic interest by all liberty loving people everywhere.[55]

Soon after his return to the United States, Hearst tried to explain Hitler and his own attitude towards him. Hitler had come upon a Germany in chaos, he said, and he "restored character and courage, ... gave hope and confidence, ... established the order, the unity of purpose which Hindenburg had proclaimed but never accomplished." Because of that, the Germans loved him and "regard him as a savior." He had made some unspecified mistakes – "some terrible ones, I think" – but "the Germans forgive Hitler much and attribute many of the existing errors and evils to the excesses of the revolution." It was too soon to say clearly whether this was so or whether, as many Germans claimed, Hitler was really "remedying mistakes and rapidly restoring privileges and liberties."[56]

What Hearst appears to have been doing here is what many of his countrymen seemed unable to do. He was distinguishing between Hitler's expression of what Hearst saw as the legitimate grievances of Germany and the Führer's methods of governing Germany, concerning which Hearst had growing doubts and ultimately strong distaste. Thus, he could allow his papers to publish the anti-Hitler editorials and cartoons that frequently appeared at this time, and simultaneously approve such actions as the reoccupation of the Rhineland in 1936, which he characterized as Germany's doing merely what everybody had known she would do all along: "namely, take possession of HER OWN TERRITORY."[57]

The two sides of Hearst's attitude towards Hitler and his methods are perhaps best summed up in an editorial published in the spring of 1938. At this point, Hearst said, Hitler still had an opportunity to prove that he had the stuff of greatness in him, which "is not made by marching troops nor by howling crowds, but by enduring records of constructive statesmanship." The opportunity, he went on, lay "in more farseeing statesmanship than he has ever yet shown, and a more liberal and broadminded attitude towards all classes and professions, all races and religions in his Reich, than seems to lie within his intellectual composition." Hitler was not the success Hearst had hoped for in giving Germany peace, order, and good government: "As a military genius he is emphatically a good corporal but as a constructive statesman he is still a bad housepainter." Hearst praised Hitler's objective of creating a united Germany: "The world is not opposed to the natural union of Germans with Germans," he said, "but it is opposed to the extension of the intolerance and the oppression which have characterized Nazism."[58]

Eight months later Hearst wrote his last appeal to the good qualities that he had earlier hoped the German dictator possessed. In a dramatic statement of the position in Europe, he cried: "Were there a voice powerful enough in the world to bring the German Government back to its senses before it is too late," it would tell Hitler that he had broken "the oppressive shackles of the Versailles Treaty" and "redeemed by diplomatic victories the inglorious peace of twenty years ago"; that he had "set out to liberate [his] country" and "to give Germany a deserved place in the sun"; but that now he was isolating Germany, "working for a German defeat more infamous than the surrender on the battlefields of France," and "making it a pariah in the family of nations ... [and] the flag of National Socialism a symbol of national savagery." Was it, Hearst asked finally, "too late to rescue Germany from the catacombs of medievalism, nay, of aboriginal tribalism, in which she is now floundering?" If it was, then Hitler and his dictatorship would "bear the responsibility for the gaping and widening gulf which is separating Germany at a perilous pace from the civilized world."[59]

Thus, as the thirties moved to their close and Europe closer to war, Hearst – at first inclined to see in Nazism and its leader a natural reaction by Germans to the disastrous situation in which they found themselves, and to hope that Hitler would be able, by acceptable means, to give Germany a fresh start – concluded that he was merely another dictator: cruel, arrogant, imperialistic, and operating from assumptions contrary to everything that Americans held dear. He saw Hitler, with his counterpart, Mussolini, and his ideological opponent, Stalin, as increasingly dangerous threats to the peace of Europe and the world.[60] To this triple menace in Europe was added the ever-present danger in Japan. These factors together led the Hearst papers to picture the United States as a nation increasingly threatened and alone in a mad world moving gradually and perhaps inevitably towards war – a perception that was not, of course, too far from the truth.

In this situation Hearst, as he had before 1917, opposed any involvement with Europe that might result in participation in a future conflict, a stance made more cogent by reinforcing the lessons of the earlier war. Thus, he opposed attempts to introduce legislation empowering the government to impose arms embargoes on nations in conflict: "The power to place an arms embargo on one or the other of nations in conflict is the power to abandon the neutrality of the United States and to take sides in the conflict. To declare an arms embargo against all nations at war does not involve us in the conflict and is not a breach of neutrality but to supply arms to one nation and to refuse to supply them to another is an overt hostile act and would assuredly involve the United States in the conflict." He concluded that the nation needed "restrictions to keep [it] out of war not unwarranted and probably unconstitutional power to involve us in war." The president had "done enough injury to constitutional government here at home," and "the Congress should not let him add this enormous damage that would ensue from the irresponsible right to involve us in foreign wars."[61]

Hearst opposed neutrality legislation, even that passed by Congress as late as 1939, characterizing it as "fantastic schemes spawned by so-called idealists" and a "curious blend of homicidal and suicidal mania."[62] He poured scorn on Roosevelt's 1937 Chicago speech, principally on the Japanese invasion of China, in which the president suggested the "quarantine" of aggressor nations and advocated common and positive action to ensure peace. It was, Hearst noted, a statement that was "studded with proof that Mr. Roosevelt is THINKING LIKE WOODROW WILSON." Neither of these presidents had wanted war, of course, but this kind of behaviour would inevitably bring it; the surest way to get into a war was to join others who were trying to keep the peace, and the surest way to stay out was "to keep clear of foreign entanglements."[63] He declaimed against any suggestion that the United States should become involved in the Far East crisis, where, with "Communist China and Communist Russia on the one side and Fascist Japan on the other," the nation had no desire or need to fight either: "America gradually became involved in the last great war by truculent notes and biased attitudes arousing undue antagonism," a mistake that it would be folly to repeat.[64] Here was the essence of Hearst's policy at this time: "to avoid a repetition of the role that the United States had played in the First World War."[65]

Finally, as war in Europe came ever closer, as it became clear that attempts like the Munich agreement between Chamberlain and Hitler were breaking down, Hearst addressed the nation in a radio broadcast, asking, "What Is America's Foreign Policy?" He quoted the secretary of state, who was in turn quoting the president, as saying that "the defense of religion, of democracy and of good faith among nations is all the same fight ... to save one we must now make up our minds to save all." But what, precisely, asked Hearst, did this mean? Must the United States, having saved democracy once, "save democracy again – and in the same way – and with the same result?" He denied that the United States had any obligation to Great Britain or France: "Must the free citizens of our genuine democracy support France and England in their desire to maintain their despotisms in Asia against the rising renaissance in that awakening continent? What common interest, what sympathy, has the free and true Republic of America with the age-old imperialism of oppression and exploitation exemplified in French and English dominion in Asia?" The strength of the United States should be gathered – but only for defence, not for "the promotion of alien principles and the perpetuation of alien despotisms and imperialisms."[66]

Thus Hearst stated his position before war broke out, and thus he continued to state it after the war began. On 5 September 1939, two days after the outbreak of war in Europe, an *Examiner* editorial was printed under the heading "Our Real Duty: To Stay Out of This World War."[67] For the next two years Hearst spoke strenuously on behalf of genuine neutrality – as distinct from what he believed to be the president's sham neutrality – and of those who seemed to him to be supporting the concept and its application to the present situation. He approved of the views of the America First Committee[68] (though he seems to have had no formal connection with them),[69] but, as so often, this was not unwavering support – as when he attacked Charles Lindbergh, by now the primary spokesman for the committee, for his "intemperate and intolerant address in Des Moines."[70] This time, at the outset, Hearst had a solid body of opinion to work with – there

Stand Fast! America

San Francisco Examiner, 8 October 1939

was more sentiment in the country for avoiding war. However, as in 1917, he eventually lost his fight to keep his nation free from European entanglements and from participation in Europe's war, holding to a position that was increasingly untenable and uncomfortable.[71]

When war came, Hearst declared his intention of again, as in 1917, supporting the war effort to the utmost: "We are in the war and we have got to win it ... there may have been some difference of opinion among good Americans about getting into the war, but there is no difference about how we should come out of it."[72] A little later he wrote that the nation had gone to war as it should: "democratically, under responsible leadership, by constitutional methods, and with the consent, approval and united support of the American people." Those who thought the country did not want war were correct, "but those who thought that Americans would not FIGHT in defense of their honor, their liberty and their free soil must feel the weight of America's wrath and America's incomparable and unconquerable arms."[73] These would now be used to maintain the position that Hearst had pursued all along – America first.

First Blood

A red spot on a white flag most appropriately flies over the country that treacherously struck under cover of solicited peace negotiations.

America has been too trusting in the past but that fault is now rectified and dire retribution for this first blood will be exacted.

San Francisco Examiner, 20 December 1941

9 America First

Perhaps the most striking and remarkable feature of the foreign policies the Hearst press advocated between 1895 and the outbreak of the Second World War is their consistency. Throughout his career Hearst was continually accused of capriciousness, of changing his mind for reasons he seldom made clear, and these charges are, to a considerable extent, justified. He never made a virtue of consistency, maintaining that it was better to be right than consistent, and on many issues he changed direction rapidly and dramatically.[1] This behaviour was true of his crusades concerning foreign policy, particularly when they were concerned with the makers of American policy. Nevertheless, it cannot be emphasized too strongly that the principles on which he based his crusades, his basic understanding of the American role in the world, never altered in over half a century.

This consistency is most clearly demonstrated by Hearst's attitudes towards the one major area of American concern not so far dealt with as a unit: the Western Hemisphere. Throughout his publishing career Hearst saw this region and the protection of American interests there as the most vital concern of his country's foreign policy. If, in its relations with the rest of the world, the United States adopted a policy in which she consulted principally her own interests, how much more must she adopt such a policy in the hemisphere in which she was the major power but where other powers had interests, influence, and even possessions? The thrust of Hearst's view of the hemisphere was that it should be an American preserve, the one region in which the United States must – aggressively if necessary – fight for her interests.

Hearst grounded his view of America's hemispheric policy firmly on what he saw as the historic basis for American action. Thus, if the pronouncements of the first president of the United States made him, for Hearst, the father of the nation's foreign policy in general, then, regarding hemispheric affairs, the pronouncements of the fifth president entitled him to the same position. The Monroe Doctrine, Hearst proclaimed as early as 1895, "is the foundation of the established public law of this hemisphere. That it has never been formally recognized by the Europeans is nothing to us." The point was not the Europeans' lack of recognition but that they had only once – disastrously – ventured to violate the policy openly. In the mid-1860s Louis-Napoleon of France, with the support of Mexican notables in exile, tried to establish a Latin empire by placing the Archduke Maximilian of Austria on the throne of Mexico – "And the result of that experiment did not encourage its repetition."[2]

A few days before he made this bald statement on the authority of the Monroe Doctrine, Hearst had spelled out the implications of his view of the affairs of the Western Hemisphere. There were "a dozen petty disputes with European powers over their aggressions on the weak Spanish-American republics." The best way to deal with this problem would simply be a formal restatement of the Monroe Doctrine to bring it into line with modern conditions. In doing this, the United States should make clear to the European powers that she herself had no wish to acquire territory in North or South America but that "the European colonies on these continents exist only on sufferance, that they are not to be considered as permanently planted here, that they are not to be increased at the expense of neighboring republics, and that in all controversies in which they and their republican neighbors are involved, the final arbiter is the United States." Acceptance of these principles would, he forecast, bring an end to friction between the United States and the European powers.[3]

Hearst spent the remainder of his life advocating that the implications of this policy be effected in the affairs of Latin America and the Caribbean. Time after time he proclaimed the determination of the United States to stay out of the affairs of the European nations and their dependencies, but with equal vehemence he declared that the corollary must be that the European powers stay out of American affairs. If this agreement was not to be secured by peaceful means, the United States must enforce it. Vigorous and expanding as were the major powers of Europe, the u.s. was the guardian of the integrity of the Western Hemisphere, where its interests were paramount and where any threat to the security of the parts or the whole became a threat to American security.

A prime example of Hearst's view of the situation in Latin America was his attitude to the construction and maintenance of an isthmian canal. Throughout his career he advocated strongly that such a canal be built and that it be regarded as the exclusive preserve of the United States. One of his most enduring and forceful campaigns – which he continued until his death, and even after an alternative route had been chosen and the Panama Canal completed – was in favour of building a canal by the Nicaragua route through Central America.[4] In 1895, when a bill to construct such a canal passed from the Senate to the House, he wrote that it would be "a work of such surpassing importance that it would be remembered to the credit of the Fifty-third Congress when all the imbecilities of the past two years had been forgotten."[5] He advocated establishment of a canal under American guarantees and free from European interference. "We want less European interference, not more, in the affairs of America. Let Europe look after Suez, and we shall not meddle, any more than we shall permit her to meddle with Nicaragua."[6]

He received with scorn suggestions that there be European participation in the building or management of the canal. "We shall build the canal because we think it best," he wrote; "[we] shall manage it according to the principles of justice as we understand them, and shall protect it by our own power."[7] This was always Hearst's view, but never was it more firmly, even violently, expressed than during the controversy over the Hay-Pauncefote Treaty. Early in 1900 the Hearst papers noted that construction of a Nicaraguan canal would seriously affect Anglo-American relations "unless our English friends clearly understand that it is to be an exclusively American affair." Because it would be "an extremely important strategic waterway, profoundly affecting our national interests," the United States proposed "to own, fortify and control it permanently." The editorial concluded that "no other country in the world will have anything to say about it."[8] A month later, however, as the proposed treaty became public, the Hearst papers rose up in patriotic indignation against the government's "attempt to surrender the Nicaragua Canal to England and the European powers." The agreement, they charged, gave away the rights of the United States over the proposed canal to Great Britain, and thus indirectly to the other European powers. Abandoning "the fruits of twenty years of diplomacy," it "puts the American Government back exactly where it was in 1850, when Great Britain secured our assent to the Clayton-Bulwer Treaty."[9]

Beginning with this pronouncement, the Hearst papers mounted an outspoken campaign against the treaty. Basing their arguments as so often on precedent, they quoted the nation's sixth president, John

Quincy Adams, who had claimed: "as to an American system, we have it; we constitute the whole of it."[10] Two days later, under the heading "NO ALLIANCES WANTED," an editorial noted that the nation desired no permanent alliances or agreements with other powers and especially "no concession to Europe to interfere with the management of affairs on this continent". "It was foolish," maintained Hearst, quoting Washington, "to look for disinterested favors from another" nation whose attachment to the United States would remain firm only so long as its own interests dictated.[11] As negotiations continued, so did the Hearst campaign, reviling the Treaty until it was rejected – and greeting the second Hay-Pauncefote treaty, which gave the United States sole right of construction, maintenance, and control, with approval. This document was acceptable because it removed "the obstacles in the way of our exclusive control of the canal," freed the nation from "the obligation never to acquire territory in Central America," and entrusted maintenance of the canal's neutrality to the United States so that "no foreign power is to have anything to do with it."[12]

Within a short time, however, the situation had changed dramatically. Obstacles to American control of the canal might have been removed, but obstacles to its construction had not. The president's answer to this dilemma produced one of the most remarkable episodes in the extraordinary career of the first Roosevelt: the 1903 revolution in Panama. This incident Hearst labelled a national scandal, asking, "Is this country, then, to be the bully of the American continent instead of [the] friend and protector the Monroe Doctrine proclaimed her to be?" His outspoken condemnation of the president's action in acquiescing in and then supporting the revolution ended with a call to dig the Nicaragua canal and "deliver us from the ugly mess at Panama."[13] Soon after this, however, Hearst obviously decided that construction of a canal was more important than its location. This view was unusual among Progressives, most of whom disagreed, though not loudly, with the president's popular action, and Hearst pleaded with the Democratic Party not to oppose the Panama route: Roosevelt had "not acted with justice, warrant of law or patriotism, but what mistakes he has made he and his party are responsible for," and the Democrats should not allow his shabby actions to blind them to the overwhelming need for a canal. Though the Nicaraguan route would be preferable, "any canal, rather than no canal," was the important consideration.[14] From this time onwards the canal became a goal of paramount importance, "one of the greatest undertakings in history" and "beyond partisan politics."[15]

When the canal was eventually completed, the Hearst papers set themselves to defend American rights against all comers. It was an

American canal, built and operated by American enterprise, and it must remain so. Shortly before the First World War the British government protested favourable treatment for American shipping on the canal. The British suggestion that the ensuing dispute be submitted to international arbitration was dismissed, but Hearst rejected as even more fantastic what he took to be the British attitude on canal tolls.[16] The British Foreign Office, he said, was taking the view that "the Americans have an exclusive right to build the Panama Canal, to care for its perpetual up-keep and defense, and to bear all the losses that may be entailed by its physical failure, or destruction." At the same time, the British considered that "the Americans have no right to make a single penny out of the canal, without sharing the profit pro rata among all the nations that may choose to make use of the waterway." A proposition so absurd did not even deserve to be discussed – though, as usual, he did.[17]

Thus the Hearst papers saw a canal across the isthmus of Central America as purely an American concern. Its use was dictated by the interests of the Western Hemisphere and therefore of the United States, and its regulation and protection were none of Europe's business. Hearst took the same view of hemispheric affairs in general.

In October 1895 a suggestion in the London *Spectator* that the United States and Great Britain guarantee each other's possessions in the Western Hemisphere was branded as a clear example of British duplicity. The United States would guarantee all the British colonies while, in return, Great Britain would guarantee American possession of the United States. This seemed neither fair nor reasonable, and in any case Hearst felt that the day would come when his country would not wish to guarantee British presence in the hemisphere.[18] At the time the United States was wrangling with Great Britain over Nicaragua and Venezuela, eager to eliminate British interference in those two nations and to limit British influence in the hemisphere as a whole. Hearst was thus content with the outcome of the Venezuelan episode the following year, applauding President Cleveland for standing up to the British and securing a solution that, since "what England has not cared to insist upon no other power will attempt," would mean "peace throughout the Western world, and when Europe becomes thoroughly accustomed to the situation ... not only peace but good will."[19]

By standing firm against the British, the United States had demonstrated the advantages of such a policy and its effectiveness in dealing even with major powers. Thus, in future – as when the Venezuelan question arose in another form – he stood firm on the principle of adherence to the Monroe Doctrine.[20] Along with this stance, however, went another that was to cause more controversy in the Western Hemisphere. This was Hearst's belief that, as well as being the guarantor of order in the region, the United States was the guardian of its nations' internal affairs. In 1908, for example, he recommended that the United States intervene in Haiti to establish order and good government. "For four hundred years," he noted, "Hayti [sic] has been the cockpit of the Western world ... a fat carcass picked to the dry bones by the eagles of all nations." Foreign powers ruled and the result was anarchy. The remedy for this regrettable situation was that it should be governed from elsewhere, and "it is obvious that Washington is the only possible quarter." He concluded: "Whatever the diplomatic name it may go by, the predominance of the United States in Hayti should be clear and conclusive."[21] Six years later, as Wilson began his abortive intervention in Haiti, he had the support of the Hearst papers.

America's attitude towards Latin America should be one of friendship, co-operation, and assistance mingled with protection to secure mutual benefit. In 1910, writing on the Pan-American Congress to be held in Buenos Aires in the following year, Hearst noted: "We should take every means of cultivating the friendship of the South American republics and making ourselves intelligible to them" so that "the dream of the younger days of our national life, that this whole continent, north and south, was reserved for some common destiny of freedom that set it apart from the feuds of the Old World, should not be permitted to end in dreamland." Thus, the nation must take every opportunity to co-operate with and make itself understood by the southern republics.[22] Almost ten years later, just after the First World War, he advocated again that – while keeping its nose out of European affairs and compelling Europe "to keep its grasping fingers out of the affairs which affect our Nation and our Western Hemisphere" – the United States should "make ... leagues and associations mainly among the nations of the Western Hemisphere, ... look out for the welfare of the Western Hemisphere, and ... prevent European nations or Asiatic nations from meddling in the matters which concern our Western Hemisphere."[23]

Again, in the thirties, Hearst supported strengthening the Pan-American movement that, he claimed, rested "on the principle of mutual helpfulness." The growing commercial and industrial strength of the Latin American republics meant that they would play a more important part in world trade, and the United States should trade with them on a just and equitable basis. The nations of the Western Hemisphere were equal partners in a common enterprise, and it was the object of the United States "to use its resources not to burden them but to assist them; not to control them but to co-operate with them."[24]

In other words, Pan-Americanism in its best sense should be made a reality. A few months before the United States entered the Second World War, Hearst wrote that the peoples of the Western Hemisphere, being united in "ideals and objectives, principles and political purposes ... do not need Europe ... Let us see the Americas first, and let us love the Americas best; and let us, while deeply enjoying ourselves in all America's wonderlands, do everything within our power to bring the peoples of the Americas into closer amity and closer unity."[25]

Few Americans – indeed, few Latin Americans – would probably have quarrelled with such statements. The trouble was that, when translated into specific situations where action was required, the desire to be helpful, co-operative, and protective often seemed something entirely different. The most obvious example of this alteration appeared in Hearst's prescriptions for American policy in Mexico. Early in his career he had expressed a desire to see Mexico (along with the other Latin American republics) "strong, happy, prosperous and well-governed,"[26] and he later supported the rule of Porfirio Diaz (president 1877–80 and 1884–1911) as the most important factor in moving the country towards this goal.[27] However, by spring 1911, in the face of growing disorder in Mexico and increasing evidence that Diaz was unable to maintain peace, Hearst was advocating United States intervention.

"The conditions now prevailing in Mexico," he wrote, "may speedily demand a great and decisive movement by the American government." Diaz should have a chance to restore order, but, if he proved unable to do so, "the responsibility resting upon this country is clear and imperative." Under normal international custom, nations assumed the responsibility of protecting their citizens at home and abroad, and under the Monroe Doctrine the United States had undertaken to protect citizens of other nations in the Americas rather than allow non-American powers to interfere to do it for themselves.[28] As the situation in Mexico became more chaotic, the Hearst papers were perhaps the nation's loudest and most consistent advocates of American intervention to protect American property and restore order there. The Taft administration declined to follow this advice.

Hearst welcomed the beginning of Francisco Madero's brief presidency in 1911, estimating that he represented "the sentiments of a very large majority – probably four-fifths – of the people of Mexico." Violence and disorder seemed to be diminishing, and under the leadership of a president who "showed courage under adversity during the revolution and moderation and self-control after his triumph ... confidence soon will be re-established and investment will once more be directed toward that marvelously rich country."[29] This euphoria was fleeting. Within a few weeks Hearst was asking, "What is the matter with this Democratic Congress of ours that it stands limp and impassive in the face of the intolerable Mexican situation?" It was for Congress to lead, because the president's neutrality proclamation had thrown the responsibility for upholding the Monroe Doctrine upon them. "The interests of this country in Mexico are greater than those of any other country ... And our moral obligation – the obligation imposed by our immemorial policy – is absolute."[30] The situation continued throughout the Taft administration, with the Hearst papers becoming more and more indignant against the president, comparing him unfavourably to Cleveland. "Even Mexico," Hearst charged, "goes on with impunity to slaughter our people and to destroy our property, and laughs at Mr. Taft and despises our country."[31]

Just before Wilson took over the presidency, Madero was assassinated, apparently on the orders of one of his generals, Victoriano Huerta, who thereupon became precariously president. With civil war now under way, as Huerta was assailed by Venustiano Carranza, Hearst pushed again for intervention. In November 1913 he noted that none of the three major Western European powers cared who governed Mexico as long as somebody did, that they had waited a long time for the United States to act, and that even Huerta had been led by American hesitation to threaten the United States publicly. A crisis was approaching, and "President Wilson will then have to choose between prolonged anarchy in Mexico, unpleasant friction with great and friendly nations, or a decisive policy of sufficient power to end more than three years of bloodshed and ruin only just across our own border."[32] Later, he detailed precisely what this meant: "There is only one course that it [the American government] can pursue, either honorably or effectively ... That course is to occupy Mexico and restore it to a state of civilization by means of American MEN and American METHODS."[33]

Wilson's Mexican policy changed direction dramatically from time to time and seldom won Hearst's support. The occupation of Vera Cruz in April 1914, undertaken without clear objectives and managed indecisively, helped minimally to bring down Carranza but exposed the United States to widespread condemnation. Later, as the Carranza government was assailed by his former lieutenant Francisco (Pancho) Villa, who tried to provoke war with the U.S., Wilson again proved indecisive, and the confusion following General John J. Pershing's pursuit of Villa into Mexico brought the two countries to the edge of war. Hearst, of course, demanded full-scale intervention. In spring 1916, a month after Pershing had entered Mexico, under the headline "Shall We Play the Fool or Play the Man in Mexico?" he demanded that "the Government of the United States shall manfully and righteously employ the full naval and military strength of the nation in effective and irresistible intervention TO PUT AN END TO TROUBLES IN MEXICO."[34]

When the situation in Mexico became more stable during the twenties and thirties, Hearst maintained that – the chaos of the second decade of the twentieth century having subsided, and strong leaders having replaced the succession of ineffective presidents and local chieftains who had succeeded Diaz – the time for armed intervention to protect American property and lives was over. The United States could best serve its own interests by working with the new leaders of Mexico to restore order, stability, and good government. He supported, for example, President Álvaro Obregón, president 1921–24: "A capable and conservative man," the new president had "largely restored law and order and civilized conditions in Mexico. He is very friendly to Americans. It would seem very difficult to secure in all Mexico a better man for President than General Obregón."[35] After a visit to Mexico in October and November 1921, during which he met the new president, Hearst noted that none of the Americans to whom he had spoken there had been able to understand U.S. recognition of the previous government, which "was indifferently permitting the killing and outraging of Americans," but that now they all realized the ability of the new administration to prevent such occurrences and were in favour of recognition.[36]

From this time on Hearst supported increased co-operation with the Mexican government. This attitude was summed up in an editorial printed in the spring of 1923, a few months before the hoped-for recognition of the Obregón government by the new Coolidge government was granted. Hearst wrote: "There should be an endeavor on the part of our Government to co-operate with the Mexican Government in such a way as sufficiently to protect the interests of Americans without seeming to desire to interfere with the just objects of the Mexican Government to benefit their people and to encourage prosperity and productivity."[37]

Franklin Roosevelt espoused a Latin-American policy that met with Hearst's approval, taking the line of developing Hoover's goodneighbour policy. FDR brought relations with the nations of Latin America to a hitherto unknown level of co-operation and confidence, culminating in the Declaration of Lima, which resulted from the eighth Pan-American Conference in December 1938. By this agreement the republics of the Americas determined to work together on a number of international issues, seeing such unity as a bulwark against threats from outside the hemisphere. Hearst continually supported the president in these policies, arguing in the spring of 1941 that FDR should keep American interests – that is, those of the U.S. and of the other republics – within their own hemisphere, giving the rest of the world a model to emulate. "We can show them how governments and nations can BEST be conducted by attending wisely to our own welfare – by forming our own democratic order in the Western Hemisphere – by establishing the Republics of all the Americas in a union not only for protection but for prosperity – by setting an example of peaceful progress and promoting peace and progress throughout the world."[38] At about the same time he released to the Mexican newspapers a statement applauding Roosevelt's policy of trying to cement relations with other American nations, particularly Canada and Mexico, and expressing the hope that "the interests and actions of the three great states of the North American continent can unite rapidly toward progress, prosperity and mutual protection."[39]

Hearst's policy towards Latin America was of a piece with his attitude to the rest of the world. It was clear to him that the United States, the strongest and most prosperous power in the region, had a legitimate interest in maintaining peace and order there. Interest, tradition, and humanity combined to make this a necessary part of American policy – and he condemned fiercely those presidents who did not live up to his concept of their duty. A corollary of this, again ordained by both interest and tradition, was that the United States had an obligation to minimize the influence of other powers. It was clearly not possible for such influence to be removed either immediately or even entirely, but the United States should permit no new colonization, no further extension of European influence in the Western Hemisphere. Beyond this the United States had the same obligation to Latin America as to the rest of the world: to assist with development – preferably towards democracy – and prosperity, and to maintain friendly political and commercial relations.

Hearst supported two presidents, Coolidge and Franklin Roosevelt, who, as he saw it, tried to pursue such a policy. He applauded the improvement in U.S. relations with Latin America that occurred during their presidencies. Yet again, however, the credibility of his position was undermined by factors quite divorced from the positions themselves. The very violence and outspokenness of his advocacy of intervention during the Taft and Wilson administrations generated suspicions that persisted into the twenties and thirties. Incidents such as the affair of the Mexican documents and the deal that Hearst was believed to have made with the Mexican government to support its recognition by the United States cast further doubt on Hearst and his motives.

In the first case, in early December 1927 the Hearst press published a set of documents purporting to show that the Mexican government had bribed four unnamed u.s. senators with a total of $1,115,000. The report followed almost a month of hints of Mexican scandal in the press and caused the kind of outcry that even Hearst seldom provoked. Senators, maintaining that they were all under a cloud until specifics were revealed, demanded and received a Senate investigation. This revealed that the senators in question, now publicly identified as William Borah, George Norris, Thomas Heflin, and Robert La Follette, had received nothing and that the documents were forged. Hearst, maintaining their validity for too long, was exposed as having been at best – and there is no evidence that this was not the case – unbelievably negligent. As one of his more loyal editors noted later, it was "one of the most embarrassing periods of his whole editorial career" and "a disgraceful performance." [40]

Hearst's alleged deal with the Obregón government is less sensational and unsupported by any real evidence, but suspicion was widespread and damaging. Rumour had it that Hearst had agreed to publish propaganda favouring recognition of the Obregón government in 1921 and 1922 in exchange for tax concessions for his properties in Mexico and, if Obregón was confirmed by May 1922, a grant of five million acres. No proof of this agreement exists, but it was widely believed that Hearst's views on Mexican affairs were based, as one newpaper put it, on "personal and political interests."[41]

Whatever the views of politicians, the press, or the public, however, Hearst's view of the correct policy for the United States in Latin America was both reasonable and consistent. He recognized that, in the Western Hemisphere, the United States possessed a legitimate sphere of influence in which her own interests should dictate much of the conduct of other nations' affairs in this area. He saw that these affairs and the way they were conducted would affect, and even threaten, vital American interests and that the United States should thus have the right and the power to ensure that these interests were upheld. However, he realized that American power should not be used to push the nation's authority any further and that, for the health of her own economic system, she should trade and co-operate with the nations of the hemisphere as fully as possible.

Writing just after the turn of the century, Hearst noted that "the Monroe Doctrine is essentially defensive. It aims to preserve the status quo. It forbids European encroachments in America, but says that we shall not interfere with the existing possessions of European powers."[42] Somewhat earlier he had noted that along with this policy should go the attempt to cultivate "not only friendly but cordial relations with all the other nations of these continents."[43] Such policies were to be tied to the development of a strong national power that would enable the United States to establish its influence over the Pacific Ocean, another legitimate American sphere of influence, and to enforce, in the Western Hemisphere, "the principles of justice and freedom on which it is founded."[44] On this basis the country should, indeed must, be able to stay away from excessive involvement in the problems of the rest of the world. It must be secure in the knowledge that its own ambitions did not extend outside its own spheres of interest – except to trade and to maintain friendly relations with the rest of the world – and that any substantial involvement in the affairs of other nations would merely produce trouble.

Throughout his career Hearst constantly turned to the words of the nation's first president to buttress his advocacy of this policy. In 1904, for example, as events on the far side of the Pacific became more violent and, with the onset of the Russo-Japanese conflict, more dangerous for the United States, he used the occasion of Washington's birthday to press home the message of the Farewell Address. "The farewell address to the people of the United States, delivered in September, 1796," he noted, "has for the present juncture a singular appositiveness. The war in the Orient has roused popular feeling, and men are permitting their sympathies to transform them into partisans in a quarrel with which we properly have no close concern as a nation. Throughout the land, among the judicious, there is fear that the Government at Washington may allow itself to become involved through a spirit of meddling, which has its motive in a wish to shine on the world's stage for the gratification of vanity and the furtherance of political ambitions." Such an attitude was entirely contrary to the injunctions of the Farewell Address, to which could be added the words of Thomas Jefferson, who had felt that the foreign policy of the United States should be "peace, commerce and honest friendship with all nations; entangling alliances with none."[45]

Such pronouncements became the rule in Hearst's recommendations for the conduct of the nation's foreign relations. The United States was a great and independent nation, built and developed through the genius of its own people, who were beholden to none in the conduct of their affairs. He proudly hailed the triumphs of American ingenuity, noting that "the inventive faculties of our people have blessed all civilization." Americans had invented the sewing machine, "the reaper, the cotton gin, the incandescent light, the steel building, the phonograph, the telegraph, the submarine cable, the

Linotype, the typewriter, the kinetoscope and the airbrake." American money had developed wireless transmission. The crowning achievement, at this point, was that two Americans, "with machines heavier than the air, fly with almost the swiftness, ease and grace of the eagle,"[46] a touch of Hearstian hyperbole that even the huge achievement of the Wright brothers could hardly justify. Blessed with such genius, and with growing power and prosperity, Americans did themselves and humanity a disservice if – as all too frequently happened – they showed themselves "too prone to depend upon others for their standards of action, their guides to conduct, too ready to accept the views of others rather than to assert and maintain their own." Such attitudes were un-American: "We are departing from our ideals just when we are most positive we are reaching toward them. We must lead, not follow."[47]

Clearly, when American democracy, technology, and enterprise were the world's finest examples of civilization, the United States should take seriously her position as the world's leading power. In the thirties, as Hearst saw the world threatened by the terrifying and alien philosophies of Communism and Fascism in Europe and by the Oriental menace in the Pacific, he proclaimed the preservation of Occidental civilization against such enemies a duty, not only to Americans but also to the world: "We must keep the torch of freedom aflame to light the feet of humanity, weary of oppression, back to civilization, back to the free exercise and enjoyment of the elemental human rights of life, liberty and the pursuit of happiness."[48]

Having recognized the existence of this high duty to itself and humanity, the United States faced the problem of translating obligation into action. As with Hearst's recommendations for American policy towards Latin America, implementation of the policies he advocated frequently departed from the concepts on which they were based. It has already been noted that Hearst fits into at least one type of American Progressivism. In many of the domestic programs he espoused, and frequently in his approach to foreign policy, he was a Progressive if he was anything at all – indeed, he saw himself as a Progressive of the Theodore Roosevelt stamp.[49] One study of Progressivism and foreign policy between the beginning of the Spanish-American War and American entry into the First World War argues that the central theme in the ideology of Progressive foreign policy was expansion. To a large section of the movement this meant "not territorial expansion so much as the extension of American political institutions into backward areas; the superimposition of American democratic ideals and values on backward peoples and 'inferior' races; the extension of American morality and Good Samaritanism into international politics; the projection abroad of America's faith in the achievement and enforceability of lasting international peace; and the expansion of American trade and commerce into world markets."[50] There could be no better description of Hearst's views on the subject.

Hearst does not fit into that wing of the Progressive movement led by people like William Jennings Bryan and Robert La Follette.[51] Rather, he should be equated with the group that believed that the United States should engage in a more active policy abroad, spreading American commercial initiative and political ideology through as large a part of the world as possible.[52] He held what have been described as the three basic foreign policy ideas of the Progressives: first, the United States, having been thrust into the competitive international arena, should be militarily strong and politically and administratively efficient if she was to play a role in the international system; second, the nation should be constantly aware of the need to keep its domestic economic system, on which its foreign trade depended, strong and vigorous; and third, American ideas and ideals should be seen as exportable commodities just as much as American goods.[53] Thus, Hearst and many of his Progressive contemporaries envisaged an America strong enough to preserve its territories inviolate and defend its legitimate interests against any other nation, able to expand foreign trade to help preserve prosperity at home, and – inspired by the strength and purity of the American political system – beneficent enough to bring the blessings of democracy, honesty, and freedom to the less enlightened nations of the earth and to relations among them.

It was a noble concept from which Hearst never departed. It lay at the root of all his statements on and policies for the conduct of the nation's foreign relations. In the 1890s he had expounded a policy of *expansion without imperialism*. This was, he said, "the policy and the practice of the United States since the original thirteen States first set up housekeeping for themselves, and it is the policy to which is due the formation of the American character, the strength of the American nation, the capacity of the American people." He believed that "the advancement of the American nation had been entirely due to the fact that there always have been other American worlds to conquer." This situation, however, no longer existed, since North America had "been pretty well surveyed, explored, conquered and policed," but this did not mean that future generations should not have fresh worlds to conquer: it would be folly to "attempt to set back the onward march of our manifest destiny." There must, however, be no thought that future American acquisitions should be regarded as colonies to be exploited or private fiefdoms "to be plundered by a President's favorites, to be ruled by a statesman's incompetent sons." The United States, more enlightened, more vigorous, and more ingenious than other colonizing powers, must do its best to set up a system "under which men can live and thank God they are alive."[54]

Accordingly, Hearst supported the expansion that resulted from the Spanish-American War. Acquisition of the Philippines, for example, had made the United States "a world force that must be reckoned with ... [and would] spangle Asiatic seas with the white sails of our commerce ... broaden the national character ... give a new impetus to our business life."[55] It also gave the nation an unparalleled opportunity to spread the benefits of the American system. Failure to take advantage of this would redound to the detriment of the peoples whom the United States was coming to rule and constitute a threat to the continuation of the system at home.[56] Curiously, the distinction between expansionism and imperialism as one not of substance but of semantics – as, in fact, an entirely specious distinction – never occurred to Hearst as he praised the efforts of American administrators and wondered at the intractability of men like Aguinaldo in the Philippines, who rebelled against the civilizing mission of his country's American rulers.[57] The view from San Simeon seemed somehow to preclude such a conclusion.

Before the First World War, Hearst had espoused a foreign policy whereby the United States, keeping free from entanglements, particularly in Europe, must attempt to expand her economic system and disseminate American political and moral ideals. This belief led him to oppose American entry into the war because this would reduce the nation's commercial opportunities, reduce its freedom to use its influence to achieve a just and lasting peace, and – by contact with the corrupt and oppressive regimes of the Old World – contaminate the American system. This same belief led him to unwavering opposition to American involvement in European affairs and in the international organizations set up after the treaty of 1919. And it was this belief that led, during the interwar period, to his being branded an isolationist.

Hearst had not stopped believing that the United States had an obligation to itself and the rest of the world to ensure "the extension of our civilizing influence, of our beneficial and benign activities, of our uplifting and inspiring ideals." Geographically, the nation was ideally situated for this: it was "at the conflux of the world's activities," with the Atlantic and Europe to the east, the Pacific and Asia to the west, and the growing republics of South America to the south. "Such a commanding and controlling location," he felt, "should make our country as it made Venice in former times and under former conditions, the center of the world's commerce, the custodian of the world's wealth."[58] From this favoured position the United States would be able to extend her beneficent influence throughout the world.

Hearst argued that the United States should lead the world by example. He believed that only "general and genuine democracy," a system that tended to produce peace rather than conflict, would cure the situation in Europe and in the rest of the world: "The democracies – the peaceful nations will lead the march of progress and prosperity ... The United States has a great mission ... It can show the way."[59] To achieve this, however, the United States must try not to involve itself in the quarrels of the rest of the world, since contact with these conflicts and with the alien and corrupt systems that produced them would only weaken the American system and its ability to achieve its objectives.

This was not, however, isolationism. In 1923 Hearst argued that those who maintained that the United States must not hold aloof from the world and must abandon its isolated position were mistaken in making such an argument, mistaken in the very terms in which they argued. For politically, commercially, financially, the nation was and could by no means be isolated, and all that those charged with isolationism had done was to urge that the nation maintain its sovereignty intact and retain its freedom of action in international affairs.[60] They were rather seeking to ensure that the United States placed its own interests first. Quoting the conclusion of an article in an unnamed magazine that "the ultimate aim of the foreign policy of the United States is the preservation of world peace," Hearst noted that this was "the exact opposite of the truth," since the ultimate aim was no more nor less than "the safety and welfare of the United States." He prophesied: "The day when this nation ceases to shape its foreign policy primarily for the safety and welfare of the American people will be the day on which its national doom is sealed – and its international doom, too." He concluded that "only by being strong, great and wisely self-devoted can a nation fix a standard which other nations will seek to emulate. Any 'others first' theory in international affairs is claptrap."[61]

Ten years later, in answer to a request for a statement of his views on foreign policy, Hearst wrote: "I personally believe in nationalism AND internationalism, each in its proper place." This belief he defined as follows:

I believe in promoting the public welfare, but I do not believe it necessary in doing so to be entirely indifferent to the needs of my own family and associates. I believe in peace and all sane measures to promote peace at home and abroad and among nations – BUT PARTICULARLY AT HOME. I believe that the best way to insure peace at home is to keep out of wars abroad and out of unnecessary international complications which may lead to war. I believe in disarmament when nations are willing to disarm. I believe in sustained efforts to persuade nations to disarm. But I do not believe that a rich and envied country like our own should place itself in the position of a shortsighted and misguided nation like China, and leave itself open to attack and exploitation by other nations which are ambitious, unscrupulous and ARMED.[62]

These were the precepts on which Hearst's ideas about foreign policy up to the beginning of the Second World War were based. They do not fit with isolationism as it is customarily defined – or as Hearst has been accused of advocating. They give substance to the distinction proposed in an article on American isolationism in the 1920s, which saw use of the terms *interventionism* and *isolationism* as "not merely useless but positively misleading" and argued that the real distinction, both in the United States and in Europe, was between the "idealist" and the "realist," between those "who wished to see America act as the leader of the world towards a millennial order based on morality and law, right rather than might; and those who on realist grounds believed this to be impossible, undesirable, and likely to impose upon America demands contrary to her tradition and beyond her strength."[63] This second view was held by many, probably including Johnson and Borah, whose policy positions Hearst frequently supported.[64] Substantially, too, it was Hearst's position – although, as with other attempts to force him into a mould or make him conform to the beliefs of a specific group, he does not quite fit this description.

The foreign policy he advocated was, broadly, that of the realists, though he also believed that it was part of the nation's duty to lead the world towards a better future. To him this aim was both desirable and possible, although he considered the methods proposed by the internationalists of the Wilson-Hoover school to be wrong: they were contrary to American tradition and likely to weaken the nation at home and ultimately abroad. For Hearst, this was the final consideration. Nothing must be allowed to interfere with the growth, strength, and prosperity of the United States. The nation, and those who governed it, had no higher duty than to the nation itself, and the national interest, defined in this way, was the overriding consideration in deciding what course to follow in international affairs. The constant concern of William Randolph Hearst was for the welfare, domestic and foreign, of the United States, for America first, a policy he held up to his readers and to the ten presidents who served during his journalistic career.

10 Hearst and United States Foreign Policy

The period covered by this study contains all or part of the administrations of ten presidents of the United States, from the later years of Grover Cleveland's second term to the first half of Harry S Truman's second term. In between, the Hearst newspapers provided commentary on the presidential policies and conduct of William McKinley, Theodore Roosevelt, William Howard Taft, Woodrow Wilson, Warren Harding, Calvin Coolidge, Herbert Hoover, and Franklin Roosevelt. Hearst's relations with all except two were almost invariably bad.

The exceptions were Harding and Coolidge. As a veteran campaigner against corruption in government, Hearst was appalled by and loudly critical of the scandals of the Harding years but managed to maintain generally good relations with the administration. This was largely because of the president's opposition to the League of Nations.[1] As for Coolidge, the Hearst press supported his policies so unvaryingly that at least one Hearst editor enjoyed a good deal of influence at the White House.[2] Otherwise, however, relations with the White House were almost unrelievedly strained. Theodore Roosevelt's view of Hearst has already been discussed, and his opinion was shared by both his predecessor[3] and his successor, the latter referring to him on one occasion as "this knight of evil."[4] So it continued almost for the rest of Hearst's life.

Wilson, branded a "sham progressive" while still governor of New Jersey, received a few accolades from the Hearst press in late 1917 and early 1918 as he tried to lay down the terms of the peace, but this was a brief interlude only.[5] Partly because of his strong antipathy for

Al Smith, the Democratic candidate, Hearst supported Hoover in the 1928 campaign, but before long the president had become that "dangerous man in the White House."[6] The pattern was repeated with Franklin Roosevelt, whose nomination Hearst was said to have engineered, whose victory he greeted effusively, and who soon became and remained just another blighted hope for the Hearst papers.[7] And despite moderate approval in his early years, Truman was quickly condemned to the kind of vituperation that presidents must by then have come to expect from Hearst.

Given the clear hostility between Hearst and successive occupants of the White House, it is reasonable to expect that the overt influence of his papers on American foreign policy would be small. There is, for example, little evidence – indeed, none from most of the presidents or their intimates – that Hearst was regarded as a figure whose support was worth having or whose opposition was to be feared on most issues. Where they agreed with Hearst's campaigns, presidents would take his side and accept his support, but only reluctantly. One of Hearst's biographers notes Theodore Roosevelt's comment to Secretary of State John Hay over the isthmian canal: "John, I love you and I despise Hearst. But, dammit, this time Hearst is right! We must have a fortified canal."[8] Nevertheless, he still kept his distance, and his namesake was not prepared, for example, to accept Hearst's support for his Latin American or preparedness policies in the late thirties, firm and enduring as it was.

The one exception was Hoover, who occasionally acted as if he was prepared to go some way towards pacifying Hearst and securing his support. For most of his term, however, Hoover was a worried and uncertain man, anxious to reduce the political risks he was obliged to take, particularly if this meant bringing on further attacks from the nation's largest newspaper chain. During the furor over Hearst's expulsion from France in 1930, Stimson noted that the president "despised Hearst but did not evidently want to have any trouble with him."[9] Although he made no concessions to Hearst in the way of policy changes, Hoover remained concerned about the effect Hearst was having on national policy. On the question of the moratorium on war debts, for example, Stimson noted that "it was the same old situation … the President allowed himself to become very much disturbed by the attacks which were made upon it by the Hearst press and by the Democrats."[10] But even in this situation, where the president clearly demonstrated concern about the attacks of the Hearst press, there is evidence for hesitation but not for changes in policies or directions. The conclusion is inescapable that, during the whole period from 1895 to 1951, no Hearst campaign on foreign issues forced such changes.

This conclusion is entirely consistent with modern theoretical studies of the relationship between presidents and the press in the formulation of foreign policy. Most writing in the last twenty to thirty years has emphasized both the fragile relationship between the White House and those who cover its occupants' policies, and the special position of the president himself in foreign relations. As Bernard C. Cohen, one of the major commentators on the relationship between presidents and press, notes, "the President is especially powerful as a shaper of public opinion, since he is the acknowledged symbol and spokesman for the country in foreign affairs. He commands attention from the media whenever he wants it; he formulates policy alternatives with an authority which no one else possesses."[11]

Cohen and others have also commented, however, that although, "from the standpoint of the State Department, the White House, and the Pentagon, the press is looked on as a dangerous, unattractive beast, which can lead you along for a little bit of the way, but which is likely to turn and bite you at the slightest opportunity,"[12] there are undoubtedly cases in which distinguished foreign correspondents have close relations with the White House or the State Department and are informed and consulted on issues of importance. But such relationships are limited to those whose reputation for probity and responsibility has been consistently demonstrated; there is also fairly general agreement over who these individuals are. The majority of the press has only limited influence on the administration, and such a relationship is at best wary.[13] This, of course, is a perfectly proper situation because, as one recent commentator has noted, "the government must base its policies *primarily* on its own more sophisticated and fully informed understanding of the world," and this will normally – whatever the rhetoric of public officials about public participation – mean the use of the press as a means of disseminating information.[14]

William Randolph Hearst would not, however, fit into either of these categories – that is, successive presidents and their officials undoubtedly regarded neither him nor his commentators as people it was appropriate to consult on foreign issues, nor could he see his newspapers as mere disseminators of information on behalf of the White House. Hearst, who read the wire services every day[15] and whose own travels and correspondents around the world kept him well informed of overseas developments, regarded himself as having just as much competence in the realm of foreign relations as the average president or secretary of state. If administrations did not see fit, therefore, to heed his words, then those words would be directed towards the other participants in the making of u.s. foreign policy, the Congress and the people.

In his classic study *Public Opinion and Foreign Policy* James Rosenau differentiates between the mass public, which is both uninformed and unconcerned about foreign policy, and the attentive public, which is the opposite.[16] As the name implies, the first group, at whom the Hearst papers were largely aimed, make up between 70 and 90 per cent of the American people, the rest being what James Reston rather snootily referred to as "the saving remnant" of educated and articulate Americans who may beneficently influence the nation's foreign policy.[17] Rosenau's view is that the primary function of the mass public is to set the boundaries, to identify the limits within which decision-makers should normally feel constrained to operate.[18]

Given the general agreement on the power of the presidency to manipulate public opinion on foreign policy matters, these limits are wide to the point of vanishing. This is emphasized by the point, made by Rosenau and others, that "the mass public does not respond to specific arguments, only to emotional ones."[19] Kenneth Younger, a junior minister in the British Foreign Office in the fifties, makes the same point more graphically, when he speaks of the basic disinterest of the mass public in foreign policy issues: "Only a major international crisis suffices to knock the cheesecake off the front page."[20]

This comment, however, could not be levelled against the Hearst papers. It has been at least implicit in previous chapters of this study that the amount of coverage given to foreign policy matters by Hearst was unusually high. His view of the United States as a unique and precious experiment led him to a strong belief, frequently expressed in his newspapers, that it was constantly threatened both internally and externally, and that such threats must be vigorously resisted. Thus he reminded his readers of this threat and bombarded them with his views on the proper conduct of American foreign relations. His influence over the public and its representatives in Congress must therefore be examined with this in mind.

A recent commentator on the public's perception of the Middle East has suggested that "there exists the possibility that a few owners will exert their personal political perspectives on the majority of the media," and this exemplifies Hearst's position. The same author quotes an American journalist's remark that "nothing prevents a publisher from buying a newspaper and turning it into a vehicle for one side or the other" and Winston Churchill's pronouncement that "there is no such thing as public opinion, … there is only published opinion."[21] Hearst knew this and attempted to exploit it for the benefit of the causes he supported. He also knew, as Cohen has observed, that "the press is a significant part of the public audience for foreign policy,"[22] precisely because it is the way most people find out what is happening abroad: "If we do not see a story in the newspapers (or catch it on radio or television), it effectively has not happened as far as we are concerned." Thus, Cohen concludes that the press "may not be successful much of the time in telling people what to think, but it is stunningly successful in telling people what to think about."[23] This view is consistent with that expressed in the best recent summary of the role of journalists in influencing policy – that, however much officials may try to circumvent the media, "the day-to-day flow of information still depends primarily on the news media. Journalism's chief effect accumulates through this daily process."[24]

How does this view of the role of the press stand up to examination through the career of William Randolph Hearst? Preceding chapters of this study have examined the major campaigns fought by Hearst through his newspapers, usually against the foreign policies of successive administrations. In most of them he was unsuccessful in changing the path the nation followed. Presidents tended to ignore him, and even – as with Herbert Hoover – when they did not, there was no discernible change in their policies. Hearst's constant attempts to change American policy on war debts, one of Hoover's major problems and one of Hearst's principal campaigns in the twenties and thirties, is perhaps the clearest example of this. Hoover continued to worry about Hearst's charges even as he prepared to leave the White House, but he remained firm in his policies.[25]

On at least three occasions, however, it can be argued – indeed was argued by the Hearst press itself – that it clearly affected the course of U.S. foreign relations by mounting effective campaigns against particular actions. In the first case, that of the Spanish-American War, not only the Hearst papers – "How do you like the *Journal's* war?" – but also a number of contemporary and later commentators – "Mr. Hearst Seems to Own a War" – credited them with pushing the country into a war, claims that were greatly exaggerated. The second occasion occurred soon after the war, when Hearst mounted a fierce campaign against the first Hay-Pauncefote Treaty, which would have settled the isthmian canal question on terms unfavourable to the United States. The third came more than thirty years later, when Hearst, having constantly pursued the supporters of American entry into the League of Nations and the World Court, apparently delivered the final blow with his unyielding opposition to the court in 1935.

In February and March 1900 the Senate was called upon to ratify a treaty signed by Secretary of State John Hay and the British ambassador to Washington, Sir Julian Pauncefote. This document amended the earlier Clayton-Bulwer agreement of 1850 by allowing the United

States to build and control a canal across the Isthmus of Panama. It also agreed that the proposed waterway should be neutralized, and expressly prohibited the United States from fortifying it. These provisions provoked strong opposition in many quarters – even from some supporters of the government – and a storm of protest from the Hearst papers. When the Senate amended the first treaty in ways that the British would not accept, the *Journal*, which had carried the burden of Hearst's campaign, claimed credit.[26] From this time onwards, until the issue was finally settled by the second Hay-Pauncefote agreement in November 1901 and its Senate ratification the following month, the Hearst papers maintained a ceaseless and strident campaign against the original agreement.

Hearst took credit for this victory, claiming that he had brought the Senate round when other newspapers and most politicians had either given up or not bothered to fight. It is hard, however, to take issue with the author of the most complete study of this episode, who notes that Theodore Roosevelt had earlier despaired of changing the first treaty and that Hearst had mounted a sustained and powerful two-year campaign. He nevertheless concludes that its apparent success could only have been achieved with the help of several other factors.[27] Hearst's sustained coverage of the isthmian canal and its fortification helped to create public awareness of the issue, maintained this awareness through the long debate on the canal treaty, and thus "contributed to the formation of the patriotic Senatorial consensus in a favorable nationalistic atmosphere of the day."[28] But other factors helped Hearst's cause, and these will be examined with reference to the third campaign.

This was the final struggle over the 1935 proposal of Franklin Roosevelt's government that the United States should join the World Court. The question of entry had arisen from time to time since the end of the First World War and had sometimes gained a fairly broad measure of agreement: in 1924, for example, both the Republican and Democratic presidential platforms endorsed entry. However, there had always been sufficient opposition in the Senate, led by influential men like Borah and Johnson, to provide an effective counter. Hearst, as has been seen, maintained ferocious opposition and did his best to keep the court issue before the public.[29]

However, in late 1934 and early 1935 the matter came before the Senate for what proved to be the last time. Hearst, aided by the radio priest Father Charles E. Coughlin, weighed in again with his usual flood of editorials. He combined these with pleas to readers to deluge their senators with demands that they vote against the court, and with "a platoon of lobbyists" on Capitol Hill assigned "to harass senators personally." The apparent result was that, when the issue finally came to a vote on 29 January 1935, the proposal was defeated, with fifty-two senators in favor and thirty-six against, seven less than the two-thirds majority required for approval.

Again the Hearst papers loudly claimed credit for this victory. In this they were joined by others. After Hearst's death the *New York Times* noted that "as much as any other single man he was responsible for the defeat of resolutions to make the United States a party to the World Court covenant."[30] At the time Senator Borah, one of the irreconcilables who had engineered the defeat of the proposal, sent him and Coughlin congratulatory messages. But Borah privately believed that their campaigns had not materially affected the Senate vote, that he had had enough support to ensure the proposal's defeat before the Hearst campaign began, and that support on both sides had held firm throughout.[31] Borah was not, of course, a man to make such judgments lightly, nor did his estimates of the voting tendencies of his Senate colleagues lack shrewdness and perception. His view of the situation in 1935 is borne out by the evidence of previous and subsequent Senate votes on such questions; until it was swept away by Pearl Harbor, there was always a substantial minority that could be mustered to defeat measures that smacked of internationalism.

Yet Hearst and his editors believed that, on this occasion, they had affected the votes of the senators. Four years later Coblentz, writing to a colleague, spoke of the value of the tactics of bombarding legislators "with letters and wires of protest ... I do not think they are influenced by a smattering of letters and wires. It is the deluge that they respect." He used the fight against the World Court as the principal example of successful use of this technique.[32] The evidence suggests, however, that he was wrong, that even when a major fight by the Hearst papers was successful, their real influence over the course of events was minimal. There were, in other words, always other factors to explain the outcome.

The relationship between the messages received from the populace and the actions taken on the subjects of those messages by the legislators who represent them is at best imprecise. It cannot be assumed that mass communication is a one-way process. More than twenty-five years ago Joseph Klapper showed that what he called the "hypodermic syringe" model – which saw mass communication as "pure stimulus, like the serum in a hypodermic syringe, which, when injected, would either produce a response or would fail to do so" – was fallacious. He found that the mediating factors of selective exposure, retention, and interpretation, through which individuals filter communications, are of equal or greater importance in determining how messages from the mass media are received. Additional factors, like sense of self, current situation, and social and political reference groups, are also vital determinants of how individuals interpret such messages.[33]

These findings tend to confirm the earlier work of P.F. Lazarsfeld and his associates, most notably on the 1940 presidential election. In their study of the election that returned Roosevelt to the White House for the third time, they concluded that, notwithstanding the opposition to Roosevelt of the majority of the press, voting was largely determined by personal influence, in the form of family and friends, and by the presence of a strong leader of opinion – that is, the mass media had little effect on individual voters, either in changing their votes from previous elections or in maintaining them for the same parties or individuals.[34] The cumulative effect of work like this is to propose two primary effects of the mass media in making public opinion. First, the filtering of messages through personal mediating processes tends to reinforce existing individual and group attitudes. Second, the mass media only create opinion where individuals are themselves uncertain, where opinion leaders take no strong stand on specific issues, or where groups have no standards by which to judge particular events. In other words, the role of the mass media is limited to forming opinions where none exist.

The implication for assessing the influence of the Hearst press on popular views of American foreign policy is clear. In both the campaigns discussed here the president failed, either deliberately or inadvertently, to take a strong stand on the issue at hand – McKinley on the first Hay-Pauncefote Treaty and Franklin Roosevelt on entry into the World Court – thus leaving a vacuum in which the Hearst campaign could have some effect. On other occasions, where the presidential lead was stronger or where a clear choice was presented by other leaders of opinion, the effect was negligible. In these contexts, the lack of effect of the frequently published stories of atrocities in the First World War is instructive.[35] Only perhaps in the area of influencing long-term attitudes would the Hearst press and organizations like it play a part.

The Hearst press's own estimate of its readership has been cited earlier in this study;[36] at its most extensive it could claim between 12 and 14 per cent of total newspaper readership.[37] The press was by far the largest single influence in the United States at this time. Hearst's tactics of continually pounding away on subjects that exercised him, of reminding readers in the clearest and most unequivocal terms of his position on particular issues, must have affected the views of his readers, must have left them with impressions and prejudices, perhaps unconsciously held, that would influence their reactions to foreign policy questions as they arose.

Many studies have shown that foreign relations are seldom cited as a major interest of the American public – that, for example, the conduct of foreign affairs is rarely a deciding factor in national elections.[38] Nevertheless, the media are the major source of the views that the mass public hold of the rest of the world. As one scholar has noted, to the unconsciously acquired views of other places and peoples "we have to add all that gets communicated ... through the mass media, books, journals, newspapers, films, and radio and television, each bit becoming part of the process of creating and summoning up relevant images in people's minds, an item in the intimate interaction in the ways people perceive other people, how they interpret others' behavior, and how they behave themselves."[39]

It is in this sense that the Hearst press had its greatest influence over the mass public in the United States. Though that public changed or was manipulated in ways that will be discussed in the next chapter, in the first three decades of this century most Americans held hostile attitudes to other countries, attitudes that were fostered by many agencies, the Hearst press among them. In the early forties the Office of War Information, seeking to establish the views of Americans about the prospects of peace and world-wide stability and cooperation, noted that there was an increase in support for "such general statements of America's war goals as the Atlantic Charter and the Four Freedoms" but that "distrust and suspicion of other nations may once again cause Americans to shy away from international collaboration."[40] The report concluded that "similarly, we may fear that our diplomats are certain to be outsmarted by the suave representatives of other countries ... there is the notion that the attempt to achieve a better world is visionary and impractical ... that internationalism is incompatible with Americanism ... that policies which have served America in the past will necessarily be appropriate under the changed conditions of today."[41] It appeared that "suspicion and hostility toward England and Russia have by no means been eliminated ... and many Americans still talk about Russia, England, and other nations in stereotyped, unrealistic terms." Such views were being "sedulously fostered by a small but powerful minority of America's newspapers."[42]

11 Epilogue: 1941–1951

Although the Hearst papers were not mentioned by name in the intelligence reports quoted at the end of the previous chapter, there can be no doubt that they were foremost among those regarded as "sedulously fostering" suspicion of America's allies. As the war began for the United States, the Hearst papers advocated support for the administration and the war effort.[1] Before long, however, Hearst was taking issue with the policies of the government and its allies. He regarded it as "our duty, as a now open and declared ally of England in this war, … [and] to our selfish advantage" to give all possible aid to Great Britain, but he objected to Winston Churchill's suggestion that the war in Europe take priority over that in the Pacific.[2] This argument was, however, primarily with the Roosevelt government, which Hearst regarded as very short-sighted in failing to understand the urgency of the fight against the Japanese, rather than with America's allies.[3]

Hearst maintained the view of Russia that he had held throughout the thirties, even though she, too, was now an ally against Germany. In October 1942, for example, commenting on demands from the British Communist Party that a second front be opened in France immediately to take pressure off Russia, he noted that "the best military authorities of both countries say that such a second front now might mean utter disaster but that is of no consequence to the Communists, for they are not interested in the fate of 'capitalistic' America and England, but seek only to draw Hitler's hordes out of Russia." Stalin had said in effect that, when this had been accomplished, he would make peace with Hitler: clearly, "the greatest enemies of harmony and efficiency among the United Nations are the Communists."[4] This view of the Russians and their motives continued throughout the war, as Hearst constantly warned of the dangers of not taking firm and calculated steps to curb Russian ambitions and counter Russian subversion.[5]

At the same time Hearst fought proposals that smacked of a revival of the League of Nations or any similar threat to American freedom of action after the war. The "great issue that is crystallizing in the consciousness of all thinking Americans," he declared in 1943, "is not 'isolationism' versus 'internationalism' ... It is AMERICAN NA-TIONALISM versus the INTERNATIONALIZATION OF THE UNITED STATES." There was a conspiracy led by "New Deal interventionalists of the Wallace-Willkie-Hopkins-Frankfurter-Laski-Cripps stripe" – an unlikely conspiracy! – to make the nation part of an international federation, "an atom of an INTERNATIONAL AXIS."[6] A little later, in an editorial that could have been written at any time in his life, he pleaded with the American people to "keep free to do whatever we believe to be our duty ... to protect the welfare of the American people as well as of other peoples ... free from compacts and commitments."[7] Or again, along the same lines, "international cooperation is indeed an ideal of human brotherhood ... But any surrender of sovereignty, in any measure, by the one government on earth that best exemplifies the freedom and dignity of mankind would be unwise and unthinkable."[8]

The reader who has come this far will hardly be surprised to learn that Hearst's views on American foreign policy in the post-war world amounted largely to more of the same. In the last decade of his life Hearst saw no reason to change his ideas about American conduct in the world, even though he was living through events that changed that world and, more to the point, changed the way in which many Americans – including many of the strongest opponents of internationalism – regarded their country's relations with it. Almost alone, Hearst went on thundering his warnings and his anathemas from his mountaintop. The last ten years of his life were in every sense an epilogue for William Randolph Hearst and for his view of American conduct in the world.

Many of the legislators Hearst had supported in the twenties and thirties, as they tried to keep the United States out of the League or the court and to stop other manifestations of a policy that would reduce or remove the country's freedom of action and perhaps lead to a repetition of the First World War, were either passing from the scene or being obliged to change their minds. Borah died before the United

States entered the war in 1941. Others remained to be defeated. In the Senate, Gerald Nye of North Dakota and George Norris of Nebraska were both defeated in 1944, and Robert La Follette, Jr, of Wisconsin, Burton Wheeler of Montana, and Henrick Shipstead of Minnesota followed in 1946, for reasons often closely related to their stand on foreign affairs.[9] Others simply changed their minds, the most notable convert from isolationism to internationalism being Senator Arthur Vandenburg – although, as one scholar has noted, Vandenburg remained a militant nationalist and fervently anti-Soviet, so that "few 'conversions' have been made with so many previous assumptions intact."[10] Hiram Johnson retained his position to the end: one of his last political acts was to vote against American participation in the United Nations,[11] although he was joined in this by only a few of his former allies.

So, as those whom he had supported since the end of the First World War fell away, Hearst was increasingly alone in his long-held views on American foreign policy. The verdict of one scholar on those he categorized as the "Old Progressives" in the Congress could also apply to Hearst: "The old progressives had become political as well as spiritual refugees in modern America ... And so they grew old and querulous and perhaps a little bitter toward a world that had constantly defied their hopes and expectations."[12]

Nevertheless, Hearst continued the crusades to which he had so long devoted himself. As FDR came home from Yalta, Hearst greeted the idea of a United Nations conference to be held in San Francisco as "a project to which all people look with hope," even though he doubted the "moral pattern of the 'peace and security' proposed."[13] Three weeks later, in an editorial suggested by Neylan, he invoked the shade of Neville Chamberlain as he described British Foreign Minister Anthony Eden's view of the conference as a victory for peace and security and wondered what the people of Estonia, Latvia, Lithuania, and Poland thought of this idea. Once again the United States had permitted itself to be hoodwinked by more cynical and selfish powers.[14]

As the San Francisco conference became a reality over the next few months, Hearst left no doubt about where the next threat to world peace would come from, now that Germany was defeated and Japan soon would be. "Even before the [San Francisco] meeting has convened and with the ink hardly dried on the Big Three agreement at Yalta, Moscow has forced Romania to oust its recently installed government and to set up a leftist regime," thus negating its promises about consultation.[15] The threat of international Communism still loomed.

In the establishment of the United Nations, however, Hearst saw much that was encouraging. When Herbert Hoover greeted the conference as a great opportunity to establish conditions for lasting peace, Hearst agreed but hoped that the United States would not blindly support whatever came out of the conference.[16] Similarly, he approved of President Truman's closing speech to the conference: "The new charter is not in itself the final instrument of the world's hopes, he very solemnly observed, and is capable of becoming so only upon the fulfillment of challenging conditions to be confronted by the nations of the world." The United States would have no problems with the new organization and its aspirations if it accepted the president's "sound appraisal ... that the new United Nations Charter is a good thing well begun but only begun."[17]

But there was to be no lessening of Hearst's demands for vigilance in the post-war world. Between 1945 and his death he campaigned to make his countrymen realize the dangers of their situation on three fronts – the menace of foreign and domestic Communism; the jeopardy of undue participation in the UN or other organizations that would restrict America's freedom of action; and the risk of unpreparedness incurred by not increasing the defence establishment and maintaining it at an effective level.

He first returned to the attack on domestic Communism, a doctrine that he continued to picture as irreversibly alien and thus a menace to everything precious and important about America. This view was never better stated than in an editorial in 1945, when the American Communist Party withdrew its support for the war effort. Only so long as Russia had been involved had the party *pretended* to support the war. Now that Russia was no longer active, neither were they. Conclusively this demonstrated that "there is no such thing, and never has been any such thing, as an AMERICAN Communist or Communist Party."[18] From this time on Hearst maintained his unrelenting pursuit of the enemy of U.S. labour, education, government – of everything American.[19]

The international policies of the Soviet Union were a concurrent and equal danger. Stalin was portrayed as at best dishonest and untrustworthy, at worst "the new Ghenghis Khan," bent on world conquest.[20] As he pursued his "relentless" way through Eastern Europe, gained "frightening" footholds in the West, toppled the "heroic" government of Chiang Kai-Shek in China, Hearst was equally relentless in his reaction.[21] Nothing seemed immune from the machinations of the master of the Kremlin, and even the United Nations would soon degenerate into his instrument. Stalin and his evil system had become the single gigantic threat to American and world peace and security.[22]

The Little Red School Teacher

San Francisco Examiner, 16 August 1946

In the face of such a threat there was only one path open to the United States – that which Hearst had advocated between the wars. His initial hopes for the United Nations were destroyed by its ineptitude in the face of Russian aggression, and by 1947 he was calling it an international debating society of no practical value.[23] Far better, he now maintained, to remain aloof, preserve American freedom of action, and remember that Washington's maxims were still valid.[24] The country must be firm with Russia and ready to resist her whenever and wherever necessary, but it must be free to pursue its own goals and its own security in its own way. Thus, in the spring of 1947 Hearst applauded the Truman Doctrine as a welcome return to sound principles after a period of flabby uncertainty in foreign policy.[25] He did not, however, extend his approval when the Marshall Plan was proposed: this he regarded as an unwarranted intervention in European affairs. The only sure way to European recovery was for the Europeans to save themselves. In any case the United States had rescued them twice before in this century and should not, Hearst noted in an editorial headed "How Much for Europe?"[26] have to do so again.

Faced with what he saw as an increasingly dangerous situation, Hearst returned to his old cry that the only guarantee of American security was American strength. He continued to ask for co-operation, even unity, for the Americas, regarding this as contributing to safety.[27] But in the end the United States had only herself to rely on, and she must be ever watchful and maintain her defences in constant strength and readiness. The atomic bomb was one of the great benefits of the Second World War for the United States because it gave the nation a unique opportunity to use what was clearly the ultimate weapon for its own defence and that of world order.[28]

Even this in itself was not sufficient. With the war scarcely over, Hearst was advocating that the armed forces be maintained at sufficient strength to secure the United States against any threat.[29] Universal military training, a cause he had championed before the war, was also an indispensable part of national preparedness.[30] The outbreak of the Korean War a few years later served to emphasize the need for constant preparedness, the government's inability to see this, and the fulfilment of what Hearst had been prophesying for years.[31]

There is evidence from this period for modifying some of the conclusions discussed earlier about the influence of the press on American foreign policy and on those who participate in its making. James Rosenau, however, offers two primary assumptions about the making of u.s. policy. First, he regards the president and his officials as the primary source of the information on foreign affairs communicated to the mass public. Second, he argues that the only function of the mass public in policy-making is to set "the outer limits within which decision-makers and opinion-makers feel constrained to operate and interact."[32]

These assumptions about attitudes of the mass public in the United States towards Russia seem to have been correct. Hearst may never have let up in his criticism and suspicion of the Soviet Union and its rulers, but most other American publishers did. The result, as traced in a study by historian Melvin Small, was a substantial softening in the attitudes of significant sectors of the American public towards the Russians and in their expectations of Russian-American relations after the war. At the beginning of the war prospects for co-operation

with the Soviet Union seemed dim: "many minds had to be opened
before Russia could be accepted as an honorable member of the international system."[33] But despite this grim outlook, "a generally positive image did emerge," so that "in 1943 and 1944 close to half the
population believed that Russia could be trusted while only a third
registered a dissenting opinion. This was a remarkable turnabout in
public opinion."[34] Thus, by the end of the war most Americans, "despite earlier anti-Bolshevik crusades, ... were prepared to live in
peace with the Soviets," and "preparations for rapprochement had
been made."[35] The majority of the media – notably excluding the
Hearst papers, which are not included in Small's review – had followed the government line and helped to prepare the mass public for
the post-war future.

This development emphasizes the point of Rosenau's first assumption, that the administration, particularly in a crisis, has the power to
ensure that its own version of events is placed before the public. As
soon as the war ended, however, the situation changed. The anti-
Communist press, the Hearst papers prominent among them, returned to the attack, mounting a widespread and sustained offensive
against Russia and Communism. In the short period between the end
of the war and the point at which – with the Truman Doctrine – the
administration itself publicly adopted a view of the Soviet Union as
evil, the anti-Communist press had been "so successful in presenting
a cohesive view of the Soviets as evil that this view provided Truman
with a base of anti-Communist attitudes which made the Truman
Doctrine readily acceptable to the mass public."[36] Here the opposite
of what had happened at the beginning of the war occurred – the
anti-Communist press, acting as an alternative supplier of information to the president and reminding its readership of the anti-Bolshevik campaigns of the past, helped in a substantial way to move
American foreign policy in a direction for which the war years had
not prepared it. In other words, the assumptions about the long-term
effects of concentrated and long press campaigns on public attitudes
discussed earlier are probably valid. As Small's study concludes, the
consequences of this may have led to widespread acceptance of the
Truman Doctrine and the Marshall Plan in the short run, but in the
long run they helped to produce an era in which the United States,
supported by a firmly anti-Communist public, became trapped by its
own rhetoric in commitments that were too broad and too expensive
to maintain.[37] This was, of course, precisely what Hearst – and the
Old Progressives who, unlike him, were in silent retreat in the forties
– had warned against. Subsequent events have, in a sense, vindicated
them.[38]

But this cannot, of course, be the last word on William Randolph Hearst, his influence on and views about American foreign policy. The principal theme of this study is that his view of American conduct overseas was basically sensible and reasonable, one that came closer than many of his contemporaries recognized to meeting some of the dicta he was so fond of quoting from the Founding Fathers. His isolationism was by no means a blind insistence on a self-sufficient Fortress America: so far as can be ascertained, he really believed in maintaining not merely American sovereignty and freedom of action but also good relations with the rest of the world. He wanted the United States to be in a position where, consulting its own interests but recognizing that these necessarily included much that brought benefit to other nations, it could live in peace and prosperity while leaving others – indeed, often helping others – to do the same. To accomplish this the United States, blessed as it was with unusual resources, had merely to be strong and independent.

It is hard to take issue with such principles, and it is arguable that, had the United States followed a course closer to that proposed by Hearst, it would have been in a more secure position for much of the present century. But this argument is, in the end, made irrelevant by lack of evidence that such principles form the invariable basis for Hearst's views on United States foreign policy. His real ideas, whatever they were, became obscured by the style in which he presented them: the style became everything – or at least everything that the public and the politicians saw.

The comparison to Charles Foster Kane comes to mind again. As one critic has noted, "Kane is a summary of America ... a frontier innocent that grew into international wealth and power but stayed hollow ... Both want to be loved but feel they must buy acceptance."[39] The faults of Kane – and Hearst – are those of the United States writ larger than life; in Hearst's case, flashed across thousands of front pages over more than fifty years. None of this detracts perhaps from the merit of what Hearst was; it merely means that the effect was nullified by his excesses of style. As in the case of Citizen Kane, "the thing is: we can't condemn [Hearst] because [his] intentions are so good; but we can't condone [him], because [he's] so forceful in imposing [his] principles."[40]

All that comes to mind when the expression "yellow journalism" is used, or, more precisely, when the name William Randolph Hearst is mentioned, militated (and more so, as time went on) against Hearst's views' being taken seriously by politicians and statesmen inside or outside the United States, against their having – except on his readers, "brainwashed" by the constant repetition of them over half a century – any marked or overt effect at all. It served no useful purpose for Hearst to protest his regard for the British, the French, the Germans, the Japanese, to ask them to believe, in the words of Euripedes' Hippolytus, "'twas but my tongue, 'twas not my soul that swore," when the swearing was voiced over and over and over again. Quite early in Hearst's career the world came to believe that the view from San Simeon, from Xanadu, was a crabbed, narrow, intolerant, xenophobic American view that allowed no room for the rights and interests of others, that brooked no argument from opponents, American or otherwise. Long before he died Hearst was one more proof of the truth of the comment of the eighteenth-century English writer Richard Bentley: "I hold it as certain, that no man was ever written out of reputation but by himself."

Notes

INTRODUCTION

1 Lindsay Chaney and Michael Cieply, *The Hearsts: Family and Empire – The Later Years*, 28–9.
2 W.A. Swanberg, *Citizen Hearst*, 526–7.
3 Frank MacShane, "The Romantic World of William Randolph Hearst," 299.
4 Ibid., 296.
5 Ibid., 304–5.
6 On this view of Hearst, see also Ferdinand Lundberg, *Imperial Hearst*, 19. Lundberg noted that Hearst was born in 1863, when San Francisco produced a thousand murders a year and "the Barbary Coast was wide open." As the only child of overindulgent parents, he grew up with the loose morals and ruthless methods of San Francisco in the 1870s and 1880s.
7 MacShane, "Romantic World," 299.

CHAPTER ONE: PROLOGUE

1 In 1895 one of the editors of the *Pittsburgh Press*, noting the rapid increase in the circulation of the *New York Journal*, wrote to ask if he could buy some of its features for his own paper. The result was the organization of the Hearst syndicate, with Curtis J. Mar as general manager. Elmo Scott Watson, *A History of Newspaper Syndicates in the United States, 1865–1935*, 55–6.

2 For a description of the techniques used by Hearst to build up the circulation of the *San Francisco Examiner*, see Donald J. Wood, *William Randolph Hearst: His Early Years in Journalism*.

3 For an account of the editorial policies of the Hearst press, see chap. 2 below. Because of the existence of these policies, the author used the method described in the bibliography to ascertain the views expounded by the Hearst press on foreign policy issues.

4 Editorial, *San Francisco Examiner*, 8 Aug. 1895 (cited hereafter as *SFE*).

5 Ibid., 13 Aug. 1895.

6 Ibid., 13 Sept. 1895.

7 Ibid., 20 Sept. 1895.

8 Ibid., 1 Feb. 1896.

9 Ibid., 1 Mar. 1896.

10 Ibid., 1 June 1896.

11 One account of Hearst's involvement in national politics in the early twentieth century argues that it was the campaign of 1896 that first made the *New York Journal* a nationally known newspaper. See James Otis Wheaton, "The Role of William Randolph Hearst in the Prenomination and Presidential Campaigns of 1912," 2.

12 Editorial, *SFE*, 14 Nov. 1896. See also Charles H. Brown, *The Correspondents' War: Journalists in the Spanish American War*, 54–5.

13 See, for example, editorials, *SFE*, 14 Dec. 1896; 2 Jan. 1897; 22 May 1897, in which it was argued that "humanity, trade, self-interest call on the United States to interfere to stop the reign of murder and pillage in Cuba"; and 8 Aug. 1897, which asked, "When is the Administration going to open its eyes to the distress of Cuba and its ears to the pleadings of its own people, and do what humanity and interest dictate?" Editorials like these were printed throughout 1897 and the early months of 1898, increasing in ferocity as the situation worsened. Editorial comment was allied with increased space on the front pages being given to events in Cuba.

14 *SFE*, 2 Feb. 1897.

15 See Lloyd Cecil Minear, "William Randolph Hearst and Foreign Affairs, 1914–1920," 6.

16 John K. Winkler, *William Randolph Hearst: A New Appraisal*, 95–6. Winkler also notes here that Hearst "later privately denied that his telegram was couched quite in the epigrammatic form quoted." Another Hearst biography states that, whereas probably no such telegram was sent, "unquestionably this was the substance of Remington's commission." Oliver Carlson and Ernest Sutherland Bates, *Hearst, Lord of San Simeon*, 97.

17 Brown, *Correspondents' War*, 95.

18 The intercession of the Pope was reported in *SFE*, 25 Aug. 1897.

19 See Brown, *Correspondents' War*, 102. It should be noted that Brown here quotes from Willis J. Abbott, *Watching the World Go By*, 215–16, on Hearst's

attitude during the Cisneros affair. "I was at the office during the progress of this comedy and in daily contact with Hearst. He took the whole affair with the utmost seriousness ... If ever for a moment he doubted that he was battling a powerful state for the life and liberty of a sorely persecuted girl martyr, he gave no sign of it. It was the one dominating, all compelling issue of the moment for him ... Hearst felt himself in the role of Sir Galahad rescuing a helpless maiden."

20 For an account of the de Lôme incident, see Sidney Kobre, *The Yellow Press and Gilded Age Journalism*, 287–8.

21 See David F. Healy, *The United States in Cuba, 1898–1902: Generals, Politicians and the Search for a Policy*, 18–19.

22 On the three days following the sinking of the Maine, the circulation of the *Journal* broke all records. Willard G. Bleyer, *Main Currents in the History of American Journalism*, 374.

23 Editorial, *SFE*, 4 May 1898.

24 Ibid., 21 July 1898.

25 Ibid., 23 July 1898.

26 Ibid., 6 Aug. 1898. For a discussion of alternatives envisaged at this time for the future of the Philippines, see Ernest R. May, "American Imperialism: A Reinterpretation," 124.

27 "The United States cannot leave any foot of ground in her [Spain's] possession within reach of our shores. To leave Puerto Rico in the possession of Spain would mean that in twenty or thirty years we would have the same work to do over again that we are now doing in Cuba. We can do it more cheaply now than then." Editorial, *SFE*, 14 July 1898.

28 Ibid., 23 July 1898.

29 Ibid., 7 Aug. 1899.

30 Ibid., 21 May 1902.

31 Ibid., 5 Sept. 1902.

32 Ibid., 24 Nov. 1908. For many years, however, Hearst continued to believe in a special relationship with Cuba. "Cuba is not merely our friend and neighbor. The relationship is closer than that. Cuba is more like a younger brother." Hearst to Clarence Lindner, np, 9 Nov. 1928, Lindner file, 1928, box 6, William Randolph Hearst Papers, Bancroft Library.

33 *SFE*, 10 Oct. 1908.

34 "Everybody at all cognizant of the conditions in the Philippines knows that it would be mere madness to fix today any time at which the authority of the United States shall be withdrawn from these islands. An overwhelming majority of their people are mere savages, unable to govern themselves except in the savage, tribal way, and certainly unfit to have anything to say in the government of Luzon and other more civilized parts of the archipelago. That condition will not change in the life of the present generation." Hearst thus applauded President Wilson's refusal to

make a firm commitment on the date of Filipino independence. Ibid., 6 June 1914.

35 William Randolph Hearst, *Obligations and Opportunities of the United States in Mexico and the Philippines*, 10–11.

36 Brown, *Correspondents' War*, v.

37 Ibid.

38 H. Wayne Morgan, *America's Road to Empire: The War with Spain and Overseas Expansion*, 14.

39 See, for example, Mark M. Welter, "The 1895–98 Cuban Crisis in Minnesota Newspapers: Testing the 'Yellow Journalism' Theory," 719–24.

40 *New York Times*, 15 Aug. 1951.

41 *San Francisco Chronicle*, 15 Aug. 1951.

42 "Pulitzer's journals rejected Hearst's rambunctious cowboy chivalry … the pro-war *World* was closer to the anti-imperialist *Nation* than either was to Hearst's antiprofessional romanticism." David Axeen, " 'Heroes of the Engine Room': American 'Civilization' and the War with Spain," 495–6.

43 Carlson and Bates, *Hearst, Lord of San Simeon*, 92–109.

44 John K. Winkler, *William Randolph Hearst, an American Phenomenon*, 146; and Winkler, *New Appraisal*, 97. Most of the material contained in the latter work under this section is a repetition of the first. In the best Hearst biography, the author entitled his chapter on the war "The War Maker," and mentioned, almost in passing, that it was Hearst's war. Swanberg, *Citizen Hearst*, 79–169.

45 Winkler, *New Appraisal*, 97.

46 Brown, *Correspondents' War*, 440. In this section Brown engages in what is probably the most comprehensive and reasonable discussion of the role of the press among the causes of the Spanish American War. See 440–6.

CHAPTER TWO: HEARST AND HIS NEWSPAPERS

1 Edwin Emery and Henry Ladd Smith. *The Press and America: An Interpretive History of Journalism*, 537.

2 Institutional data for the year 1937, Hearst Organization File, Edmond D. Coblentz Papers, Bancroft Library.

3 Figures as at 30 June 1941. List of newspapers covered by Press Intelligence Bulletin of the Division of Press Intelligence, Washington, DC, 1 Jan. 1942. Executive Division: Records of the Assistant Director, Katherine C. Blackburn, 1941–43, Records of the Office of Government Reports, Record Group 44, National Archives.

4 See Chaney and Cieply, *The Hearsts*, 43–5. Under the bank-imposed trusteeship of "the Napoleonic Shearer from 1937 to 1945," what saved Hearst was Hearst – "dictating orders to papers that only occasionally failed to respond and, unknown to the bankers, directing a quiet guerrilla war

against the alien force that had invaded his institution." This view is modified somewhat by one scholar who notes that, while Hearst suffered "some diminution of control over news … he still exerted predominant influence." William Quayle Parmeter, "The News Control Explanation of Newsmaking: The Case of William Randolph Hearst, 1920–1940," 200.

5 W.R. Hearst, Jr, to author, New York, 5 Mar. 1976. In this letter Mr Hearst indicates that his father's active interest extended to "possibly the last six months of his life." This is confirmed by evidence from the Hearst papers. In January 1951 he wrote to his son that "I am tired of seeing the *New York Journal* go down in circulation while the *Los Angeles Examiner* goes up." Hearst to W.R. Hearst, Jr, Los Angeles, 14 Jan. 1951, W.R. Hearst, Sr, file, 1951, box 43, William Randolph Hearst Papers, Bancroft Library. The last instruction included in the Hearst Papers is a detailed comment on the cover of the *American Weekly* for 20 May 1951, less than three months before his death. Hearst to Walter Howey, np, 24 May 1951, Howey file, 1951, box 43, Hearst Papers.

6 W.R. Hearst, Jr, to author, 5 Mar. 1976.

7 "Mr. Hearst has instructed me to call your attention to the fact that the *New York Evening Sun* prints financial tables very well. Mr. Hearst asks that you kindly use the *Evening Sun's* style and type." J.A. Murray, secretary to Hearst, to managing editors of all Hearst evening papers, np, 1 Dec. 1922. He also issued instructions to use the *Los Angeles Examiner* style of dividing comics in all papers. Murray to managing editors of all Hearst papers, np, 29 Dec. 1922, Series 5, box 63, folder 2, John Francis Neylan Papers, Bancroft Library.

8 Hearst to Van Hamm, np, 23 Nov. 1915, Editors file, 1915, box 1, Hearst Papers.

9 Hearst to F.W. Kellogg, publisher of the *San Francisco Call*, np, 5 June 1916, series 5, box 66, folder 18.5, Neylan Papers.

10 John Willicombe, secretary to Hearst, to editors of all Hearst papers, np, 17 Mar. 1920, series 5, box 63, folder 1, ibid.

11 Hearst to publishers of all Hearst papers, np, 23 Oct. 1922, series 5, box 63, folder 2, ibid.

12 Hearst to Coblentz, Los Angeles, 2 Aug. 1926, Incoming, Coblentz Papers.

13 Hearst to Coblentz, San Simeon, 23 May 1933, ibid.

14 Hearst to Coblentz, np, 1 Aug. 1932, ibid.

15 Edmond D. Coblentz, *Newsmen Speak*, 102–3.

16 Hearst to Neylan, np, 5 May 1933, series 5, box 65, folder 14, Neylan Papers.

17 Reminiscences of James T. Williams, in the Oral History Collection of Columbia University, 4: 788–9.

18 Ibid.

19 Ibid., 789–90

20 See, for example, 38, n 29.

21 Williams, OHC, 4:770. Hearst's son described the practice of sending out a number of editorials on the same subject by saying that, after the first Hearst editorial, "not infrequently he would send along a second or third or fourth signed editorial – never in rapid succession – but often enough to keep the fires burning and to reiterate, in his forceful language, his point and arguments." W.R. Hearst, Jr, to author, New York, 5 Mar. 1976. See also Rodney Parker Carlisle, "The Political Ideas and Influence of William Randolph Hearst, 1928–1936," 22. Hearst apparently occasionally wrote letters as if they came from others. See John Willicombe to editors of all morning papers and afternoon papers where no morning paper exists, np, 9 Oct. 1938, Editors (misc.) file, 1938, box 27, Hearst Papers. This contained a letter to be printed on the editorial pages of all papers from "A Practical American." The telegram is stapled to a copy of the letter in Hearst's handwriting.

22 Reminiscences of John T. Hettrick, in the Oral History Collection of Columbia University, 64. Brisbane spoke of Hearst to a colleague as "a sincere man, and a courageous man ... He has done more for this country, in the last fifteen years, than any single man. He has been the educator of such men as Wilson and Roosevelt and others, big and little, of about their size. And he has not only TAUGHT THEM, but he has made it possible for them to repeat safely and to loud applause, the things that he said, when the sayings meant hatred and criticism." Brisbane to Fremont Older, New York, 10 Mar. 1913, vol. 1, Fremont Older Collection, Bancroft Library.

23 Claude G. Bowers went to work for Hearst for a short time after the *New York World* went out of business. He noted that "they never knew what I was going to write about until I turned it in. They never made a suggestion as to anything I should write about. I selected my own subjects altogether, all national political subjects. They never changed anything I wrote." Bowers recalled that at one point, he made favourable comments about Al Smith in an editorial, but when he raised the question of printing it with his editor, he was told that it should go in – in spite of the long-standing feud between Smith and Hearst. He closed his comments on the association with the Hearst papers by saying: "That was the spirit I encountered all the two years I was with Hearst. It was a little different from the usual stories you hear." Reminiscences of Claude G. Bowers, in the Oral History Collection of Columbia University, 70–1. This view is confirmed by Fremont Older. See Older to Hearst, San Francisco, 11 Aug. 1932, Editors (misc.) file, 1932, box 15, Hearst Papers. See also Gibb and Bean, "John Francis Neylan", 172–4, for a favourable view of Hearst.

24 Williams, OHC, 4:747–51.

25 Ibid., 750–1.

26 Emile Gauvreau, *My Last Million Readers*, 293–305. In this section Gauvreau describes his dismissal by Hearst for publishing material favourable to the USSR. The statement quoted was made by Brisbane, who told Gauvreau that, if Hearst decided Russia was no good, then those who wrote for him must write that way and that was Hearst's prerogative. He was, said Brisbane, "the last of his kind in the newspaper business. The days of palaces in Democracy are over. I've tried to tell him that but he's going to die a king … A king has his whims. But you offended him which is the reason you are no longer one of his well-paid courtiers." See also Rodney Carlisle, "William Randolph Hearst's Reaction to the American Newspaper Guild: A Challenge to New Deal Labor Legislation," 77.

27 *News Chronicle*, 15 Aug. 1951.

28 *Manchester Guardian*, 15 Aug. 1951.

29 *The Times*, 15 Aug. 1951.

30 *Christian Science Monitor*, 15 Aug. 1951.

31 *Washington Post*, 15 Aug. 1951

32 *Los Angeles Times*, 16 Aug. 1951.

33 *San Francisco Chronicle*, 15 Aug. 1951.

34 Will Irwin, *The American Newspaper*, 15. See also Swanberg, *Hearst*, 59–76.

35 See Robert L. Duffus, "The Tragedy of Hearst," 626–7.

36 For a discussion of Hearst and yellow journalism, see Brown, *Correspondents' War*, 16 and 19. For a more general discussion of yellow journalism, see Frank Luther Mott, *American Journalism: A History of Newspapers in the United States through 250 Years, 1690–1940*, 539.

37 See Sidney Brooks, "The Yellow Press: An English View," 11.

38 See 150–1.

39 Philip C. Jessup, *Elihu Root*, 1:83.

40 Ibid., 82

41 Ibid., 2:347.

42 Also see 97. "Root is a very able man and his presence in this World Court proposition means that the big interests which usually employ Root are now employing him on something that they think of benefit to themselves." Hearst to J.T. Williams, np, 29 Mar. 1929, Williams file, 1929, box 10, Hearst Papers.

43 Theodore Roosevelt to Elihu Root, Oyster Bay, 4 Sept. 1906, Special Correspondence with Theodore Roosevelt, 1904–24 and undated, box 163, Elihu Root Papers, Library of Congress.

44 Ibid.

45 Roosevelt to R.W. Gilder, Washington, DC, 31 Oct. 1906, series 2, vol. 68, 191–2, Theodore Roosevelt Papers, Library of Congress. In a letter to his biographer Root noted that he had written his speech and then shown it to the president, who, when he came to the section giving his own view of Hearst, "took his pencil and made it stronger." Root to Philip C. Jessup,

np, 15 Sept. 1930, in Jessup, *Root*, 2:116. The president wrote to his son that he and Root "went all over it together and made up our minds that that was the best way in which I could interfere." Roosevelt to Kermit Roosevelt, Washington, DC, 4 Nov. 1906, series 2, vol. 68, 198–9, Roosevelt Papers.

46 The full text of the speech can be found in Speeches, 1894–1953, box 22, Root Papers. It is also quoted extensively in Jessup, *Root*, 2:118–20.

47 Roosevelt to Kermit Roosevelt, Washington, DC, 11 Nov. 1906, series 2, 68:295–6, ibid. See also a letter from Senator John Coit Spooner to Root, congratulating him on the speech and expressing the belief that Hearst would probably be the Democratic nominee in 1908. Spooner to Root, Madison, Wisc., 9 Nov. 1906, Correspondence, 17 Sept. to 18 Dec. 1906, box 189, John Coit Spooner Papers, Library of Congress. Spooner had earlier co-operated with Root and Roosevelt in the production of the speech. Like both of them, he clearly believed in the connection between the Hearst papers and the McKinley assassination. Spooner to Root, Madison, Wisc., 15 Oct. 1906, ibid.

48 See, for example, Roosevelt to Timothy L. Woodruff, Washington, DC, 4 Nov.; to Judge T.H. Gary, Washington, DC, 5 Nov.; and to Alice Longworth, Washington, DC, 7 Nov. (all 1906), series 2, 68:196, 231, and 293–4, Roosevelt Papers.

49 See chap. 10.

50 Carlisle, "Hearst," 193–4.

51 Ibid., 32–3.

52 See, for example, Oswald Garrison Villard, *Some Newspapers and Newspapermen* 23–4. In this chapter Villard notes that all the good that Hearst had achieved has been "tarnished by self-interest, by self-seeking, and arouses the never-failing and justified suspicion of his sincerity. For at the very moment when he has been crying out most loudly for the people's rights, he has never hesitated to strike hands with the worst of the politicians who rob the people of their rights at the behest of big business, their real masters."

53 "Make the paper helpful and kindly. Don't scold and forever complain and attack in your news columns. Leave that to the editorial page ... Be fair and impartial ... PLEASE BE ACCURATE ... Don't allow exaggeration." Signed by Hearst, marked "Circulation, June, 1922," Editors (misc.) file, 1922, box 1, Hearst Papers. For attempts to soften the constant attack on FDR, see "Our criticism is almost too uninterrupted to be effective" and "we are nagging Roosevelt annoyingly and ineffectively," Hearst to Coblentz, np, 5 Mar. 1934, Coblentz file, 1934, box 18, and 10 Jan. 1940, Coblentz file, 1940, box 29, ibid.

54 John R. Tebbel, *The Life and Good Times of William Randolph Hearst*, 157–8 and 164–5.

55 See, for a favourable and early view (though from a former employee) of Hearst's concern for the working man, Charles Edward Russell, "Mr. Hearst as I knew him," 9. For a discussion of Hearst's method of appealing to the masses, see Irwin, *American Newspaper*, 24–7.

56 Theodore Bonnet, "William R. Hearst: A Critical Study," 369–73.

57 See Villard, *Some Newspapers*, 23–4.

58 H.L. Mencken, for example, argued that Hearst lost his crusading zeal as he grew older. Carlisle, "Hearst," 27. It has also been argued that the change in Hearst and his methods was the result of changing times rather than changes in Hearst himself. See Walter Millis, "Hearst," 707.

59 Hearst wrote to one of his editors, J.D. Gortatowsky, that "I always feel that it is not as important to be consistent as it is to be correct. A man who is completely consistent never learns anything. Conditions change, and he does not." W.R. Hearst, Jr, to author, New York, 11 Nov. 1975.

60 See MacShane, "Romantic World," 300.

61 Raymond Moley, "The Hearst Tradition."

62 See David Sarasohn, "Power without Glory: Hearst in the Progressive Era," 474–82.

CHAPTER THREE: HEARST AND EUROPE

1 See *New York Times*, 15 Aug. 1951, for a summary of British press reactions to Hearst's death. See also *The Times* and the *Manchester Guardian*, 15 Aug. 1951.

2 See article from a British weekly, *Britannia*, enclosed with Henry M. Stanbury, Universal News Service, to John Willicombe, np, nd, series 5, box 65, folder 13, Neylan Papers. The article is by Gilbert Frankau and entitled "Hearst and I With Some Reflections on America." It had been sent to Stanbury by one of the London representatives of Universal in a letter dated 5 May 1928, and passed on to Hearst's secretary with the request, "Please sir show this to chief." The article begins by saying "William Randolph Hearst! The name in England ... still conjures up hatred, misunderstandings, distrust. Because for so many years Hearst, the super-Northcliffe of America, and his great chain of newspapers which links the Transatlantic continent from east to west, stood for all that was most anti-English in ... the United States." According to the author, Hearst had protested that "I was never anti-English, ... I was pro-American ... With me, America comes first. And because of that, I could not tolerate your old patronizing attitude towards us ... You used – I felt – to look down on us. And, being an American, I couldn't stand for it." See also signed statement published in the *Melbourne Herald*, 27 Jan. 1939, in the *Daily Express*, 28 Jan. 1939, and in the Hearst newspapers, 29 Jan. 1939. E.F. Tompkins, ed., *Selections from the Writings and Speeches of William Randolph Hearst*, 285.

3 Editorial, *SFE*, 21 May 1907.
4 Ibid., 6 Jan. 1902. See also other editorials in the *Examiner*, 8 Feb.; 21 Feb.; 9 Apr.; 30 Apr.; 12 May; 29 May (all 1902). The series culminated with an editorial the day after the coronation that asked happily, "Aren't we lucky we're not like that?"
5 Ibid., 9 Dec. 1907.
6 In an editorial headed "Civilization demands that Turk should be driven from Europe," the *Examiner* made the reference to Cuba. *SFE*, 27 Aug. 1903. This was only one of many discussions of Turkish tyranny, especially in Armenia, and the duties of the European powers in that area. See, for example, ibid., 6 June 1895; 25 Jan. 1896; 1 Sept. 1903; 7 Aug. 1908. The last of these also greeted the triumph of the Young Turks and hoped that their advent would presage more civilized government for the country and its empire, a hope that was quickly quenched. See ibid., 7 May 1909; 19 June 1909; 29 July 1911.
7 See chap. 5 below for a discussion of Hearst's view of the government of pre-revolutionary Russia.
8 Editorial, *SFE*, 31 July 1908.
9 See W.C. Reuter, "Anglophobia in American Politics, 1865–1900," passim.
10 See, for example, editorial, *SFE*, 14 May 1910.
11 R.L. Burgess, "Working for Hearst," 341–2.
12 Editorial, *SFE*, 14 July 1895. This view is confirmed by John Francis Neylan. Speaking of Hearst and the British, he noted that "he wasn't anti-British; he liked the British ... But he was afraid, as I am, that every time the British sit down with our politicians, they take our shirt and we pay for it." Gibb and Bean, "John Francis Neylan," 174.
13 Editorial, *SFE*, 1 July 1896.
14 Ibid., 7 Apr. 1902. In these years, too, the Hearst papers took many opportunities to poke fun at the British and their institutions. See, for example, an editorial entitled "England's Lack of Brain Power," which reported a speech by the president of the British Association attacking the antiquated nature of the British educational system. The editorial hoped that the nation would learn, before it was too late, that "the spirit of modern education is essentially democratic and altogether inconsistent with her cherished medieval ideas of class and caste." Ibid., 23 Oct. 1903. See also "The Majestic Mind of England's King," ibid., 17 Aug. 1904.
15 Ibid., 14 May 1910.
16 See, for example, editorial headed "Fifty Labor Men in the British Parliament," ibid., 7 Feb. 1906. Following the general election in Great Britain, Hearst drew the attention of working men in the United States to the strength, unity, and effectiveness of the union movement that had been instrumental in returning fifty members of the Labour Party to the House of Commons.

17 Ibid., 17 Mar. 1906.

18 See, for example, ibid., 17 Mar. 1907, 1908, and 1909.

19 Ibid., 11 Jan. 1906.

20 Ibid., 3 July 1916. See also editorial, "England Faces Eternal Infamy in Putting Casement to Death," ibid., 27 July 1916.

21 Ibid., 27 Apr. 1917. See also ibid., 18 Dec. 1918 and 21 Jan. 1919.

22 Ibid., 21 July 1916.

23 See, for example, "American Apathy Toward British Censor Insults," ibid., 18 Sept. 1916, and "England Offers One More Insult to the United States," ibid., 5 Oct. 1916.

24 Ibid., 7 Dec. 1918.

25 Ibid., 16 Sept. 1919.

26 Ibid., 5 Feb. 1920. See also editorial, "British Propagandists Here Are Defamers of America in England," ibid., 11 Feb. 1920. In this, Hearst condemned the attacks of the Beaverbrook press on the United States as the sort of propaganda-mongering that had got the United States into the war. "It was their SECRET, undermining, insidious propaganda of pretended friendship and admiration and proposed alliance that sensible Americans feared. Now that they have shown themselves in their true character of American-haters, sensible Americans fear nothing and rejoice greatly."

27 Ibid., 1 Apr. 1920.

28 William Randolph Hearst, *Original Proposal for Anglo-American Understanding*, 7–8. This was based on an address given at Oglethorpe University in May 1927. See W.R. Hearst file, Aug.–Dec. 1927, box 4, Hearst Papers.

29 Signed editorial letter, published in the Hearst newspapers, 2 Jan. 1927. See Tompkins, ed., *Selections*, 197.

30 Statement published in the Southam papers in Canada, a number of Australian papers, and, in England, in the *Morning Post, The Times,* the *Daily Herald,* and the *Manchester Guardian* on 1 June 1930. See also *SFE* of same date.

31 Signed editorial published at the editor's request in the *Sydney Sun*. Reprinted in *SFE,* 7 Oct. 1933. Hearst continued to support Anglo-American co-operation, however. See Hearst to Coblentz, San Simeon, 23 Oct. 1938, Coblentz Papers, Incoming.

32 The *Daily Express* stated that the view of Hearst's anti-British standpoint was greatly exaggerated.

33 Editorial, *SFE,* 1 Aug. 1901.

34 Ibid., 10 June 1909.

35 Ibid., 2 May 1910.

36 Ibid., 2 Apr. 1923. A week later another editorial appeared on the same subject, headed "Tell France Plainly U.S. Is Disgusted With Her Militarism," ibid., 9 Apr. 1923.

37 A signed statement on Hearst's ejection from France appeared on the front page of *SFE*, 3 Sept. 1930. See also Edmond D. Coblentz, *William Randolph Hearst: A Portrait in His Own Words*, 96–101, and Winkler, *New Appraisal*, 236–45.

38 The attitude of the administration towards Hearst's expulsion from France may be seen in the diary of Secretary of State Henry L. Stimson, who believed that the government should not become officially involved since the French were doing something that they had a perfect right to do. The president, however – in line with what appeared (from Stimson's viewpoint) to be a considerable fear of the Hearst press – wanted to make some gesture to the publisher when he returned to the United States. He finally agreed merely to ask him to lunch and to be careful to make no comment about the French incident. See entries for 4 Oct. 1930, Diary of Henry L. Stimson, Yale University Library, vol. 10 (1 Mar. 1929 to 31 Dec. 1930), 50–1. Stimson here noted that the president "despised Hearst but did not want to evidently have any trouble with him."

It is moot whether Hearst took the incident seriously or not. In public he spoke lightly of the whole affair, even stating that he would do the same again. See above, n 37, and "French Episode," an address at the last of a series of receptions for Hearst given by his friends, this one in Oakland: nd, Hearst, W.R., Sr, Writings (4), Coblentz Papers. There is also, however, the evidence of the much-quoted note to his valet: "Joseph – Don't ever get me any socks or anything else made in France. *WRH*," Incoming, ibid.

39 See chap. 8 for a discussion of Hearst's involvement with Germany before each of the world wars.

40 Editorial, *SFE*, 15 Apr. 1899.

41 Ibid., 11 Dec. 1901.

42 Ibid., 12 May 1905.

43 Ibid., 1 Jan. 1904.

44 Ibid., 6 Feb. 1905. Some months earlier Hearst had printed another editorial discussing the inequalities between officers and men in the German army and suggesting that the arrogance and brutality of the officer corps and their like benefited the United States to the extent of driving out the best Germans. Ibid., 8 July 1904. He returned to this theme a few years later in an editorial explaining why the rulers of Europe were opposed to emigration to the United States. Ibid., 13 Sept. 1907.

45 Ibid., 4 Jan. 1908.

46 Ibid., 21 Jan. 1908. This editorial, by John Temple Graves, praised the Kaiser, who had stated that "the Japanese are the scourge of God, like Attila and Napoleon" and that it was just as well that they were on the side of the United States, the only nation on earth they feared.

47 Ibid., 5 Aug. 1911.

48 Ibid., 5 Mar. 1896.

49 Interview published in the Manchester *Evening News*, 24 Sept. 1934. Tompkins, ed., *Selections*, 561–2. See also *SFE*, 25 Sept. 1934.

50 Statement made for the *Brooklyn Eagle* and published in the Hearst Sunday papers, 30 Sept. 1934. Tompkins, ed., *Selections*, 277.

51 Editorial in Hearst newspapers, 11 Mar. 1934. Tompkins, ed., *Selections*, 205–6.

52 Editorial, *SFE*, 23 Feb. 1922. The "twice" in the above quotation refers to the negotiations leading to the Treaty of Versailles and to the Washington Naval Treaty of 1922.

53 Ibid., 10 Aug. 1928. The latter reference is to an *SFE* editorial, 18 May 1924.

54 Ibid., 3 June 1920.

55 Ibid., 2 Feb. 1923.

56 Ibid., 6 Feb. 1923.

57 Ibid., 8 Apr. 1926.

58 Ibid., 13 Oct. 1939.

59 Ibid., 2 Feb. 1940.

60 William Randolph Hearst, *Statements on International Affairs*, 4.

61 Article published in the *Daily Express*, 24 June 1931, with a similar one in the same day's *News Chronicle*. Cable 206, United States Ambassador Atherton to Secretary of State, London, 24 June 1931. Two days later, Atherton reported that the two British papers had published an "explanatory recantation" over Hearst's signature. Cable 216, same refs., 26 June 1931. Official File OF 1275, AG 5/915, Hoover Papers.

62 The Hoover Papers also contain a memorandum of a conversation between Secretary Stimson and Sir Ronald Lindsay, the British ambassador, in which the former explained the campaign of the Hearst press against debt reduction. Stimson recorded that he told Lindsay that "a powerful set of newspapers, like the Hearst press, was deliberately attempting to make difficult any decent relations on these subjects and that I hoped that he would believe that I was using all my influence to prevent anything being said or done which would tend to impair the frank and friendly relations which had been established between our two governments." Stimson noted that he regarded this as of great importance, and the ambassador replied that "he realized that and that he understood perfectly." Ibid.

63 On Bainbridge Colby, see Coblentz to Hearst, 23 Sept. 1931, Outgoing, Coblentz Papers. On Hiram Johnson, see Hearst to James R. Nourse, San Simeon, 16 Oct. 1931, part III, box 43, Hiram W. Johnson Papers, Bancroft Library. Nourse was managing editor of the *Examiner* at this time, and Hearst wrote congratulating him on Johnson's article of that day and asking whether he could arrange for the senator to write regular articles.

64 Editorial, *SFE*, 10 Oct. 1931. See also ibid., 4 Jan. 1932; 10 July 1932; and 21 Dec. 1932.

65 Editorial, *SFE*, 8 Nov. 1933.

66 Ibid., 2 Jan. 1934. The germ of this idea came perhaps from Colby, who had written an article entitled "Dealing with Debtors," published in the Hearst papers on 11 Nov. 1933. Some days before this appeared, Hearst wrote saying that "I like greatly your editorial of our applying France's policy of high duties against defaulting debtors to France itself. Was not that the threat which Jackson made and which finally brought France to terms? Moreover why should we limit the embargo to wines? Why not make it against all French products?" Hearst to Colby, Los Angeles, 3 Nov. 1933, box 5, 1933, Bainbridge Colby Papers, Library of Congress.

CHAPTER FOUR: HEARST AND THE YELLOW PERIL

1 William Randolph Hearst, *Statements on International Affairs*, 16–17.

2 See chap. 6.

3 For a comment on this from Hearst himself, see chap. 5, n. 16.

4 In 1911 Hearst warmly greeted the Chinese revolution. The *Examiner* noted that "Chinese patriotism under the old regime was mainly manifested in a cordial hatred of "the foreign devils." … But now it seems … that the living and moving part of China has revolutionized the character of its patriotism. The best news of the Chinese revolution is that the insurgents act as if they felt an affinity for foreigners. If this sign does not fail, if it brightens into an assured and undeniable fact, the fortune of the Chinese revolution is made." Editorial, *SFE*, 18 Nov. 1911. Later, he recommended that "the Chinese Republic should be kept intact; and to this end the United States should make haste to welcome the new democracy to the family of nations." Ibid., 19 Feb. 1912. He also criticized the administration's slowness to recognize officially a sister republic who needed American support to survive. Ibid., 12 Aug. 1912.

5 Ibid., 3 Jan. 1895.

6 Ibid., 7 Feb. 1895.

7 Ibid., 1 Dec. 1897.

8 Ibid., 12 Jan. 1898. See also ibid., 17 Mar. 1898.

9 "The Japanese are so numerous and aggressive in Hawaii that they are not inclined to submit quietly to the laws." They had appealed to their government for protection, and "it is understood that a Japanese force is on its way to the islands to back up the demands of the Mikado's representative." This could not be allowed to occur: "We like them in their own country and sympathize with their desire to expand," but "when they come halfway across the Pacific and undertake to supersede us in a country that has been substantially an American protectorate for more than half a century, we draw the line." Ibid., 3 Apr. 1897. See also "THE NEW HAWAIIAN QUESTION," ibid., 9 Apr. 1897.

10 Hearst later wrote, in an editorial headed "Jap Lessons From Hawaii," that "Hawaii is a laboratory of America's Japanese problems" and used the example to justify further and stronger Japanese exclusion from the continental United States. "The cure is to chalk the cracks of the Golden Gate with drastic laws, so that no Japanese can slip through." Ibid., 2 July 1923. See also Neylan to Hearst, np, 30 Jan. 1934, series 5, box 65, folder 14, Neylan Papers.

11 In an 1895 editorial the *Examiner* noted that 28,000 new arrivals had been processed during the week at New York and that such unrestricted immigration was a threat to American workers, who already did not have enough work to go around. *SFE*, 17 May 1895. Eighteen months later Hearst proposed a five-year moratorium on immigration to help solve the unemployment problem. Ibid., 15 Dec. 1896.

12 In an editorial headed "Exclude Prejudice From u.s. Immigration Policy," Hearst charged that the bill favoured the Nordic races over those from Eastern and Southern Europe. Ibid., 1 May 1924.

13 In December 1930 President Hoover asked for the co-operation of the Hearst papers in advocating the "strengthening [of] the immigration laws by more selective and restricted immigration." Hoover to Williams, np, 10 Dec. 1930. Williams replied by saying that he would bring the request to the attention of his superiors. Williams to Hoover, np, 11 Dec. 1930, President's Personal File 1120, AG 5/, Hoover Papers.

14 Signed letter, published in the Hearst newspapers, 3 Sept. 1933. Tompkins, ed., *Selections*, 258–60.

15 Editorial, *SFE*, 12 Dec. 1897.

16 Ibid., 3 Apr. 1900. See also ibid., 10 Apr. 1900.

17 Ibid., 10 Oct. 1900.

18 Ibid., 31 Jan. 1902.

19 Ibid., 25 Sept. 1902.

20 Editorial, *Los Angeles Examiner*, 30 July 1904. See also editorial, *SFE*, 2 June and 22 Sept. 1904.

21 Editorial, *Los Angeles Examiner*, 27 Sept. 1904. This editorial also appeared in *SFE*, 11 Oct. 1904.

22 *SFE*, 3 Sept. 1904.

23 Ibid., 28 June 1905. See also a front-page news story on the arrival of the Chinese commissioners in Washington, headed "MR. ROOSEVELT OVERRIDES THE LAW." *SFE*, 13 Jan. 1906.

24 "COOLIES ARE 'SCHOOLING' IN MEXICO," ibid., 10 Apr. 1906.

25 For a discussion of the views on immigration of another newspaper often advocating views similar to those of the Hearst press, see Jerome E. Edwards, *The Foreign Policy of Col. McCormick's Tribune, 1929–1941*, 50.

26 Editorial, *SFE*, 20 Feb. 1907.

27 *SFE*, 4 Feb. 1909. It should be noted that this commentary, though it follows closely the line taken by this paper and others in the Hearst chain, was written by Alfred Henry Lewis.

28 Editorial, *SFE*, 4 Feb. 1909.

29 Ibid., 20 Aug. 1919. For later editorials on Oriental exclusion, see ibid., 18 Aug. 1921 and 2 Feb. 1923. In a signed editorial letter, published in the Hearst newspapers 15 Apr. 1924 under the heading "Japanese Exclusion Vital To u.s., says Mr. Hearst," he drew on the example of Australia and stated, "I am strongly in favor of Japanese exclusion, to prevent these Orientals from swarming into the country and absolutely overrunning it." Tompkins, ed., *Selections*, 256.

30 Editorial, *SFE*, 23 Aug. 1916.

31 See Robert W. Jones, *Journalism in the United States*, 460. Jones makes the point that, as so often in his unpopular campaigns, Hearst stuck to his guns and later events justified his opinions. See also D.W. Riegel, *Mobilizing for Chaos: The Story of the New Propaganda*, 142–3. This section of the work attacks strongly the kind of campaign mounted by Hearst, maintaining that "any kind of obscure event or crackpot utterance is used by the Hearst press to build up a Japanese bogy in the United States."

32 See the "Life of George Hearst," in Hubert Howe Bancroft, *Chronicles of the Builders of the Commonwealth*, 2:396–9.

33 See Robert Seager, "The Progressives and American Foreign Policy, 1898–1917," 26.

34 Raymond A. Esthus, "The Changing Concept of the Open Door, 1899–1910," 440.

35 Hearst's views on Oriental immigration and the Japanese school question provoked the government and offended the Japanese and Chinese, but the difference between him and the administration was one of style rather than substance.

36 For a discussion of this question, see Esthus, "Changing Concept," 440 and 451–2; and Charles Vevier, "The Open Door: An Idea in Action, 1906–1913," 54–5.

37 Editorial, *SFE*, 20 Apr. 1895.

38 Ibid., 1 May 1895.

39 Ibid., 12 Feb. 1899.

40 Ibid., 18 May 1899.

41 Ibid., 6 Jan. 1900.

42 Ibid., 17 July 1900.

43 Ibid., 8 June 1900.

44 Ibid., 20 Aug. 1904.

45 Ibid., 18 Sept. 1905.

46 Ibid., 27 Feb. 1906.

47 *SFE*, 7 May 1906.

48 Ibid., 9 Aug. 1906

49 Ibid., 11 Nov. 1906.

50 Ibid., 2 Dec. 1906.

51 Ibid., 4 Dec. 1906.

52 Ibid., 5 Dec. 1906

53 Editorial, *SFE*, 21 June 1907.

54 Ibid., 20 Apr. 1908. See also ibid., 7 Aug. and 24 Nov. 1909.

55 Signed editorial published in the Hearst newspapers, 4 Mar. 1918. Tompkins, ed., *Selections*, 576–8.

56 See, for example, editorial letter published in the Hearst newspapers, 9 Mar. 1918. Tompkins, ed., *Selections*, 580–2.

57 Editorial, *SFE*, 13 and 14 May 1919.

58 Ibid., 22 Oct. 1922.

59 Signed editorial published in the Hearst newspapers, 12 Feb. 1922. Tompkins, ed., *Selections*, 193–4.

60 For a discussion of the attitudes of the Hearst newspapers in the late thirties and the period between the outbreak of the Second World War in Europe and Pearl Harbor, see below, 118–19.

61 See Theodore Roosevelt to Elihu Root, Washington, DC, 10 Mar. 1907, and Oyster Bay, 13 July 1907, Special Correspondence with Theodore Roosevelt, 1904–24 and undated, box 163, Root Papers. In April 1907 Root made the presidential address to the American Society of International Law at Washington. In this speech he noted that "one great and serious question" underlay all the points at issue between the United States and Japan. This was not war, for "all the foolish talk about war was purely sensational and imaginative." The question was "what state of feeling would be created between the great body of the people of the United States and the great body of the people of Japan as a result of the treatment given to the Japanese in this country? What was to be the effect upon that proud, sensitive, highly civilized people across the Pacific, of the discourtesy, insult, imputation of inferiority and abuse aimed at them in the columns of American newspapers and from the platforms of American public meetings? What would be the effect upon our people of the responses that natural resentment would elicit from the Japanese?" He answered this by saying that, "in this modern day, through the columns of the myriad press and messages flashing over countless wires, multitude calls to multitude across boundaries and oceans in courtesy or insult, in amity or in defiance … The people who permit themselves to treat the people of other countries with discourtesy and insult are surely sowing the wind to reap the whirlwind, for a world of sullen and revengeful hatred can never be a world of peace. Against such a feeling treaties are wasted paper and diplomacy the empty routine of idle form." Address delivered in Washington, DC, 19 Apr. 1907, Speeches, 1894–1933, box 221, Root Papers.

CHAPTER FIVE: HEARST, THE CZAR, AND THE BOLSHEVIKS

1 Editorial, *SFE*, 26 July 1902.
2 Ibid., 28 May 1903. This is but one editorial among a number on the same subject published at this time.
3 Ibid., 14 Oct. 1903. See also a further editorial on the Kishinef situation, ibid., 28 Dec. 1903. It should be noted that the Hearst papers were, at this time, the most vociferous section of the American press in their protests against the killing of the Jews in Russia and in their arguments for armed intervention to stop it. See Thomas A. Bailey, *America Faces Russia*, 180–1.
4 Editorial, *SFE*, 23 Feb. 1904.
5 Ibid., 6 July 1904. The same piece appeared in the *Los Angeles Examiner*, 1 July 1904.
6 Editorial, *SFE*, 2 Dec. 1904.
7 Ibid., 24 Jan. 1905. See, however, the cartoon published in *SFE*, 6 Jan. 1906.
8 Editorial, *SFE*, 21 Apr. 1905.
9 Ibid., 8 Sept. 1905.
10 *SFE*, 29 Apr. 1906. For similar atrocity stories, see ibid., 2 Jan., 21 June, 8 and 25 July 1906.
11 Editorial, *SFE*, 11 May 1906.
12 Ibid., 30 July 1906. News stories about the 1906 revolution appeared on the front page of ibid on, for example, 2, 3, 4, and 5 Aug. 1906.
13 Editorial, *SFE*, 9 Aug. 1906.
14 See, for example, ibid., 17 June and 3 Nov. 1907 and 1 July and 22 Nov. 1911. For a discussion of Hearst's views on Russia before the First World War and on her role in the causes of the war, see Minear, "Hearst and Foreign Affairs," 16–18. The reader should be aware, however, that this study adopts a strong anti-Hearst stance on most issues.
15 Signed editorial letter, *SFE*, 21 Mar. 1917.
16 Editorial, *SFE*, 22 Mar. 1917.
17 Ibid., 24 Mar. 1917.
18 Ibid., 22 May 1917.
19 See below, nn. 34, 35, and 36.
20 Editorial, *SFE*, 20 Oct. 1917.
21 Ibid., 22 Jan. 1918.
22 Editorial, *New York American*, 28 Jan. 1918.
23 Signed editorial letter published in Hearst newspapers, 1 Mar. 1918. Tompkins, ed., *Selections*, 102–3. This and the editorial cited in the previous note are quoted at length in Joseph Wershba, "I Hold Here in My Hand …," 131–47. This is an account of Hearst's early reactions to the Bolshevik revolution and its aftermath in which the author attempts to demonstrate Hearst's early sympathy for Bolshevism and to contrast it with his later vehement opposition to Soviet Russia and to Communism.

24 Editorial, *New York American*, 11 Mar. 1918. Also quoted in Wershba, "I Hold Here in My Hand ...," 137–8.

25 Ibid.

26 Editorial, *SFE*, 14 Mar. 1918. The presidential message in question was reported by the *Examiner* on its front page on the same day, under the dateline "Washington, 11 March 1918."

27 Wershba, "I Hold Here in My Hand ...," 139.

28 Editorial, *New York American*, 3 June 1918.

29 Editorial, *SFE*, 15 July 1918.

30 Bailey, *America Faces Russia*, 234–5.

31 Ibid.

32 Ibid.

33 Peter G. Filene, *Americans and the Soviet Experiment, 1917–1933*, 32.

34 Ibid., 26.

35 Christopher Lasch, *American Liberals and the Russian Revolution*, 77.

36 Ibid., 79 and 100.

37 Editorial, *SFE*, 25 Nov. 1918.

38 Ibid.

39 Ibid., 29 Jan. 1919; see also 27 Feb. and 1 Dec. 1919.

40 See Filene, *Americans and the Soviet Experiment*, 42.

41 For discussions of American intervention in Russia, see ibid., 53–4; Lasch, *Liberals and the Revolution*, xii and 110, and "American Intervention in Siberia: A Reinterpretation," 206–8 and 217; and, for the views of a California Progressive, Peter Gerard Boyle, "The Study of an Isolationist: Hiram Johnson," 146–7.

42 For a discussion of the importance of the directions for United States foreign policy laid down by Wilson at this time, see N. Gordon Levin, Jr, *Woodrow Wilson and World Politics: America's Response to War and Revolution*, passim.

43 Hearst to Fremont Older, np, 2 Jan. 1919, vol. 1, Older Collection.

44 Editorial letter published in the Hearst newspapers, 20 Dec. 1919. Tompkins, ed., *Selections*, 108–9. This letter appeared in *SFE* on 2 Jan. 1920.

45 See chap. 8 below for a discussion of the change in Hearst's view of Wilson's foreign policies during and immediately after the First World War.

46 Editorial, *SFE*, 1 Jan. 1921.

47 Ibid., 10 Jan. 1921.

48 "March of Events," *SFE*, 20 Aug. 1921. See also an editorial in a similar vein, 27 Aug. 1921.

49 Ibid., 6 Apr. 1922.

50 For a discussion of the debate on trade with and recognition of the Soviet Union, see Joan Hoff Wilson, *Ideological Economics: US Relations with the Soviet Union, 1918–1933*, 103–32.

51 Ibid., 10 July 1923. See also similar editorials, 2 Jan. and 20 Feb. 1924 and 2 Apr. 1925.

52 Editorial, *New York American*, 18 Feb. 1924. For a discussion of the basis for American non-recognition of Russia, see Claude E. Fike, "Aspects of the New American Recognition Policy Towards Russia Following World War I," 3–4.

53 Editorial, *SFE*, 10 Nov. 1933.

54 Editorial, *New York American*, 22 Nov. 1933. See also Arthur Brisbane, "Interviews," 19 Nov. 1933.

55 The Progressive movement "was not an attempt to remold the world anew, to discard the old system for a new society. The Progressives were completely part of American life, accepting the traditional values and ideals, cherishing the aspirations of middle-class America, including the new sense of delight in the rise of the United States as a world power." William E. Leuchtenberg, "Progressivism and Imperialism: The Progressive Movement and American Foreign Policy," 503. See also John Milton Cooper, Jr., "Progressivism and American Foreign Policy: A Reconsideration," 263; and Otis L. Graham, *An Encore for Reform: The Old Progressives and the New Deal*, 46.

56 Editorial letter published in the Hearst newspapers, 19 June 1918. Tompkins, ed., *Selections*, 224–5.

57 Address at a dinner in his honour, 5 Apr. 1923, Tompkins, ed., *Selections*, 301.

58 For an illuminating discussion of this question, see Emily S. Rosenberg, *Spreading the American Dream: American Economic and Cultural Expansion, 1890–1945*.

59 Editorial letter to Senator James A. Reed, published in the Hearst newspapers, 10 Feb. 1919. Tompkins, ed., *Selections*, 103–7. See *SFE*, 11 Feb. 1919.

60 Ibid. This view was shared by Hiram Johnson. See Boyle, "Johnson," 108–9.

61 Editorial, *SFE*, 28 Mar. 1919.

62 Ibid., 23 Apr. 1919.

63 Ibid., 9 Apr. 1919. See also ibid., "The Remedy for Unsound Radicalism Is Genuine and Liberal Democracy," 20 Jan. 1920.

64 See Frederick Henrotin, General Staff, American Expeditionary Force, Advance General Headquarters, to Assistant Chief of Staff, Treves, 2 June 1919. Enclosed with and discussed in Brig.-Gen. D.E. Nolan, Asst. Chief of Staff, to Military Intelligence Division, Washington, DC, 8 June 1919, file 10058–385, General Staff Military Intelligence Division 1917–41, War Department General and Special Staffs, Record Group 165, National Archives.

65 Editorial, *SFE*, 27 June 1923.

66 Ibid., 8 Oct. 1930.

CHAPTER SIX: HEARST AND THE RED MENACE

1 See chap. 5.
2 See Swanberg, *Citizen Hearst*, 471. See also Bonnie Sharp Jefferson, "The Rhetorical Restrictions of a Devil Theory: The Anti-Communist Press's View of Communism, 1945–47," 67.
3 Editorial, *SFE*, 21 Apr. 1934. This editorial appeared on page 1; another entitled "The Reds Exposed" was printed on the editorial page.
4 Hearst to Coblentz, London, 13 Sept. 1934, Incoming, Coblentz Papers.
5 Instructions to editors of Hearst newspapers, San Simeon, 24 Nov. 1934. Published in the Hearst newspapers on 26 Nov. Tompkins, ed., *Selections*, 181–3.
6 Signed editorial published in the Hearst newspapers, 9 Dec. 1934. Tompkins, ed., *Selections*, 110–11.
7 Willicombe to Coblentz, San Simeon, 17 Dec. 1934, Incoming, Coblentz Papers. This telegram was marked for the attention of all Hearst editors.
8 *New York World-Telegram*, 25 Feb. 1935, series 5, box 66, folder 15, Neylan Papers. In his address to a meeting of nearly a thousand school and college educators, Beard noted that he had never found "one single person who, for talent and character, commanded the respect of the American people who has not agreed with me that William Randolph Hearst has pandered to depraved tastes and has been the enemy of everything that is noblest and best in the American tradition." The anti-professor campaign also attracted a good deal of journalistic comment. See, for example, Hamilton Basso, "Mr. Hearst Sees Red," 269–71.
9 The address was given from San Francisco on 5 Jan. 1935. Tompkins, ed., *Selections*, 112–20. It was reprinted in *SFE*, 6 Jan. 1935. See also William Randolph Hearst, *On Communism and Fascism*, 8 and 11–13.
10 Willicombe to Coblentz, Los Angeles, 16 and 17 April 1935, Outgoing, Coblentz Papers.
11 Editorial, *SFE*, 20 July 1935.
12 Hearst to Coblentz, Wyntoon, 15 July 1935, Incoming, Coblentz Papers.
13 Editorial, *SFE*, 12 Aug. 1935.
14 Ibid., 4 Sept. 1935.
15 Coblentz to editors of all Hearst papers, np, 31 Dec. 1935, Outgoing, Coblentz Papers. See editorial "America Should Get Rid of ALL Foreign-Born Revolutionists!" *SFE*, 21 Apr. 1936.
16 See below, chap. 7.
17 Editorial, *SFE*, 27 Jan. 1936.
18 Hearst to Coblentz, np, 13 Feb.1936, Incoming, Coblentz Papers. In this letter Hearst specifically mentioned the *March of Time* newsreel, which, he claimed, had "a completely bolshevik line of propaganda in its latest issue."

19 Coblentz to Hearst, np, 28 Feb. 1936, Outgoing, Coblentz Papers. This letter refers to a projected program featuring Earl Browder and, a week later, Rep. Hamilton Fish, on "Communism vs. Americanism." See also Willicombe to Coblentz, np, 27 Feb. 1936, instructing Coblentz to produce an editorial entitled "Columbia Broadcasting Company Goes Communist." Incoming, Coblentz Papers.

20 Editorial, *SFE*, 18 Mar. 1936.

21 Editorial published in the Hearst newspapers, 3 July 1936. Tompkins, ed., *Selections*, 126–8.

22 Editorial, *SFE*, 10 July 1936.

23 See also editorial headed "World Treason," ibid., 14 July 1936, and "Communism: A Universal Conspiracy,", 25 July 1936. The editorial "The 'Leftist' Mask" appeared 5 Aug. 1936.

24 For an account of the role played by the Hearst press in the build-up of Governor Landon's candidacy, see George Wolfskill, *The Revolt of the Conservatives: A History of the American Liberty League, 1934–1940*, 202–4. See also Williams, OHC, 4:841 and 846–50. It was the opinion of Harold Ickes that Landon would not have been nominated had it not been for Hearst. Entry for Monday, 27 July 1936, Ickes Diary, 1652.

25 Coblentz to Hearst, np, 23 Sept. 1936, Outgoing, Coblentz Papers.

26 Hearst to Coblentz, np, 9 April 1937, Incoming, Coblentz Papers.

27 Editorial, *SFE*, 21 Apr. 1937.

28 Ibid., 22 Feb. 1938.

29 See, for example, Coblentz to Hearst, np, 19 Apr. 1937, and Hearst to Coblentz, np, 3 May 1937, Outgoing and Incoming, Coblentz Papers.

30 Editorial published in the Hearst newspapers, 27 Apr. 1938. Tompkins, ed., *Selections*, 16–18.

31 Editorial, *SFE*, 27 Aug. 1938.

32 Ibid., 20 Aug. 1940.

33 Ibid., 20 May 1941.

34 On Hearst's view of Hoover and Roosevelt in 1932, see Carlisle, "Hearst," 76. For Hearst's praise of Hoover before the latter became president, see, for example, editorials, *SFE*, 5 Feb. and 5 May 1927.

35 Carlisle, "Hearst," 80–5.

36 Ibid., 88 and 95–100.

37 Roosevelt to Hearst, White House, 3 Oct. 1934, in Elliott Roosevelt, ed., *FDR: His Personal Letters, 1928–1945*, 1:424. As far as the president was concerned, this was almost certainly a political attachment rather than a personal note. Less than a year later he privately expressed the opinion: "I sometimes think that Hearst has done more harm to the cause of Democracy and civilization in America than any three other contemporaries put together." Roosevelt to Robert M. Hutchins, np, 1 July 1935, President's Personal File 1834, Franklin D. Roosevelt Library, Hyde

Park, NY. A year later, during the presidential campaign, he wrote to a friendly editor, "Keep up the good work. We are up against a pirate's crew." Roosevelt to Norman Hapgood, on presidential special, 10 Oct. 1936, President's Personal File 2278. FDR also had material gathered by the secretary of the interior, consisting of unfavourable comments on Hearst's current and earlier political activities, in case he should wish to go after him in person during the campaign. Ickes to Roosevelt, Department of Interior, 25 Sept.1936, President's Personal File 2278, Roosevelt Papers.

38 Carlisle, "Hearst," 95.

39 For a discussion of the divisions between some of those who had earlier been identified as Progressives and the supporters of the New Deal, see Graham, *Encore for Reform*, 183 and 185–6. Graham seeks to establish that, while many of the old Progressives accepted the directions laid down by the Roosevelt administration, supporting him in his moves towards centralization of the national government, higher government spending, and more government intervention in the economy, a significant minority – of whom Hearst was one – refused to accept these moves. They preferred to wait for the economy to right itself and to practise what Hearst called "the principles of Jeffersonian democracy."

40 Hearst, *Communism and Fascism*, 28–9. One scholar argues plausibly that what precipitated the final break was the wealth tax. At this point, with the creation of a tax bracket that seemed to apply only to him, Hearst decided "that the President, after all, was at the root of the social changes which disturbed him ... [and] was personally offended when Roosevelt implied that his own accumulation of great wealth was a threat to social stability." Rodney Carlisle, "William Randolph Hearst: A Fascist Reputation Reconsidered," 132.

41 Coblentz, *Hearst*, 169–72, quoting from a letter to the author from Hearst, dated 9 Apr. 1935.

42 Signed editorial headed "A Reply to the President," published in the Hearst newspapers, 21 Sept. 1936. Tompkins, ed., *Selections*, 130–1. Hearst cabled the editorial from Amsterdam on 20 Sept.

43 "I understand that the Hearst papers this morning came out with an editorial denouncing me as a communist on the basis of the speech I made last week to Great Britain. What crooks or fools some newspaper publishers and writers are." Entry for Wednesday, 2 Mar. 1938, Ickes Diary, 2636. See also entries for Friday, 15 Nov, and Sunday, 22 Dec. 1935, ibid., 1248–9 and 1308–9.

44 Editorial, *SFE*, 26 May 1938.

45 Ibid., 22 Aug. 1941.

46 Ibid., 15 Feb. 1940.

47 Ibid., 1 May 1940.

CHAPTER SEVEN: HEARST AND PEACE

1 Editorial, *SFE*, 18 Feb. 1911.
2 Hearst, *Original Proposal*, 6–7.
3 Editorial, *SFE*, 18 Sept. 1899.
4 Ibid., 4 June 1907.
5 Ibid., 24 Oct. 1907.
6 Ibid., 12 May 1910. During the interwar period Hearst supported move-
   ments for imposing peace in Europe such as the Locarno Pact, which, he
   said, was a conference where "responsible statesmen sat undisturbed by
   dreams of personal immortality, [and] ... worked out a system of defi-
   nite, easily enforced individual pledges among the nations." Ibid.,
   5 Nov. 1925.
7 Signed statement appearing in the London *Evening Standard*, 3 Sept. 1912.
   Tompkins, ed., *Selections*, 192–3.
8 Brisbane to Johnson, np, 26 July 1923, part III, box 25, Johnson Papers.
   The letter enclosed an editorial, from which the quotation is taken, and a
   cartoon supporting a Johnson speech on the World Court. See below, n 10.
9 For a discussion of Borah's attitude towards the court, see Robert D. Accinelli, "The United States and the World Court, 1920–1927," 119. For
   Johnson's view of the court question, see Boyle, "Johnson," 275. La Follette also saw the court as a "cleverly-conceived plan of the International
   Bankers to entangle the United States" in European affairs to protect their
   investments. John A. Ziegler, "The Progressive's Views on Foreign Affairs,
   1909–1941: A Case Study of Liberal Economic Isolationism," 204.
10 Editorial, *SFE*, 26 July 1923.
11 Ibid., 15 Jan. 1926.
12 Ibid., 1 Mar. 1926.
13 Ibid., 3 Mar. 1926.
14 Ibid., 9 Mar. 1926.
15 See, for example, ibid., 10 May, 1 July, 3 July, 9 Aug., and 4 Sept. 1926.
16 Ibid., 15 Feb. 1927.
17 See, for example, ibid., 3 Apr. 1929.
18 See editorials, *SFE*, 3, 9, and 11 Apr., and 6 Sept. 1929. Another metaphor
   employed was "International Schemers Try to Get Uncle Sam to Put One
   Foot on League of Nations' Flypaper," ibid., 10 Apr. 1929.
19 Ibid., 8 Apr. 1929.
20 Hearst to Coblentz, San Simeon, 27 Mar. 1933, Incoming, Coblentz Papers. This instruction is marked for the attention of all papers. Just before, Coblentz had written to Hearst with the suggestion that "we
   should revive immediately anti-World Court campaign in view of possible Senate action." Coblentz to Hearst, New York, 12 Dec. 1932, Outgoing, Coblentz Papers. Hearst continued to try to keep up the pressure.

See, for example, Hearst to Coblentz, np, 3 May 1934, Coblentz file, 1934, box 18, Hearst Papers. This telegram, too, was marked "attention of all papers."

21 See, for example, page 1 editorial, *SFE*, 13 Apr. 1934, where Hearst agreed with Johnson, who had recently stated that it was impossible to assert (as some still did) that the court was not the back way into the League.

22 Ibid., 29 Jan. 1935.

23 Ibid., 5 Jan. 1935. For a discussion of the role of Roosevelt and Hull in this final campaign for entry into the court, see Wayne S. Cole, "Senator Key Pittman and American Neutrality Policies, 1933–1940," 651–2.

24 For a further discussion of Hearst's anti-court campaign at this time, see chap. 10.

25 Signed editorial, *SFE*, 10 May 1919.

26 Ibid., 14 Feb. 1920.

27 Minear, "Hearst and Foreign Affairs," 135–9. See also Hearst, *International Affairs*, 22.

28 Signed editorial in the London *Evening Standard*, 20 June 1922. Tompkins, ed., *Selections*, 608–10.

29 Editorial, *SFE*, 24 Sept. 1934. See also ibid., 9 June 1936.

30 Ibid., 19 Feb. 1919.

31 Ibid., 25 Feb. 1919.

32 Hearst to H.H. Tammen, New York, 29 Mar. 1919, Outgoing, Coblentz papers.

33 Hearst to Neylan, np, 16 June 1919, series 5, box 63, folder 1, Neylan Papers. Hearst was disturbed by some pro-League articles that had appeared in the *San Francisco Call*, of which Neylan was publisher; he noted that, although his papers were permitted some independence, on important matters such as this, where his own views were well known, they should follow his lead.

34 The final reference is to editorial, *SFE*, 21 Nov. 1919. For examples of Hearst editorials during the debate over the peace treaty, see ibid., 8, 11, 12, 13, 17, 22, 23, 24, 25, 27 Sept. 1919, etc.

35 Signed editorial, *SFE*, 3 Nov. 1920.

36 Editorial, *SFE*, 6 Sept. 1923.

37 Ibid., 20 Sept. 1923.

38 Ibid., 11 Oct. 1924.

39 Ibid., 8 Nov. 1924. On the question of the Democratic platform in 1924, see Charles A. Beard, *American Foreign Policy in the Making, 1932–1940: A Study in Responsibilities*, 48–50.

40 Hearst, *Original Proposal*, 24.

41 Editorial, *SFE*, 14 Jan. 1926.

42 See, for example, ibid., 4, 5, 6, and 7 Jan. 1926.

43 Ibid., 29 Nov. 1927.

44 For a contemporary scholar's account, see Denna F. Fleming, *The United States and World Organization, 1920–1933*. See also Victor L. Albjerg, "Isolationism and the Early New Deal, 1932–1937," 204; and Coblentz, *Hearst*, 120–3. Some years later, in a private letter, Hearst wrote an account of Roosevelt's repudiation of the League in 1932, noting that, although the latter had stated publicly his opposition, Hearst was "sure he never honestly meant it." Hearst to Neylan, Wyntoon, 6 Oct. 1937, series 5, box 66, folder 20, Neylan Papers.

45 Editorial, *SFE*, 4 Apr. 1932.

46 Ibid., 12 Dec. 1933.

47 See, for example, ibid., 12 Mar. and 10 Apr. 1934. Both these editions of the *Examiner* included forms for a petition to be addressed to members of Congress, protesting the proposal to join the League.

48 Coblentz to Hearst, np, 25 May 1936, Outgoing, Coblentz Papers.

49 Editorial, *SFE*, 17 July 1937.

50 Ibid., 2 Mar. 1938.

51 Ibid., 1 Nov. 1895.

52 Ibid., 13 Jan. 1898.

53 Ibid., 23 June 1898. See also ibid., 11 Nov. 1898.

54 Ibid., 4 June 1901.

55 Ibid., 4 Dec. 1901.

56 Ibid., 26 Dec. 1902.

57 Ibid., 14 June 1905.

58 Ibid., 4 Apr. 1906.

59 See, for example, ibid., 14 Oct. 1906; 8 July 1907; and 14 Jan. 1908.

60 Ibid., 12 Jan. 1908.

61 Ibid., 2 and 21 Feb. 1908.

62 Ibid., 20 Mar. 1908. At this point the fleet had just arrived in Magdalena Bay after the trip around South America.

63 Ibid., 2 Nov. 1908.

64 Speech by Hearst at the National Independence Party banquet in New York, 9 May 1908. Reprinted in *SFE*, 19 May 1908. The quotation is from President Grant's memoirs; Hearst also quoted Washington and Lincoln on this occasion to the same effect.

65 Editorial, *SFE*, 19 July 1913.

66 Editorial letter published in Hearst newspapers 19 Mar. 1917. Tompkins, ed., *Selections*, 377. See also other editorials on universal military training, *SFE*, 5, 10, 28, and 29 Mar., 1917.

67 Signed editorial published in Hearst newspapers, 27 Oct. 1915. Tompkins, ed., *Selections*, 375–7.

68 Editorial, *SFE*, 11 Jan. 1918. Although the Progressives were split on preparedness, Hearst had support from some of the more conservative Republican sections of the press. See Thomas G. Paterson, "California

Progressives and Foreign Policy," 334; and Richard B. Rice, "The California Press and American Neutrality," 216.

69 Editorial, *SFE*, 10 Nov. 1919. In 1925 Hearst, continuing to support military training, instructed his editors to keep the words *war* and *preparation for war* out of stories and editorials about military training, instead using phrases like *national defense* and *preparation for national defense*. "Our people and our nation do not want war," he wrote, "and [they] do want national defense and they must realize that certain preparations are necessary" to make that defense effective. Hearst to editors of all Hearst newspapers, 28 Nov. 1925, series 5, box 64, folder 28, Neylan Papers.

70 On reducing naval expenditure, see editorials, *SFE*, 21 and 30 Nov. 1918, 5 Mar. 1919, and 3 Jan. 1921.

71 "March of Events," *SFE*, 29 Oct. 1921.

72 Editorial headed "England Recaptures Her Colony," *SFE*, 1 Apr. 1922. For other statements on the Washington Conference, see, for example, ibid., 5, 6, 10, and 21 Jan, and 10, 15, 16, 22, and 23 March 1922. Hiram Johnson was one of the few from among Hearst's customary allies on foreign questions who supported his fight against ratification of the Washington Treaty. See Boyle, "Johnson," 270.

73 Editorials, *SFE*, 3 July 1923 and 27 May 1924.

74 Ibid., 17 May 1924.

75 Ibid., 29 May 1924.

76 Neylan to Hoover, San Francisco, 24 Sept. 1929, series 3, folder 54, Neylan Papers. In this letter Neylan indicated to the president that he had just discussed the parity question with Hearst. "He told me he was heartily in favor of real naval parity ... I was present while he dictated instructions to his editors and managers to do everything possible to aid your negotiations for naval parity." Neylan went on to say that Hearst "was terribly disgusted with the Washington Conference, which really put us at a great disadvantage as compared with England," and that he was also "fearful of the pacifists and well-meaning people who would disarm their own country as a Christian gesture, while the rest of the world is making thorough-going preparations to protect itself in case of armed conflict." This letter is also in the presidential papers: President's Personal File 405 AG5/, Hoover Papers.

77 Editorial, *SFE*, 28 Oct. 1929.

78 Ibid., 2 Mar. 1930.

79 Ibid., 4 June 1930. For other editorials attacking the treaty and the president, see ibid., 2 and 3 June; 2, 4, 15, and 18 July 1930.

80 Johnson to his sons, np, 21 July 1930, part VI, box 5, Johnson Papers. Once again, Johnson had opposed the treaty. He noted that "the fact that the Eastern press, with the exception of the Hearst press and the *Chicago Tribune*, have berated me outrageously would no more deter me from

entering into the struggle again, than it affected me in the slightest in pursuing my way in these past weeks. Hearst may be all we sometimes think of him. We may have for him the utmost contempt in some of his activities, but he made here a real American fight. He did not make it as intelligently as it might have been made, but this was due not to him but to lack of intelligence of the subordinates."

81 Editorial, *SFE*, 2 Mar. 1925. Later the same year General Mitchell would be court-martialed for criticizing the War and Navy departments' mismanagement of aviation service.

82 See, for example, the signed editorial published in Hearst newspapers on 9 Sept. 1925 and 27 Mar. 1938. Tompkins, ed., *Selections*, 382–3 and 385–8. In the spring of 1938 Hearst instructed his papers to "emphasize special need of biggest air force," and he later gave support to a Borah speech calling for "more planes and air defenses." Hearst to Coblentz, San Simeon, 19 Apr. 1938, and Willicombe to Coblentz, Los Angeles, 27 Apr. 1938, Incoming, Coblentz Papers. See also Tebbel, *Life and Good Times*, 159.

83 Editorial, *SFE*, 1 Feb. 1934.

84 Ibid., 17 Jan. 1936.

85 Ibid., 25 Oct. 1937.

86 Ibid., 15 Jan. 1938.

87 Ibid., 9 May 1940. In an article in his "In the News" column Hearst urged liberality in supplying European nations with airplanes but also caution in being sure that the United States had all the planes she needed. Ibid., 2 May 1940.

88 Baruch to Coblentz, np, 23 Jan. 1941, Incoming, Coblentz Papers.

89 "In the News," *SFE*, 13 Mar. 1940.

CHAPTER EIGHT: HEARST AND WAR

1 Editorial, *SFE*, 5 Aug. 1914.

2 Ibid., 8 Aug. 1914.

3 Signed editorial published in the Hearst newspapers, 3 Sept. 1914. Tompkins, ed., *Selections*, 566–70.

4 Ibid.

5 Cable to the publishers of *The Times* and *London Daily Telegraph*. Published in the Hearst newspapers, 10 Sept., 1914. Tompkins, ed., *Selections*, 570–2.

6 See 112–13.

7 Rice, "California Press," 28.

8 Editorial, *SFE*, 9 Oct. 1915. See also 1 and 5 Jan. 1916.

9 Ibid., 12 May 1916. See also 18 Oct. and 12 Dec. 1916.

10 Ibid., 21 Dec. 1916.

11 See chap. 7 above.

12 Editorial, *SFE*, 23 Jan. 1915.

13 Ibid., 2 Feb. 1915.

14 Ibid., 3 Mar. 1915. A few weeks later Hearst admitted again that such protests were probably useless unless they were backed by force. "International Law Is Mere Academic Theory," ibid., 23 Mar. 1916.

15 The reaction of the Hearst papers to the *Lusitania* incident was to brand it "wholesale murder." Along with this, however, they saw the affair as demonstrating that the nation had only itself to depend on for protection and should thus step up its preparations for defence. Rice, "California Press," 105.

   When, in mid-May 1915, the president sent his first protest on the *Lusitania* to the German government, the *Examiner* noted that, while the situation obviously called for strong protest, and demands for reparation and assurance that the affair would not be repeated were justified, the extension of the protest, into one on the use of submarines in all circumstances overstepped the mark. In doing this, Wilson risked forfeiting America's just demands and moving into a position where his moralizing would endanger vital American interests. Ibid., 111–13.

   When Germany replied, Hearst expressed the widespread dissatisfaction with the response and again noted (in a signed editorial) that it was time for the neutral nations to band together as the only possible way to protect their rights. Ibid., 116–18. See also Edwin Borchard and W.P. Lage, *Neutrality for the United States*, 177–83, which notes that the stand taken by the Hearst papers at this time was legally correct. On the *Sussex* case, see Rice, "California Press," 196–9.

16 Editorial, *SFE*, 21 Mar. 1916.

17 Ibid., 28 Sept. 1916.

18 Ibid, 1 Feb. 1917.

19 Ibid., 13 Apr. 1917.

20 Ibid., 27 June 1917. See also 10 July 1917.

21 Reminiscences of Keats Speed, in the Oral History Collection of Columbia University, 22.

22 Part of file 10175–334 in the records of the War Department, General Staff, Military Intelligence Division, 1917–1941 (Record Group 165, National Archives), contains a report on the pro-German activities of William Randolph Hearst and his associates. The report is unsigned and undated, though the last date mentioned is 27 July 1918. The report consists of a detailed account of Hearst's contacts with Bolo Pasha, with Count von Bernstorff, the German ambassador, and with Count Oscar Bopp von Obestadt, vice-president of the Peter Schoenhoefer Brewing Company of Chicago. It also lists Hearst articles "used by enemies of the United States for propaganda purposes favorable to Germany." The report concludes thus:

Hearst has done everything to undermine the morale of the American public, to discourage enlistments, to an attack on America's allies, to editorial after editorial of abuse of Great Britain, to an attack on Japan, the picturing of a coming war between Japan and America and the prophecy that the German war is of no particular moment and that a much more terrible conflict with Japan confronts us, to the statement of the chance of America's allies deserting her and of America deserting her allies.

An examination of the news and editorial matters in the Hearst papers throughout the country will show that he has consistently done everything he could to aid Germany in this war, both before and after the entrance of the United States into the war.

If he had been some little foreign newspaper or some German citizen and had been heard to speak as he has spoken in the Hearst newspapers, his papers not only would have been suppressed, but he would probably be serving a term in the penitentiary.

23 See Proceedings of the Subcommittee of the Senate Committee on the Judiciary: Investigation re Brewing and Liquor Interests and German Propaganda (Washington, DC, 1919), vol. 2, passim.

24 See Mrs Fremont Older (Cora Miranda Baggerly), *William Randolph Hearst, American*, 411–12.

25 Rice, "California Press," 8.

26 See Swanberg, *Citizen Hearst*, 299–300 and 315–16; and Brewing and Liquor Interests, 2:2342 and 2462.

27 Tebbel, *Life and Good Times*, 232–3.

28 Editorial letter published in the Hearst newspapers, 13 Dec. 1918. Tompkins, ed., *Selections*, 599–600. See also Tebbel, *Life and Good Times*, 234.

29 Tebbel, *Life and Good Times*, 232. For a discussion of opposition to the war in the Senate, see Barton J. Bernstein and Franklin A. Leib, "Progressive Republican Senators and American Imperialism, 1898–1916," 167–8 and 203–4. See also Norman L. Zucker, *George W. Norris: Gentle Knight of America Democracy,* 128; Marian C. McKenna, *Borah,* 141–3; Seager "Progressives," 255–6; and J.A. Thompson, "An Imperialist and the First World War: The Case of Albert J. Beveridge," 133–50.

30 Winkler, *American Phenomenon*, 262.

31 See chap. 1 above.

32 See chap. 7 above.

33 Editorial, *SFE*, 3 Sept. 1917.

34 Signed editorial published in the Hearst newspapers, 8 Mar. 1918. Tompkins, ed., *Selections*, 579–80.

35 Ibid., 14 Oct. 1918; 594–5.

36 Ibid., 14 Aug. 1929; 611–12.

37 Signed article written for (but not published by) the London *Daily Express*. Published in the Hearst newspapers, 23 June 1931. Tompkins, ed., *Selections*, 560.

38 Editorial, *SFE*, 3 Feb. 1925.

39 Ibid., 5 Oct. 1931.

40 Ibid., 1 Feb. 1932. Although this was the dominant theme on Manchuria, it should be noted that the *Examiner*, mostly through Brisbane's contributions, expressed indifference about who owned Asia (7 Oct. 1931) and predicted eventual Chinese victory anyway (19 Sept. 1932).

41 Signed editorial published in the Hearst newspapers, 30 Aug. 1933. Tompkins, ed., *Selections*, 421–2.

42 Editorial, *SFE*, 2 Sept. 1933.

43 Published in *SFE*, 11 Jan. 1934.

44 See, for example, editorials, *SFE*, 28 July 1939; 2 Jan. and 1 Feb. 1940. In the first of these Hearst criticized the administration for ending the Japanese commercial treaty, an action that could only further endanger world peace. In the second he welcomed indications of a more conciliatory attitude on the part of both the Japanese and the American governments; in the third he again inveighed against the president for his severance of normal trade relations with Japan, which was also seen as an action likely to lead to war. All along, however, Hearst had carried on his campaign against the yellow peril and had sounded a loud warning against the danger from Japan.

45 Editorial, *SFE*, 22 Jan. 1936.

46 Ibid., 18 Aug. 1937.

47 Ibid., 9 May 1934. It should be noted that Hearst had visited Mussolini in 1931. See John Diggins, *Mussolini and Fascism: The View from America*, 48–9.

48 Ibid., 11 Apr. 1924.

49 Tebbel, *Life and Good Times*, 254–6.

50 Hearst to Coblentz, np, 2 July 1934, Incoming, Coblentz Papers. Two days later an editorial, presumably written in response to the instructions contained in this letter, appeared in the *Examiner* under the heading "Lesson in Despotism."

51 Editorial, *SFE*, 4 Aug. 1934. In the same edition a page-one news story had appeared under the headline "Hitler Regarded As Planning to Put Himself on Throne." This followed a similar report (also on page one) headed "HITLER SEIZES ABSOLUTE POWER!" *SFE*, 3 Aug. 1934.

52 *SFE*, 8 Aug. 1934. The cartoon was headed "How the Gods Must Tremble – With Scorn."

53 Coblentz, *Hearst*, 103–5.

54 Ibid., 106.

55 Hearst to Dr Ernest Hanfstaengl, Munich, 22 Aug. 1934, Incoming, Coblentz Papers.

56 Interview in the *Brooklyn Eagle*, published in *SFE*, 30 Sept. 1934.

57 Editorial, *SFE*, 11 Mar. 1936.

58 Signed editorial published in *SFE*, 16 Mar. 1938.

59 Editorial published in the Hearst newspapers, 16 Nov. 1939. Tompkins, ed., *Selections*, 33–5.

60 Hearst had earlier supported the Italian conquest of Ethiopia on much the same grounds that he supported Hitler's moves into the Rhineland. Italy needed room to expand and – though it had not, as Germany had, taken what was rightfully Italy's to take – its entry into Ethiopia was the conquest of a country that was savage, uncivilized, and oppressed in order to redeem it for civilization by colonization. Editorials, *SFE*, 12 and 16 May 1936. See also 26 Jan. 1938, in which Hearst praised British recognition of the conquest of Ethiopia, saying that "the progress of civilization in the savage sections of the globe should be encouraged by all civilized countries."

Later, however, this view changed, as Mussolini became more belligerent and Italy came closer to resembling the growing menace of Hitler's Germany. See ibid., 12 Jan. 1939, though, even at this date, Hearst felt that Mussolini's demands had some justice in them.

61 Hearst to Coblentz, Wyntoon, 22 Aug. 1935, Incoming, Coblentz Papers.

62 Editorial, *SFE*, 7 Feb. 1936.

63 Ibid., 6 Oct. 1937. For a discussion of press reaction to the quarantine speech, see Albjerg, "Isolationism," 210.

64 Editorial, *SFE*, 4 June 1938.

65 See Rodney Carlisle, "The Foreign Policy Views of an Isolationist Press Lord: W.R. Hearst and the International Crisis, 1936–41," 220.

66 Nation-wide radio address, 18 Feb. 1939, published in the Hearst newspapers, 19 Feb. 1939. Tompkins, ed., *Selections*, 210–17.

67 Editorial, *SFE*, 5 Sept. 1939.

68 In Sept. 1940 the formation of the AFC was greeted with a rather patronizing statement that all this was, after all, just what the Hearst papers had been advocating for years. Ibid., 21 Sept. 1940.

69 The files of the committee contain a letter to Hearst, inviting his co-operation in their campaign – but there is no reply in this collection or in Hearst's papers. The letter is marked as having also been sent to Pulitzer and Howard, of whom only the latter replied. R.E. Wood to Hearst, Chicago, and file marked "Important People Who Supported AFC," box 291, Papers of the America First Committee, Hoover Institution.

70 See Wayne S. Cole, *Charles A. Lindbergh and the Battle against American Intervention in World War II*, 177, and *America First: The Battle against Intervention, 1940–1941*, 148.

71 See Carlisle, "Isolationist Press Lord," 226.

72 "In the News," *SFE*, 8 Dec. 1941.

73 Editorial, *SFE*, 9 Dec. 1941.

CHAPTER NINE: AMERICA FIRST

1 See chap. 3, n. 59. James T. Williams comments on Hearst's changes of mind. He notes that "the Chief" was very firm in pursuing men whom he felt had done him an injury, that "it was very difficult to change him on that." He continues: "On the other hand, he didn't hesitate to reverse his policy. Here again was a very cunning understanding of the mass mind. He seemed at times to operate on the theory that nobody read yesterday's newspapers. It is amazing how often the Hearst newspapers could get away with a reversal of policy, because nobody remembered what they had been saying a few years before." Williams, *OHC* 4:789–96.

2 Editorial, *SFE*, 20 Apr. 1895.

3 Ibid., 14 Apr. 1895.

4 In an editorial of 26 Jan. 1895 Hearst commented favourably on the passage through the Senate of a bill to provide for the construction of a canal through Nicaragua. Although he eventually supported, the building of the Panama Canal, he returned to the question of the Nicaragua route from time to time when it became obvious to him that the existing waterway could not handle the traffic imposed on it or that other advantages would proceed from construction of a new canal. See, for example, editorials in *SFE* of 8 Feb. 1929; 15 Aug. 1940; 3 Dec. 1946; and 4 Apr. 1949.

5 Ibid., 16 Feb. 1895.

6 Ibid., 2 July 1895.

7 Ibid., 7 July 1895.

8 Ibid., 16 Jan. 1900.

9 Ibid., 11 Feb. 1900.

10 At this time, editorials against the treaty appeared almost daily. See, for example, ibid., 14, 15, 17, 19, 20 Feb. 1900. The reference to Adams is to be found in a signed editorial published 3 Mar. 1900.

11 Ibid., 5 Mar. 1900.

12 Ibid., 7 Dec. 1901. The Hearst papers claimed credit for the defeat of the first Hay-Pauncefote Treaty and for the successful negotiation of a new treaty. In November "the journalism that has acted" was credited with helping to achieve this. Ibid., 19 Nov. 1901. For an excellent discussion of this campaign, see Soon Jin Kim, "An Anatomy of the Hearst Press Campaign to Fortify an American Isthmian Canal."

13 Editorial, *SFE*, 7 Nov. 1903. A few days later Hearst discussed "this theft of Panama, which, if successful, will deprive us of moral standing before the world" and which was "as needless as it is criminal." Ibid., 11 Nov. 1903.

14 Ibid., 15 Jan. 1904. The reference to "any canal, rather than no canal" is in an editorial printed 24 Feb. 1904. Hearst was, however, rather unusual in Progressive circles in this view of the taking of Panama. Progressives did "little more than mutter something about the 'immorality' of it all.

Roosevelt's actions in Panama were too well received by the American people to warrant an open political attack on the Government's Isthmian policy." In any case, the big stick was rather popular among Progressives. Seager, "Progressives," 93.

15 Editorial, *SFE*, 15 Mar. 1907.

16 Ibid., 12 Dec. 1912. The editorial was headed "America Knows Her Rights in Her Own Canal, and Knowing Dares to Maintain Them." This campaign continued through to 1914. See, for example, an editorial headed "Jackson, Lincoln and Cleveland vs. Wilson: Americanism Contrasted With the Policy of Surrender," published 7 Mar. 1914.

17 Editorial, *SFE*, 10 Apr. 1913.

18 Ibid., 15 Oct. 1895.

19 Ibid., 11 Nov. 1896. For comment on Hearst's views on Venezuela, see chap. 3.

20 Ibid., 15 Dec. 1902 and 24 Jan. 1903.

21 Ibid., 7 Dec. 1908.

22 Ibid., 1 Jan. 1910.

23 Signed editorial published in the Hearst newspapers, 31 Jan. 1919. Tompkins, ed., *Selections*, 426.

24 Editorial, *SFE*, 12 Jan. 1933.

25 "In the News," 24 Apr. 1941.

26 Editorial, *SFE*, 25 Jan. 1895.

27 Ibid., 31 May 1907.

28 Ibid., 16 May 1911.

29 Ibid., 22 Jan. 1912. Some months before this editorial appeared, Hearst had asked Madero about his aspirations. Madero replied that he felt it was necessary to allow the 1911 election to demonstrate the abuse of the system before resorting to open revolt. See Madero to Hearst, Ciudad Juarez, 25 Apr. 1911, in Jerry W. Knudson, "When Did Francisco I. Madero Decide on Revolution?" 529–34.

30 Editorial, *SFE*, 12 Mar. 1912.

31 Ibid., 3 Jan. 1913.

32 Ibid., 4 Nov. 1913.

33 Ibid., 17 Nov. 1913.

34 Ibid., 15 Apr. 1916.

35 Signed editorial, *SFE*, 23 Aug. 1921.

36 William Randolph Hearst, *Why We Should Recognize the Mexican Government*, 17–19.

37 Signed editorial letter published in the Hearst newspapers, 22 Apr. 1923. Tompkins, ed., *Selections*, 428–9.

38 "In the News," 17 Apr. 1941.

39 *Mexico City Post*, 1 Mar. 1941. Enclosed with Josephus Daniels to Secretary of State, Mexico City, 10 Mar. 1941, 032/1481, Department of State, Record

Group 59, National Archives. Hearst had made the same point earlier in his own papers when he said that "one of President Roosevelt's most useful achievements is his wise development of the utmost of fraternal relations with Mexico." "In the News," 14 Feb. 1941.

40 Williams called the affair "one of the closest calls Mr. Hearst ever had. It was a disgraceful performance, and yet it was a performance that showed how gullible perfectly honest men can be." He added that Hearst, too, was deceived, though he ought not to have been – and would not have been had he not been "so anxious to get something on the Calles government." Williams, OHC 4:773–7. See also McKenna, *Borah*, 232. Hiram Johnson, a member of the Senate committee set up to investigate the charges, noted that "the entire country, as evidenced by the press here, is in full cry after Hearst." Johnson to his sons, Washington, DC, 24 Dec. 1927, part IV, box 3, Johnson Papers. He later noted that "the bitterness, hostility and hatred of the rest of the press for Hearst was the most remarkable thing to me. Outside of the testimony actually taken, this bitterness and hatred has no limits, and I am thoroughly convinced that the rest of the press would commit any crime to fasten one upon Hearst." He also noted that the respectable *Philadelphia Ledger* and *New York Times* had apparently been willing to pay to have the Mexican government offices burgled to get what they wanted. "There is little difference in the ethics of these newspaper men." Johnson to Hiram Johnson, Jr, Washington, DC, 7 Jan. 1928, part VI, box 5, Johnson Papers.

41 On the question of a deal between Hearst and the Mexican government, see C. Dennis Ignasias, "Propaganda and Public Opinion in Harding's Foreign Affairs: The Case for Mexican Recognition," 47. A Justice Department report had noted the rumour of the Hearst-Obregón deal. A similar rumour appeared early in 1922 in a military intelligence report, which noted that a Villista agent from El Paso, Texas, had published a report that Hearst had received tax concessions for his existing Mexican properties in exchange for pro-Obregón propaganda and that, if the latter was recognized by May 1922, Hearst would receive an additional five million acres of land. Summary of Mexican Intelligence, 8–15 Mar. 1922, Headquarters, 8th Corps Area, Fort Sam Houston, Texas, General Staff, Military Intelligence Division, 1917–41, 10640–2361 (222), War Department, Record Group 165, National Archives.

The Mexican newspaper report noted that Hearst had no direct relations with the present Mexican government but that his campaign for recognition was based on "personal and political interests." It also took a very serious view of the interference of Hearst, who was felt to be dangerous to both Mexican stability and prestige. *Democrato*, 10 Mar. 1922, enclosed with George F. Summerlin to Secretary of State, Mexico City, 10 Mar. 1922, State Department, Mexico, 711.12/407.

Hearst has frequently been accused of suiting his opinions to the needs of his own Latin American interests. Lundberg, for example, charged that, in 1928, Hearst secured the appointment of Alexander Moore as ambassador to Peru to protect his mining interests there. Moore served until Hearst no longer needed him and in 1931 was transferred to Poland. *Imperial Hearst*, 174–81. He has been accused of advocating strong action when his properties were endangered and of toning down his attitude when the danger passed. See, for example, George Seldes, *Lords of the Press*, 32. Villard notes that Hearst's views cannot have been "wholly uncolored by the fact that he is the alien and absentee owner of hundreds of thousands of Mexican acres which he is holding for future exploitation and is also the credited holder of mining interests in that country." *Some Newspapermen*, 27–8. Another author also suggests that Hearst's motive for demanding intervention was a venal one and couples this with the nonsensical opinion that Hearst wished the United States to take over Mexico and incorporate it into the United States. Minear, "Hearst and Foreign Affairs," 161. It is of course true that, in periods such as 1911–16, when Hearst was advocating intervention, his properties were often in danger and even threatened with confiscation; and it is also true that, when the dangers subsided, his demands did the same. There is no evidence, however, that his demands for intervention were merely a function of his concern about his property.

42 Editorial, *SFE*, 6 Oct. 1901.

43 Ibid., 10 Mar. 1896.

44 Ibid., 5 July 1898.

45 Ibid., 22 Feb. 1904.

46 Ibid., 11 Sept. 1908.

47 Ibid., 1 Nov. 1913.

48 Signed editorial published in the Hearst newspapers, 3 Mar. 1935. Tompkins, ed., *Selections*, 143.

49 See chap. 5, n. 55.

50 Seager, "Progressives," 31. See also Axeen, "Heroes of the Engine Room," 490ff.

51 On Bryan and foreign policy, see Kendrick Alling Clements, "William Jennings Bryan and Democratic Foreign Policy, 1896–1915," passim; and, on one particular incident in Bryan's career, Paolo E. Coletta, "Bryan, McKinley and the Treaty of Paris," 132. See also, for another survey of Bryan's views on foreign affairs, Coletta, "Bryan, Anti-imperialism and Missionary Diplomacy," 167–87. On La Follette, see Padraic Colum Kennedy, "La Follette's Foreign Policy: From Imperialism to Anti-Imperialism," 287–93. See also Seager, "Progressives," 29 and 203.

52 See Seager, "Progressives" 66; and Leuchtenberg, "Progressivism and Imperialism," 483–5. Though the implication of this study, in discussing the relationship between the progressives and foreign policy, is that

Leuchtenberg's attribution of a unified view of foreign policy is not a valid one, nevertheless his analysis does hold up for a large portion of those who labelled themselves Progressives. For a criticism of Leuchtenberg, see Thomas G. Paterson, "California Progressives and Foreign Policy," 329–42.

53 Seager, "Progressives," 2–3.
54 Editorial, *SFE*, 17 Nov. 1898.
55 Ibid., 4 July 1899.
56 Ibid., 6 Aug. 1900.
57 See chap. 1.
58 Hearst, *Obligations and Opportunities*, 12–13.
59 Hearst to Coblentz, np, 7 Oct. 1934, Incoming, Coblentz Papers. This was a letter written by Hearst to a reporter for the newspaper *Der Tag* of Amsterdam, and dated Amsterdam, 4 Aug. 1934.
60 Editorial, *SFE*, 13 Apr. 1923. "Although Hearst used the traditional language of isolationism – a tradition, he loved to remind his readers, that had its origins with George Washington and Thomas Jefferson – his actual set of ideas, his own foreign policy, envisioned a kind of interest in international concerns which is hardly implicit in the term 'isolationist.'" Carlisle, "Hearst and the International Crisis," 218–19.
61 Ibid., 7 May 1924.
62 Hearst to the President of the Association of College Editors, np, 17 Nov. 1934. Tompkins, ed., *Selections*, 410–11. The letter was also printed on page one of *SFE*, 21 Nov. 1934.
63 D.C. Watt, "American 'Isolationism' in the 1920's: Is It a Useful Concept?" 15.
64 See Boyle, "Johnson," 176, 260–1, and 367–8; and McKenna, *Borah*, 288–9, where the author quotes William Appleman Williams, *The Shaping of American Diplomacy*, 655–9.

CHAPTER TEN: HEARST AND U.S. FOREIGN POLICY

1 See Tebbel, *Life and Good Times*, 242.
2 Williams, OHC, 3:607; and Neylan to Coolidge, np, 16 Oct. 1924, series 3, folder 27, Neylan Papers.
3 See, for example, Hearst to McKinley, New York, 28 Dec.1897, in which even Hearst admitted that there was animosity between them. William McKinley Papers, series 1, Library of Congress.
4 Taft to Root, Fort Leavenworth, Kansas, 10 Nov. 1906, in which Taft congratulated Root on his anti-Hearst speech, ascribing to it great influence in Hearst's defeat. Special Correspondence with William Howard Taft, 1904–28 and undated, box 166, Root Papers.
5 For the comment on Wilson, see Carlson and Bates, *Lord of San Simeon*, 177. Secretary Lansing accused Hearst and other members of the press of

being "venomously hostile to the President" and of "conducting an insidious campaign to cause trouble between the President and officials of the
Administration." "The Press Campaign to isolate the President," 2 Jan.
1920, notebook 6, 1920–21, box 66, Robert Lansing Papers, Library of Congress. Wilson simply refused to discuss the publication of Ray Stannard
Baker's book about him in the Hearst papers. George Creel to John Randolph Bolling, New York, 3 Aug. 1921, Woodrow Wilson and cpi Material,
1918–30 and undated, vol. 2, George Creel Papers, Library of Congress.

6 Hearst to Coblentz, San Simeon, 29 Jan. 1932, Coblentz file, 1932, box 14,
Hearst Papers, and Incoming, Coblentz Papers. The same words appeared
in an editorial a few days later. sfe, 1 Feb. 1932. The president was finally
goaded into striking back in an election-day speech in Sacramento in
1932. Herbert Hoover Literary Productions 2048, ag1, Hoover Papers.

7 There are several accounts of Hearst's role in the 1932 Democratic conven-
tion, at which Stimson, for example, believed that fdr was nominated "by
a deal engineered by McAdoo and Hearst." Entry for 4 July 1932, Stimson
Diaries, vol. 23 (27 June to 3 Oct. 1932), 21. Most of them are contradictory,
emphasizing the writer's role in swinging what was seen as a Hearst-
dominated California delegation to Roosevelt. See, for example, Thomas
M. Storke, *California Editor* 299–301, 318–19, and 333; and Gibb and Bean,
"John Francis Neylan," 21. Hearst greeted the nomination with an editorial headed "Roosevelt Will Make Great President," sfe, 3 July 1932; and
his inauguration with another headed "Franklin Roosevelt's Inauguration
Brings Hope to American People," sfe, 4 Mar. 1933. Relations deterio-
rated rapidly, however, so that by the 1936 election fdr had made it clear
that "Hearst is persona non grata as far as the Administration is concerned." Entry for 14 Nov. 1936, Diary of Harold L. Ickes, Library of
Congress, 1825. The Ickes diary is an excellent source for tracing the
deterioration of relations between fdr and Hearst.

8 Quoted in Winkler, *New Appraisal*, 183.

9 Entry for 4 Oct. l930, Stimson Diaries, vol. lo (1 Mar. 1929–31 Dec. 1930),
50–1. Stimson advised Hoover that he should invite Hearst to lunch at the
White House "as long as it was not an official action and as long as it was
not anything that protested against France's right to do what she had a
right to do." The lunch took place but apparently to no effect. Entry for
8 Oct. 1930, 56.

10 Entry for 20 Nov. 1932, ibid., vol. 24 (4 Oct.–14 Dec. 1932), 111–12. Earlier,
Stimson noted that Hoover had hesitated for a long time over American
entry into the World Court and that what the discussions came down to
was "whether or not the President would be willing to take the hounding
from the Hearst papers which would begin as soon as the World Court
was submitted." Entry for 7 Nov. 1930, vol. 10 (1 Mar. 1929–31 Dec. 1930),
132.

11 Bernard C. Cohen, "The Relationship Between Public Opinion and Foreign Policy Makers," in Melvin Small, ed., *Public Opinion and Historians*, 71. For discussion of the special position of the president and his top officials in the making of foreign policy, see also, for example, Ralph B. Levering, *American Opinion and the Russian Alliance, 1939–1945*, 11; and Montague Kern, Patricia W. Levering and Ralph B. Levering, *The Kennedy Crises: The Press, the Presidency, and Foreign Policy*, 195. Some scholars modify this picture in detail, and this will be discussed later in this chapter.

12 Bernard C. Cohen, *The Press and Foreign Policy*, 167–8. See also Montague Kern, "The Press, the Presidency, and International Conflict: Lessons from Two Administrations," 65–6. Although Kern reviews a period after Hearst's death in which television had become a larger factor, the conclusions are essentially the same.

13 See Cohen, *Press*, 143–6. A revealing comment on this question comes from a British politician who had been a junior minister in the Foreign Office in the early 1950s. Kenneth Younger noted that he could not "immediately recollect any occasion when I or my superiors had been greatly affected by public opinion in reaching important decisions." "Public Opinion and Foreign Policy," 169. Cohen has also argued that this view is consistent with that of American policy-makers: "My own researches into the public opinion perceptions of State Department officials persuade me that most of their talk about the power of public opinion is ritualistic." "Public Opinion and Policy Makers," 79.

14 Michael Ledeen, "The Press and Foreign Policy: Public Opinion, Press Opinion, and Foreign Policy," 19.

15 See chap. 2 above.

16 James N. Rosenau, *Public Opinion and Foreign Policy*, passim.

17 James Reston, *The Artillery of the Press: Its Influence on American Foreign Policy*, 99–108.

18 Rosenau, *Public Opinion*, 35–6.

19 Ibid.

20 Younger, "Public Opinion", 172.

21 Jack G. Shaheen, "Media Coverage of the Middle East: Perception and Foreign Policy," 169–71.

22 Cohen, *Press and Foreign Policy*, 253

23 Ibid., 13. Other scholars have confirmed this view. See, for example, Jennifer Tebbe, "Print and American Culture," 259–79, which emphasises the role of "consensus formation" and of creating and maintaining public awareness of issues.

24 James Boylan, "Journalists and Foreign Policy" in Alexander De Conde, ed., *Encyclopedia of American Foreign Policy*, 2:513.

25 Stimson noted that, in Jan. 1933, Hoover worried over Hearst's new charge that he had "entrapped Roosevelt into these negotiations with

other countries." Entry for 27 Jan. 1933, Stimson Diaries, vol. 25 (14 Dec. 1932–1 Feb. 1933), 193.

26 The banner front-page headline in the *New York Journal* on 9 Mar. 1900 read GREAT VICTORY FOR THE JOURNAL.

27 See Soon Jin Kim, "Hearst Press Campaign." The reference to Roosevelt is on 356; the detailed analysis of the campaign's effectiveness on 360–76.

28 Ibid., 378.

29 Accinelli, "U.S. and the World Court," 262–4. Using "every time-tested Hearst device," he depicted the court as "a tool of conniving European diplomats with the British leading the pack and as a threat to American interests and independence. The motives of its foreign judges were impugned, its decisions derided, its limitations transformed into crippling weaknesses." In this he was not alone in the newspaper world. The *Chicago Tribune* defied its readers to pronounce the names of the court's judges and asked how many friends Uncle Sam could count on if he appeared before the court. Edwards, *McCormick's Tribune*, 104.

30 *New York Times*, 15 Aug. 1951.

31 Robert J. Maddox, *William E. Borah and American Foreign Policy*, 233–4. Maddox also argues in the same place that Borah, "by this time 'adreaming' of the Presidency again," simply wanted to ensure the support of those who might help him to achieve it. See also Fred L. Israel, *Nevada's Key Pittman*, 30–1; and Geoffrey S. Smith, *To Save a Nation: American Counter-subversives, the New Deal and the Coming of World War II*, 136. For a contemporary view, see Robert W. Desmond, *The Press and World Affairs*, 371.

32 Coblentz to John S. Brookes, Jr, np, 28 June 1939, Outgoing, Coblentz Papers.

33 Joseph T. Klapper, "Mass Communication, Attitude Stability and Change," in Carolyn W. and Muzafer Sherif, eds., *Attitude, Ego-Involvement and Change*, 300.

34 F. Lazarsfeld, B. Berelson, and Hazel Gaudet, *The People's Choice*, passim.

35 See chap. 7 above.

36 See chap. 2, nn. 1, 2, 3.

37 Carlisle, "Hearst and the International Crisis," 217.

38 For an excellent survey of the relationship between public opinion and foreign affairs, see May, "American Imperialism: A Reinterpretation," 123–283. See also, for example, James M. McCormick and Michael R. Coveyou, "Mass Political Imagery and the Salience of International Affairs," 498–509. One of the conclusions of this article is that "even in those groups most likely to express foreign policy concerns, a substantial majority of the mass public still fail to do so." On the question of elections and foreign policy, see Kenneth N. Waltz, "Electoral Punishment and Foreign Policy Crises," in James N. Rosenau, ed., *Domestic Sources of Foreign Policy*,

263–93. For a brief discussion of some of the exceptions to this generalization, see Farouk A. Sankari, "The Effects of the American Media on Public Opinion and Middle East Policy Choices," 109.

39 Harold R. Isaacs, "Sources for Images of Foreign Countries," in Small, ed., *Public Opinion*, 97. See also Boylan, "Journalists and Foreign Policy."

40 "America and the Post-War World," Special Intelligence Report, 12 Dec. 1942, Office of War Information, Bureau of Intelligence, 2–3, OSS files, box 162, 25668.

41 Ibid.

42 The report noted that, while about three-quarters of those questioned felt that postwar co-operation could be relied on from Great Britain, the remainder still regarded her with suspicion, as did a similar proportion with Russia. Ibid., 11–12. These findings are duplicated in other reports. See, for example, "Some Preliminary Indications of U.S. Attitude toward our Allies – Britain, Russia and China," 9 Mar. 1942, OSS files, box 149, 13823, and Intelligence Report 66, 12 Mar. 1943, Office of War Information, Bureau of Intelligence, entry 254, box 1335.

CHAPTER ELEVEN: EPILOGUE 1941–1951

1 See "In the News," 19 Dec. 1941.

2 Ibid., 2 Jan. 1942.

3 See ibid., 23 Jan. 1942, and editorial published in all Hearst papers, 20 Dec. 1942. Tompkins, ed., *Selections*, 638–42. Hearst was in fact still expressing admiration for the British in his editorials. See, for example, *SFE*, 7 July 1942.

4 Editorial, *SFE*, 2 Oct. 1942.

5 See, for example, an editorial published in all Hearst papers on 27 May 1943, in which he argued that Russian support for General Charles de Gaulle was merely a cynical move to retain pre-war Russian influence in France. This was merely a part of the influence that she intended to impose throughout Europe after the war. Tompkins, ed., *Selections*, 648–51.

6 Editorial, *SFE*, 17 July 1943.

7 Editorial published in all Hearst newspapers, 15 Sept. 1943. Tompkins, ed., *Selections*, 222.

8 Editorial, *SFE*, 18 Nov. 1943.

9 For a discussion of the fate of Progressives such as these during and after the war, see Robert Griffith, "Old Progressives and the Cold War," 334–47, and Justus D. Doenecke, *Not to the Swift: The Old Isolationists in the Cold War Era*.

10 Doenecke, *Not to the swift*, 46. See also James Gazell, "A.H. Vandenburg, Internationalism and War," 375–94.

11 Boyle, "Johnson," viii.

12 Griffith, "Old Progressives," 347.

13 Editorial, *SFE*, 14 Feb. 1945.

14 Ibid., 6 Mar. 1945. Neylan wrote to Hearst, sending a couple of editorials on Yalta that "you might find useful." One of them was printed as indicated almost verbatim and headed "Yalta and Munich." Neylan to Hearst, np, 23 Feb. 1945, series 5, box 66, folder 17, Neylan Papers.

15 Editorial, *SFE*, 10 Apr. 1945.

16 Ibid., 21 Apr. 1945.

17 Ibid., 29 June 1945.

18 Ibid., 7 June 1945.

19 See, for example, "Communism Is the Enemy of American Labor," ibid., 13 Aug. 1946, and "Communism in the Schools," ibid., 16 Aug. 1946. The latter was juxtaposed with a cartoon entitled "The Little Red Schoolteacher," showing Stalin pulling the strings of a puppet teacher.

20 Ibid., 16 Feb. 1946.

21 The British election of 1945 brought advantage only to Russia. Ibid., 27 July 1945. The Iranian crisis was, in the words of Ernest Bevin, "a brazen and unmitigated and unwarranted act of aggression." Ibid., 2 Feb. 1946. Churchill's Iron Curtain speech and Truman's support of it were taken to mean that "we have come to the end of our humiliating road of futile appeasement of Russia." Ibid., 8 Mar. 1946. "Saving China from conquest is the immediate way to save civilization from Communism," ibid., 22 July 1949.

22 Ibid., 21 Aug. 1946.

23 Ibid., 8 Apr. 1947.

24 Ibid., 2 Feb.1946.

25 He did, however, believe that the doctrine had come too late, making its implementation in Greece and Turkey more risky than it might have been. But it was necessary to stop another nation being "brought to heel under the iron heel of RED FASCISM." Ibid., 14 Mar. 1947.

26 Ibid., 14 Sept. 1947. During the congressional debate on the Marshall Plan, Hearst began calling it "Operation Rat Hole." Ibid., 13 Dec. 1947.

27 See, for example, ibid., 19 June 1945 and 27 Apr. 1951.

28 Ibid., 17 Oct. 1945. Hearst also supported Truman's refusal to share the secret of the bomb, for its possession gave the United States an advantage that must not be relinquished. Ibid., 2 Nov. 1945 and 17 June 1946.

29 Ibid., 3 Jan. and 22 Feb. 1947.

30 Ibid., 5 June, 1 Sept., and 20 Oct. 1947.

31 The editorial on the outbreak of the Korean War noted that the United States had become involved in two wars through inadequate preparation, that it was "fast asleep when the Communist invasion of China moved the borders of the Soviet Union to include a vast part of Asia," and that it

was still asleep. The heading was simply "Caught Napping Again." Ibid., 28 June 1950.

32 Rosenau, *Public Opinion*, 35–6.

33 Melvin Small, "How We Learned to Love the Russians: American Media and the Soviet Union During World War II," 466.

34 Ibid., 475–6.

35 Ibid., 478.

36 Bonnie Sharp Jefferson, "The Rhetorical Restrictions of a Devil Theory: The Anti-Communist Press's View of Communism, 1945–47," 21. In this study the anti-Communist press is represented by the Hearst papers, the McCormick papers, *Reader's Digest*, Time-Life Inc., *Saturday Evening Post*, and *Catholic World*. Two publications – the Hearst daily *Pittsburgh Sun Telegraph*, and the monthly *Catholic World* – were reviewed in detail.

37 Ibid., passim.

38 Griffith notes that, if the Progressives were to be vindicated at all, they might find justification from a later generation "which having discovered in the numbing horror of Vietnam the consequences of America's Cold War crusade, may be inclined toward a more sympathetic view of the old progressives and their critique of postwar American diplomacy." "Old Progressives," 347.

39 I am indebted to my colleague Maurice Yacowar for these comments. They are taken from his notes for a review of *Citizen Kane*, broadcast on CBC Radio in Vancouver, BC, June 1991.

40 Ibid.

Bibliography

MANUSCRIPT SOURCES

The Writings of William Randolph Hearst

THE PAPERS OF WILLIAM RANDOLPH HEARST
These are housed in the Bancroft Library at the University of California, Berkeley. They cover the period from 1903 to Hearst's death in 1951, although there is little material before 1914 and after 1945. In the fifty-seven cartons, mostly arranged chronologically, there is almost no personal correspondence. The correspondence with Hearst editors and other executives, which makes up most of the collection, presents a graphic picture of Hearst's views and of his relations with his newspapers. The collection in fact confirms the comment of William Randolph Hearst, Jr that his father was inclined to write editorials rather than letters on matters that concerned him and that his interest in his newspapers was maintained until the last few months of his life (see above, 19–20).

It should be noted, however, that many of the Hearst letters found in other collections are not included in the Hearst Papers themselves. This is sometimes the case even when the correspondence in question is not with the person concerned but with a third party. Thus, while the views expressed in copies kept in the Hearst files are consistent with those found in other places, the papers of such people as Coblentz, Neylan, and others are often as valuable as Hearst's own papers in establishing his positions.

HEARST NEWSPAPERS

The major source for this study has been the Hearst newspapers between his acquisition of the *New York Journal-American* in 1895 and his death in 1951. No attempt has, however, been made to review all the Hearst papers for this period. This exercise was restricted to the *San Francisco Examiner*, the oldest of the Hearst papers, which, on issues such as Oriental immigration and Pacific affairs, offers a sharper focus than others in the chain.

Even in the later 1930s and early 1940s, when Hearst lost much control over his empire, he still effectively controlled editorial policy and ensured that the views expressed in one paper, especially on major national issues, were duplicated in others. There is much testimony to support this conclusion (see above, 19–22), and checks of editorial comment on major issues reinforced it.

OTHER HEARST WRITINGS

There are two major selections of Hearst's writings. These are:

Coblentz, Edmond D. *William Randolph Hearst: A Portrait in His Own Words*. New York: Simon and Schuster 1952.

Tompkins, E.F., ed. *Selections from the Writings and Speeches of William Randolph Hearst*. San Francisco 1948.

In addition, Hearst published a number of pamphlets on foreign affairs. Those cited in the text are:

Obligations and Opportunities of the United States in Mexico and the Philippines. New York 1916.

Why We Should Recognize the Mexican Government. New York 1921.

Statements on International Affairs. New York 1922.

Original Proposal for Anglo-American Understanding. New York 1927.

On Communism and Fascism. New York 1935.

Documentary Sources

A wide range of documentary sources has been consulted for this study. Those cited in the text are as follows:

BANCROFT LIBRARY, UNIVERSITY OF CALIFORNIA, BERKELEY

The papers of Edmond D. Coblentz

The papers of Hiram W. Johnson

The papers of John Francis Neylan

Gibb, Corinne L., and Walter E. Bean. "John Francis Neylan, Politics, Law and the University of California." Unpublished interview, Berkeley 1971.

The Fremont Older Collection

COLUMBIA UNIVERSITY ORAL HISTORY COLLECTION
The reminiscences of Claude G. Bowers
The reminiscences of John T. Hettrick
The reminiscences of Joseph T. Mahoney
The reminiscences of Keats Speed
The reminiscences of Emily Smith Warner
The reminiscences of James T. Williams

HOOVER INSTITUTION ON WAR, REVOLUTION AND PEACE,
   STANFORD UNIVERSITY
Papers of the America First Committee

LIBRARY OF CONGRESS, WASHINGTON, DC
Papers of Bainbridge Colby
Papers of George Creel
Diary of Harold L. Ickes
Papers of Harold L. Ickes
Papers of Robert Lansing
Papers of William McKinley
Papers of Theodore Roosevelt
Papers of Elihu Root
Papers of John Coit Spooner

NATIONAL ARCHIVES, WASHINGTON, DC
Records of the Office of Government Reports, Record Group 44, Executive
   Division, Records of the Assistant Director, Katherine C. Blackburn, 1941–43.
Records of the Department of State: Record Group 59, Office of War
   Information, Bureau of Intelligence.
Records of the War Department, General and Special Staffs, Record Group
   165, General Staff Military Intelligence Division, 1917–41.

Microfilmed or photocopied documents from several collections were also
   used. Those cited are as follows:

HOOVER LIBRARY, WEST BRANCH, IOWA
Papers of Herbert Hoover

ROOSEVELT LIBRARY, HYDE PARK, NEW YORK
Papers of Franklin Delano Roosevelt

YALE UNIVERSITY
Diaries of Henry L. Stimson

SECONDARY MATERIALS

As with the documentary sources, the listing of secondary materials that follows is restricted to those cited in the text.

Abbott, Willis J. *Watching the World Go By.* Boston: Little, Brown 1933.

Accinelli, Robert D. "The United States and the World Court, 1920–1927." PhD, University of California, Berkeley, 1968.

Albjerg, Victor L. "Isolationism and the Early New Deal." *Current History* 35 (October 1958): 204–10.

Axeen, David. " 'Heroes of the Engine Room': American 'Civilization' and the War with Spain." *American Quarterly* 36 (Fall 1984): 481–502.

Bailey, Thomas A. *America Faces Russia.* Ithaca, NY: Cornell University Press 1950.

Bancroft, Hubert Howe. *Chronicles of the Builders of the Commonwealth.* Vol. 2. San Francisco: History Co. 1891–92.

Basso, Hamilton. "Mr. Hearst Sees Red." *New Republic* 81 (26 Jan. 1935): 269–71.

Beard, Charles A. *American Foreign Policy in the Making, 1932–1940: A Study in Responsibilities.* New Haven, Conn.: Yale Unversity Press 1946.

Bernstein, Barton J., and Franklin A. Leib. "Progressive Republican Senators and American Imperialism, 1898–1916." *Mid-America* 50 (July 1968): 163–205.

Bleyer, Willard G. *Main Currents in the History of American Journalism.* Boston: Houghton-Mifflin 1927.

Bonnet, Theodore. "William R. Hearst: A Critical Study." *The Lantern* 1 (Mar. 1916): 365–80.

Borchard, Edwin, and W.P. Lage. *Neutrality for the United States.* New Haven, Conn.: Yale University Press 1940.

Boylan, James. "Journalists and Foreign Policy." In Alexander De Conde, ed., *Encyclopedia of American Foreign Policy.* New York: Scribners 1978. 2:507–14.

Boyle, Peter Gerald. "The Study of an Isolationist: Hiram Johnson." PhD, University of California, Los Angeles, 1970.

Brooks, Sidney. "The Yellow Press: An English View." *Harper's Weekly,* 23 Dec. 1911, 11.

Brown, Charles H. *The Correspondents' War: Journalists in the Spanish-American War.* New York: Scribners 1967.

Burgess, R.L. "Working for Hearst." *New Republic* 71 (10 Aug. 1932): 341–2.

Carlisle, Rodney P. "The Political Ideas and Influence of William Randolph Hearst, 1928–1936." PhD, University of California, Berkeley, 1965.

– "William Randolph Hearst's Reaction to the American Newspaper Guild: A Challenge to New Deal Labor Legislation." *Labor History* 10 (Winter 1969): 74-99.

– "William Randolph Hearst, A Fascist Reputation Reconsidered." *Journalism Quarterly* 50 (Spring 1973): 125–33.

– "The Foreign Policy Views of an Isolationist Press Lord: W.R. Hearst and the International Crisis, 1936–41." *Journal of Contemporary History* 9 (July 1974): 217–27.

Carlson, Oliver, and Ernest S. Bates. *Hearst, Lord of San Simeon.* New York: Viking 1936.

Chaney, Lindsay, and Michael Cieply. *The Hearsts: Family and Empire – the Later Years.* New York: Simon & Schuster 1981.

Clements, Kendrick Alling. "William Jennings Bryan and Democratic Foreign Policy, 1896–1915." PhD, University of California, Berkeley, 1970.

Coblentz, Edmond D., ed. *Newsmen Speak.* Berkeley, Calif.: University of California Press 1954.

Cohen, Bernard C. *The Press and Foreign Policy.* Princeton, NJ: Princeton University Press 1963.

– "The Relationship between Public Opinion and Foreign Policy Makers." In Melvin Small, ed., *Public Opinion and Historians: Interdisciplinary Perspectives.* Detroit: Wayne State University Press 1970. 65–80.

Cole, Wayne S. *America First: The Battle against Intervention, 1940–1941.* Madison, Wisc.: University of Wisconsin Press 1953.

– "Senator Key Pittman and American Neutrality Policies, 1933–1940." *Mississippi Valley Historical Review* 96 (Mar. 1960): 644–62.

– *Charles A. Lindbergh and the Battle against American Intervention in World War II.* New York: Harcourt, Brace Jovanovich 1974.

Coletta, Paolo E. "Bryan, McKinley and the Treaty of Paris." *Pacific Historical Review* 26 (May 1957): 131–46.

– "Bryan, Anti-imperialism and Missionary Diplomacy." *Nebraska History* 44 (Sept. 1963): 167–87.

Cooper, John Milton, Jr. "Progressivism and American Foreign Policy: A Reconsideration." *Mid-America* 51 (Oct. 1969): 260–77.

Desmond, Robert W. *The Press and World Affairs.* New York: Appleton-Century Co. 1937.

Diggins, John P. *Mussolini and Fascism: The View from America.* Princeton, NJ: Princeton University Press 1972.

Doenecke, Justus D. *Not to the Swift: The Old Isolationists in the Cold War Era.* Lewisburg, Pa: Bucknell University Press 1979.

Duffus, Robert L. "The Tragedy of Hearst." *World's Work* 44 (Oct. 1922): 623–31.

Edwards, Jerome E. *The Foreign Policy of Col. McCormick's Tribune, 1929–1941.* Reno: University of Nevada Press 1971.

Emery, Edwin, and Henry Ladd Smith. *The Press and America: An Intepretive History of Journalism.* 2d ed. Englewood Clifs, NY: Prentice-Hall 1962.

Esthus, Raymond E. "The Changing Concept of the Open Door, 1899–1910." *Mississippi Valley Historical Review* 46 (Dec. 1959): 435–54.

Fike, Claude E. "Aspects of the New American Recognition Policy towards Russia Following World War I." *Southern Quarterly* 4, no. 1 (1965): 1–16.

Filene, Peter G. *Americans and the Soviet Experiment, 1917–1933*. Cambridge, Mass.: Harvard University Press 1967.

Fleming, Denna F. *The United States and World Organization, 1920–1933*. New York: Columbia University Press 1938.

Gauvreau, Emile. *My Last Million Readers*. New York: E.P. Dutton 1941.

Gazell, James. "A.H. Vandenberg, Internationalism and War." *Political Science Quarterly* 88 (Sept. 1973): 375–94.

Graham, Otis L. *An Encore for Reform: The Old Progressives and the New Deal*. New York: Oxford University Press 1967.

Griffith, Robert. "Old Progressives and the Cold War." *Journal of American History* 66 (Sept. 1979): 334–47.

Healy, David F. *The United States in Cuba, 1898–1902: Generals, Politicians and the Search for a Policy.* Madison, Wisc.: University of Wisconsin Press 1963.

Ignasias, C. Dennis. "Propaganda and Public Opinion in Harding's Foreign Affairs: The case for Mexican Recognition." *Journalism Quarterly* 48 (Spring 1971): 41–52.

Irwin, Will. *The American Newspaper*. Ames, Iowa: Iowa State University Press 1969.

Isaacs, Harold R. "Sources for Images of Foreign Countries." In Melvin Small, ed., *Public Opinion and Historians: Interdisciplinary Perspectives*. Detroit: Wayne State University Press 1970. 91–105.

Israel, Fred L. *Nevada's Key Pittman*. Lincoln, Nebr.: University of Nebraska Press 1963.

Jefferson, Bonnie Sharp. "The Rhetorical Restrictions of a Devil Theory: The Anti-Communist Press's View of Communism, 1945–47." PhD, University of Pittsburgh 1984.

Jessup, Philip C. *Elihu Root*. 2 vols. New York: Dodd, Mead & Co. 1938.

Jones, Robert W. *Journalism in the United States*. New York: E.P. Dutton 1947.

Kennedy, Padraic Colum. "La Follette's Foreign Policy: From Imperialism to Anti-Imperialism." *Wisconsin Magazine of History* 46 (Summer 1963): 287–93.

Kern, Montague, Patricia W. Levering, and Ralph B. Levering. *The Kennedy Crises: The Press, the Presidency, and Foreign Policy.* Chapel Hill, NC: University of North Carolina Press 1983.

– "The Press, the Presidency, and International Conflict: Lessons from Two Administrations." *Political Psychology* 5, no. 1 (1984): 53–68.

Klapper, Joseph T. "Mass Communication, Attitude Stability and Change." In Carolyn W. and Muzafer Sherif, eds., *Attitude, Ego-involvement and Change*. New York: Wiley 1967. 297–310.

Knudson, Jerry W. "When Did Francisco I. Madero Decide on Revolution?" *The Americas* 30 (Apr. 1974): 529–34.

Kobre, Sidney. *The Yellow Press and Gilded Age Journalism*. Tallahassee, Fla.: the Author, 1964.

Lasch, Christopher. "American Intervention in Siberia: A Reinterpretation." *Political Science Quarterly* 77 (June 1962): 205–23.

– *The American Liberals and the Russian Revolution*. New York: Columbia University Press 1962.

Lazarsfeld, P.F., B. Berelson, and Hazel Gaudet. *The People's Choice: How the Voter Makes Up His Mind in Presidential Campaigns*. New York: Columbia University Press 1948.

Ledeen, Michael. "The Press and Foreign Policy: Public Opinion, Press Opinion, and Foreign Policy." *Current*, no. 270 (Feb. 1985): 16–19.

Leuchtenberg, William E. "Progressivism and Imperialism: The Progressive Movement and American Foreign Policy." *Mississippi Valley Historical Review* 39 (Dec. 1952): 483–504.

Levering, Ralph B. *American Opinion and the Russian Alliance, 1939–1945*. Chapel Hill, NC: University of North Carolina Press 1976.

Levin, N. Gordon, Jr. *Woodrow Wilson and World Politics: America's Response to War and Revolution*. New York: Oxford University Press 1968.

Lundberg, Ferdinand. *Imperial Hearst*. New York: Equinox Cooperation Press 1938.

McCormick, James M., and Michael R. Coveyou. "Mass Political Imagery and the Salience of International Affairs." *American Politics Quarterly* 6 (Oct. 1978): 498–509.

McKenna, Marian C. *Borah*. Ann Arbor, Mich.: University of Michigan Press 1961.

MacShane, Frank. "The Romantic World of William Randolph Hearst." *Centennial Review of Arts and Science* 8, no. 3 (1964): 292–305.

Maddox, Robert J. *William E. Borah and American Foreign Policy*. Baton Rouge, La: Louisiana State University Press 1970.

May, Ernest R. "American Imperialism: A Reinterpretation." *Perspectives in American History* (1967): 123–283.

Millis, Walter. "Hearst." *Atlantic Monthly*, Dec. 1931, 696–709.

Minear, Lloyd Cecil. "William Randolph Hearst and Foreign Affairs, 1914–1920." MA, Stanford University 1949.

Moley, Raymond. "The Hearst Tradition." *Newsweek*, 27 Aug. 1951, 88.

Morgan, H. Wayne. *America's Road to Empire: The War with Spain and Overseas Expansion*. New York: Wiley 1965.

Mott, Frank Luther. *American Journalism: A History of Newspapers in the United States through 250 years, 1690–1940*. New York: Macmillan 1941.

Older, Fremont, Mrs (Cora Miranda Baggerly). *William Randolph Hearst, American*. New York: Appleton-Century Co. 1936.

Parmeter, William Quayle. "The News Control Explanation of Newsmaking: The Case of William Randolph Hearst, 1920–1940." PhD, University of Washington 1979.

Paterson, Thomas G. "California Progressives and Foreign Policy." *California Historical Society Quarterly* 47 (Mar. 1968): 329–42.

Pollard, James R. *The Presidents and the Press*. New York: Macmillan 1947.

Reston, James. *The Artillery of the Press: Its Influence on American Foreign Policy.* New York: Harper & Row 1967.

Reuter, W.C. "Anglophobia in American Politics, 1865–1900." PhD, University of California, Berkeley, 1966.

Rice, Richard B. "The California Press and American Neutrality," PhD, University of California, Berkeley, 1957.

Riegel, D.W. *Mobilizing for Chaos: The Story of the New Propaganda*. New Haven, Conn.: Yale University Press 1934.

Roosevelt, Elliott, ed. *FDR: His Personal Letters, 1928–1945*. 2 vols. New York: Duell, Sloan and Pearce 1947–50.

Rosenau, James L. *Public Opinion and Foreign Policy: An Operational Formulation*. New York: Random House 1961.

– ed. *Domestic Sources of Foreign Policy.* New York: Free Press 1967.

Rosenberg, Emily S. *Spreading the American Dream: American Economic and Cultural Expansion, 1890–1945*. New York: Hill and Wang 1982.

Russell, Charles Edward. "Mr. Hearst as I knew him." *Ridgeway's*, 27 Oct. 1906.

Sankari, Farouk A. "The Effects of the American Media on Public Opinion and Middle East Policy Choices." *American-Arab Affairs* (Spring 1987): 107–22.

Sarasohn, David. "Power without Glory: Hearst in the Progressive Era." *Journalism Quarterly* 53 (Autumn 1976): 474–82.

Seager, Robert. "The Progressives and American Foreign Policy, 1898–1917." PhD, Ohio State University 1956.

Seldes, George. *Lords of the Press*. New York: Julian Messner, Inc. 1938.

Shaheen, Jack. "Media Coverage of the Middle East: Perception and Foreign Policy." *Annals of the American Academy*, no. 482 (Nov. 1985): 160–75.

Sherif, Carolyn W. and Muzafer, eds. *Attitude, Ego-Involvement and Change*. New York 1967.

Small, Melvin, ed. *Public Opinion and Historians: Interdisciplinary Perspective*. Detroit: Wayne State University Press 1970.

– "How We Learned To Love the Russians: American Media and the Soviet Union during World War II." *Historian* 36 (May 1974): 455–78.

Smith, Geoffrey S. *To Save a Nation: American Counter-subversives, the New Deal and the Coming of World War II*. New York: Basis Books 1973.

Soon Jin Kim. "An Anatomy of the Hearst Press Campaign To Fortify an American Isthmian Canal." PhD, University of Maryland, 1982.

Storke, Thomas M. *California Editor*. Los Angeles: Westernlore Press 1958.

Swanberg, W.A. *Citizen Hearst*. New York: Sribners 1961.

Tebbe, Jennifer. "Print and American Culture," *American Quarterly* 32 (1980): 259–79.

Tebbel, John R. *The Life and Good Times of William Randolph Hearst*. New York: E.P. Dutton 1952.

Thompson, J.A. "An Imperialist and the First World War: The Case of Albert J. Beveridge." *Journal of American Studies* 5 (Aug. 1971): 133–50.

Vevier, Charles. "The Open Door: An Idea in Action, 1906–1913." *Pacific Historical Review* 24 (Feb. 1955): 49–62.

Villard, Oswald Garrison. *Some Newspapers and Newspapermen*. Freeport, NY: Books for Libraries Press 1923.

Waltz, Kenneth N. "Electoral Punishment and Foreign Policy Crises." In James N. Rosenau, ed., *Domestic Sources of Foreign Policy*. New York: Free Press 1967. 263–93.

Watson, Elmo Scott. *A History of Newspaper Syndicates in the United States, 1865–1935*. Chicago: Publishers' Auxilliary 1936.

Watt, D.C. "American 'Isolationism' in the 1920's: Is It a Useful Concept?" *Bulletin of the British Association for American Studies* 6 (June 1963): 3–19.

Welter, Mark M. "The 1895–98 Cuban Crisis in Minnesota Newspapers: Testing the 'Yellow Journalism' Theory." *Journalism Quarterly* 47 (Winter 1970): 719–24.

Wershba, Joseph. "I Hold Here in My Hand ..." *Antioch Review* 15 (Summer 1955): 131–47.

Wheaton, James Otis. "The Role of William Randolph Hearst in the Prenomination and Presidential Campaign of 1912." MA, Stanford University 1949.

Wilson, Joan Hoff. *Ideology and Economics: US Relations with the Soviet Union, 1918–1933*. Columbia, Mo.: University of Missouri Press 1974.

Winkler, John K. *William Randolph Hearst, an American Phenomenon*. New York: Simon and Schuster 1928.

– *William Randolph Hearst: A New Appraisal*. New York: Hastings House 1955.

Wolfskill, George. *The Revolt of the Conservatives: A History of the American Liberty League, 1934–1940*. Boston: Houghton Mifflin 1962.

Wood, Donald J. *William Randolph Hearst: His Early Years in Journalism*. Oakland, Calif. 1954.

Younger, Kenneth. "Public Opinion and Foreign Policy." *British Journal of Sociology* 6 (June 1955): 169–75.

Ziegler, John A. "The Progressive's Views on Foreign Affairs, 1909–1941: A Case Study of Liberal Economic Isolationism." PhD, Syracuse University 1970.

Zucker, Norman L. *George W. Norris: Gentle Knight of American Democracy*. Urbana, Ill.: University of Illinois 1966.

Index

Adams, John Quincy, 129–30

Aguinaldo, Emilio, 13, 141

Alliance, sinking of, 8

America First Committee, 68; WRH and, 124, 194 n 69

Baruch, Bernard, 106

Beard, Charles A., 26, 79, 183 n 8

Berens, Julius G., 71

Beresford, Lord Charles, 54

Bernstorff, Count Johann von, 114

Beveridge, Albert, 72

Bolo Pasha, Paul, 114

Borah, William E., 27, 72, 85, 92, 94, 137, 143, 149–50, 154

Brest-Litovsk, Treaty of (1918), 66, 67

Brisbane, Arthur, 20, 21, 169 n 26

Broun, Heywood, 26

Browder, Earl, 26, 82, 83

Bryan, William Jennings, 140; WRH and presidential candidacy (1896), 10; and First World War, 110

Bullitt, William C., 81

Butenko, Feodor, 83–4

Calhoun, John C., 96

Carnegie, Andrew, 91

Carranza, Venustiano, 134

Casement, Sir Roger, 35

Chamberlain, Austen, 98

Chamberlain, Neville, 99, 121, 124, 155

Chiang Kai-Shek, 156

Chicago Tribune, 71

China: WRH and Chinese immigration, 49–51; WRH and U.S. relations with, 54–5; WRH and 1911 revolution, 176 n 4

Christian Science Monitor, 22

Churchill, Winston, 43, 147, 153

Cisneros, Evangelina, 62; WRH and her escape from Cuba, 11, 164–5 n 19

Clark, Champ, 29

Clark, George N., 78

Clay, Henry, 96

Clayton-Bulwer Treaty (1850), 129, 148

Clemenceau, Georges, 69

Cleveland, Grover, 26, 32, 41, 96, 97, 131, 134, 144; resists pressure for war (1896), 10

Coblentz, Edmond D., 80, 81, 83, 86, 99, 120, 150

Colby, Bainbridge, 44, 81, 176 n 66

Comintern, 81; and international revolution, 82

Communism: as internal threat to the U.S., 24, 47, 74–6, 77–89, 156; WRH campaign to outlaw Communist Party, 84

Coolidge, Calvin, 97, 105, 136; and U.S. entry into the World Court, 92–3; and U.S. entry into the League of Nations, 98; and U.S. relations with Mexico, 135; relations with WRH, 144

Coughlin, Charles E., 149

Cox, James. M., 96

Cuba, 24, 32; WRH and U.S. policy towards, 9–10, 13–14

Daily Worker, 83
Davis, John W., 97
Davis, Richard Harding, 10
Dewey, George, 12
Diaz, Porfirio, 133
Dies, Martin, and House Un-American Activities Committee, 84
Dupuis de Lome, Enrique, resignation as Spanish ambassador to U.S., 11

Eden, Anthony, 155

Finland, repayment of war debts, 43
First World War, 25, 35–6, 37, 39, 41, 57, 63, 92, 100, 102, 105, 124, 139, 141, 149; WRH and U.S. entry into, 108–14; WRH as pro-German during, 114–15
France: WRH and, 38–9, 145; WRH's expulsion from, 39, 174 n 38

Germany, WRH and, 39–41
Great Britain: WRH on coronation of Edward VII, 32; WRH and England, 32–4, 36–8, 171 n 2; WRH and the Irish question, 34–6; WRH and union of English-speaking nations, 37–8; WRH and British war debts, 43; proposal for Anglo-American understanding, 97; British government and Panama Canal, 131; British claims in Western Hemisphere, 131–2

Harding, Warren G., 92, 105; relations with WRH, 144
Hawaii, 56, 101, 118; U.S. annexation of, 47–8
Hay, John, 145, 148
Hay-Pauncefoote Treaty (1901), 151; WRH campaign against first treaty, 129–30, 148–9; support for second treaty, 130, 149
Hearst, George, views on Orientals, 53
Hearst, William Randolph: upbringing, 5–6, 163 n 6; effect of Spanish-American War on, 17–18; view of United States, 28–9; and relations with Europe, 41–2; on U.S. relations with Western Hemisphere, 127–36; and Mexican scandal, 137, 197 n 40; and relations with Obregon government, 137, 197–8 n 41; and America First policy, 141–3, 160–1; and press influence on U.S. foreign policy, 146–52
– editorial policies: control of newspapers, 19–20, 166–7 nn 4,5,7; use of editorial comment, 21, 168 n 21; views of other newspapers on, 22–3; journalistic methods, 23–4; domestic campaigns, 27–8
Heflin, Thomas, 137
Hindenburg, Paul von, 120
Hitler, Adolf, 39, 124, 153–4; WRH and Hitler's government, 119–23
Hobson, Richmond P., 56
Hoover, Herbert, 84, 143, 144; and war debts, 44–5; and immigration, 49; and U.S. entry into the World Court, 93; and U.S. entry into the League of Nations, 98; and London Naval Conference, 104–5; and Latin America, 135; relations with WRH, 145, 148, 200 n 6
Huerta, Victoriano, 134

Hughes, Charles Evans, 25
Hull, Cordell, 81, 85, 86

Ickes, Harold L., 26, 85, 86
Immigration, Oriental, WRH and, 48–53, 177 n 10
International Court of Justice (World Court), 24, 25; WRH and U.S. entry, 91–4, 149–50; linked to League of Nations, 97–8

Jackson, Andrew, 45, 96, 97
Japan: WRH and Japanese expansionism, 48, 56–9, 117–19, 176 n 9; WRH and Japanese immigration, 49, 51–3; relations with U.S., 53–4, 179 n 61; Russo-Japanese War, 55–6, 57, 61, 101
Jefferson, Thomas, 73, 96, 97, 138
Johnson, Hiram, 27, 44, 72, 85, 92, 94, 143, 149, 155, 189–90 n 80

Kane, Charles Foster, comparison with WRH, 3–4, 160
Kellogg Pact (1925), 118
Kishinef Massacre, 60–1
Korean War, 158

La Follette, Robert, 72, 137, 140, 155
Landon, Alfred M., 83
Lansing, Robert M., 110
League of Nations, 24, 25, 39, 93, 104, 116; WRH and U.S. entry into, 94–9
Lenin, Vladimir, 66, 82
Lewis, Sinclair, 26
Liliuokalani, Queen, 48
Lima, Declaration of, 135
Lincoln, Abraham, 73, 96, 97
Lindbergh, Charles A., 124
Litvinov, Maxim, 71
Lloyd George, David, 119
London Naval Treaty (1930), 104–5, 106

London Naval Treaty (1936), 119
Los Angeles Examiner, 50
Los Angeles Times, 22
Louis-Napoleon, Mexican adventure, 128
Ludendorff, Erich von, 119
Lusitania, sinking of, 110, 112–13, 191 n 15

McKinley, William, 24, 25, 48, 55, 144, 151; first election (1896), 10; and de Lome affair, 11; and annexation of Hawaii, 48; relations with WRH, 144, 199 n 3
Madero, Francisco, 133–4
Madison, James, 96, 97
Maine, sinking of, 11–12
Manchester Guardian, 22
Marshall Plan (1948), 158, 159
Mexico, WRH and U.S. policy towards, 133–6
Mitchell, General William, 105
Monroe, James, 96, 97
Monroe Doctrine, 34, 40, 41, 100, 101, 128, 130, 131, 133, 134, 137–8
Mosley, Sir Oswald, 119
Munich Agreement (1938), 124
Mussolini, Benito, 87, 119, 123, 194 n 60

National Recovery Act (1933), 106
News Chronicle, 22
New York American, 25, 71
New York Evening Post, 47
New York Journal, 7, 8, 16, 17, 19, 24, 148, 149
New York Times, 16, 67, 71, 150
New York World, 7, 8
Nine-Power Treaty (1922), 118
Norris, George W., 27, 137, 155

Norway, WRH on Norwegian monarchy, 32
Nye, Gerald, 155

Obregon, Alvaro, U.S. recognition of, 135, 137, 197–8 n 41
Olney, Richard, 41

Page, Walter Hines, 110
Panama Canal, 50, 145; and international arbitration, 91–2; WRH and construction of, 129–31
Parker, Alton B., 26
Pauncefoote, Sir Julian, 148
Pershing, John J., 134
Philippines, 56, 101, 118; WRH and U.S. policy towards, 13, 14–15, 141
Plehve, Vyacheslav, 60
Portsmouth, Treaty of (1905), 55
Preparedness, 81; WRH campaign for, 99–107
Progressivism: WRH and, 28, 72–6; Progressives' views on Oriental immigration, 53; Progressives and Russian Revolution, 64, 67; Progressives and Panama Canal, 130, 195–6 n 14; Progressivism and U.S. foreign policy, 139–41; the "Old Progressives," 154–5, 159
Pulitzer, Joseph, 7–8, 23, 29

Reed, Thomas B., 26, 74, 95–6
Remington, Frederick, assignment in Cuba, 10–11
Roosevelt, Franklin D., 118, 144, 151, 153; and war debts, 45; and recognition of USSR, 71–2; WRH and communist tendencies in government, 81–3, 84–7; and alleged Communist support for (1936), 83; and U.S. entry

into the World Court, 93–4, 149–50; and U.S. entry into the League of Nations, 98–9; and preparedness, 106–7; and U.S. entry into Second World War, 123–4; and U.S. relations with Latin America, 135–6; and Yalta Conference, 155; relations with WRH, 145, 184–5 n 37, 200 n 7
Roosevelt, Theodore, 24, 25, 26, 38, 40, 51, 61, 72, 73, 139, 144, 149; support for Root's response to WRH, 25–6, 169–70 n 45; and Japanese school crisis, 51–2; and Japanese immigration, 52; and relations with Japan, 53, 55–7, 58; and Panama Canal, 130; relations with WRH, 145
Root, Elihu P., 27, 59; WRH's vendetta against, 24–5; Root's response (1906) and its effect, 25–6; and U.S. entry into the World Court, 93
Russia: WRH on czarist government, 32, 60–4; Russo-Japanese War, 55–6, 61, 101; Czar Nicholas II, government of, 60, 61–3
– Russian revolution: WRH and, 63–5, 67–9; American liberals and, 64, 67; recognition of revolutionary government, 65–6; Lenin and Treaty of Brest-Litovsk, 66

San Francisco Chronicle, 16, 23, 24
Second World War, 95, 106, 158; WRH and causes of, 116–23; WRH and U.S. entry into, 123–5
Shipstead, Henrick, 155
Sinclair, Upton, 83

Smith, Al, 145
Spain, WRH on Spanish monarchy (1907), 31
Spanish-American War, 100, 108, 139, 141; circulation war between WRH and Pulitzer, 7–8; Hearst coverage of Cuban situation, 8–12; outbreak of war, 12; discussion of future peace terms for Cuba, 13, and Philippines, 13; Treaty of Paris, 13–14; WRH on post-war policies towards Cuba, 14, and Philippines, 14–15; role of press in war, 15–18
Spectator (London), 131
Stalin, Josef, 43, 81, 83, 119, 123, 153; position in post–Second World War world, 156
Stimson, Henry L., on relations between Hoover and WRH, 145
Straight, Willard, 53
Sweden, WRH on death of Oscar II (1907), 32

Taft, William Howard, 144; refusal to become involved in Moroccan crisis (1911), 41; and relations with Japan, 53; and relations with Mexico, 133–4, 136; relations with WRH, 144 n 4
Thomas, Norman, 83

The Times (London), 22, 97
Trotsky, Leon, 82
Truman, Harry S., 144, 145, 156; Truman Doctrine, 157–8, 159
Tugwell, Rexford, 82, 85, 86
Turkey: WRH on Turkish government, 9, 32, 172 n 6; government compared with Russia, 60–1
Tweed, William M., and Root, 24, 25

United Nations, 155–6, 157
USSR: WRH and American intervention in, 69–70; WRH and U.S. recognition of, 70–2, 77, 78; WRH and Soviet government, 79–81, 83–4, 87–8; WRH and Soviet foreign policy, 87; WRH and Soviet policy during Second World War, 153–4, 155; post–Second World War American view of, 158–9

Vandenburg, Arthur, 155
Venezuela, boundary dispute with Great Britain, 34, 41, 100, 131
Versailles, Treaty of (1919), 122; WRH's opposition to, 94–5, 115–16
Villa, Francisco (Pancho), 134
Vinson-Trammel Act (1934), 106

Wallace, Henry, 86
War debts, 39, 145; WRH and repayment of, 42–5, 176 n 66
Washington, George, 73, 96, 97, 105, 116, 130, 157; Farewell Address, 138
Washington Naval Treaty (1922), 103–4, 105; WRH on, 58, 189 n 76
Washington Post, 22
Webster, Daniel, 96
Werner, Leo, 64–5
Weyler, Valeriano, 9, 10
Wheeler, Burton K., 155
Wilhelm II, 40
Williams, James T., and WRH's editorial policies, 20–2
Willicombe, John, 79, 80, 121
Wilson, Woodrow, 63, 65, 70, 85, 95, 116, 123, 136, 143; WRH's support for opponent (1912), 29; and Russian Revolution, 66; and U.S. intervention in Russia, 69, 76; and the League of Nations, 96–7; and First World War, 110, 111, 113; and Mexico, 134–5, 136; relations with WRH, 144, 199–200 n 5

Yalta Agreement (1945), 155